Rabindranath

# TAGORE

## AN ANTHOLOGY

# Rabindranath

# TAGORE

## AN ANTHOLOGY

EDITED BY

Krishna Dutta and Andrew Robinson

St. Martin's Press ⚮ New York

Library of Congress Cataloging-in-Publication Data

Rabindranath Tagore : a modern reader / Krishna Dutta and Andrew Robinson, editors.
    p.  cm.
  ISBN 0-312-16973-6
  1. Tagore, Rabindranath, 1861–1941—Criticism and interpretation.
I. Dutta, Krishna.   II. Robinson, Andrew.
PK1725.R2187   1997                                97-23037
                                                   CIP

First published in Great Britain by Picador an imprint of
Macmillan Publishers Ltd.

First U.S. Edition: November 1997

10  9  8  7  6  5  4  3  2  1

To the memory of
E. P. Thompson
an alien and a swadeshi homage

# Contents

# LETTERS – 131

# List of Illustrations

Rabindranath

# TAGORE

AN ANTHOLOGY

# Introduction

In Rabindranath Tagore's best-known novel, *The Home and the World,* the character who is really the author bursts out at one point with these powerful and subversive words:

> It was Buddha who conquered the world, not Alexander - this is untrue when stated in dry prose - oh when shall we be able to sing it? When shall all these most intimate truths of the universe overflow the pages of printed books and leap out in a sacred stream like the Ganges from the Gangotri?

While translating Tagore's poems into Russian in the 1960s, Anna Akhmatova made caustic gibes at them. But having finished, she declared: 'He's a great poet, I can see that now. It's not only a matter of individual lines which have real genius, or individual poems . . . but that mighty flow of poetry which takes its strength from Hinduism as from the Ganges, and is called Rabindranath Tagore.'

Readers, particularly western readers for whom this book is mainly intended, dipping into Tagore's work for the first time, are soon compelled to confront their own fundamental beliefs about the purpose of life on earth. Do we follow Buddha or Alexander, Christ or Caesar? For the spiritual values that permeate Tagore's voluminous printed works, and which brought him the Nobel prize for literature in 1913, were no second-hand religion: they were rooted both in his ancestry and in his own long and hard-fought experience, and they found constant expression in every aspect of his extraordinary life.

With this realization comes a second challenge to the reader of Tagore: which matters more, his published works - that outpouring of poetry, songs, plays, short stories, novels, essays, letters and paintings – or his human existence in India and the world, which ceased half a century ago?

Gandhi, Tagore's great contemporary, with whom he frequently and publicly disagreed, famously said of himself that his life was his message; and it is more for his actions than for his words that the world reveres him. Tagore, who first called Gandhi Mahatma, 'Great Soul', said of him:

> He stopped at the thresholds of the huts of the thousands of dispossessed, dressed like one of their own. He spoke to them in their own language. Here was living truth at last, and not only quotations from books. For this reason the Mahatma, the name given to him by the people of India, is his real name. Who else has felt like him that all Indians are his own flesh and blood? When love came to the door of India, that door was opened wide. At Gandhi's call India blossomed forth to new greatness, just as once before, in earlier times, when Buddha proclaimed the truth of fellow-feeling and compassion among all living creatures.

Though it is not now widely appreciated, much the same might be said of Tagore – with this radical difference: Tagore's medium was not that of Gandhi. He worked not on the flesh and blood but on the minds of countless individuals. He too stopped at the thresholds of thousands, thousands of minds, not just in India but worldwide, and entered them. 'I feel like a painted pict with a stone war-club,' Ezra Pound told a friend after spending the afternoon with Tagore. 'Briefly, I find in these poems a sort of ultimate common sense,' he wrote of Tagore's *Gitanjali* soon after, 'a reminder of one thing and of forty things of which we are over likely to lose sight in the confusion of our western life, in the racket of our cities, in the jabber of manufactured literature, in the vortex of advertisement.' That is why Gandhi, in his turn, called Tagore the Great Sentinel. 'I regard the Poet', he said, 'as a sentinel warning us against the approach of enemies called Bigotry, Lethargy, Intolerance, Ignorance, Inertia and other members of that brood.'

And so Tagore's life, the way he developed his mind and the manifold channels by which he flowed into other human beings, matters very much – as much as his published legacy. In fact the two are indivisible. As with Tolstoy, and more than with most writers, Tagore's art cannot be properly understood without understanding his life. Jawaharlal Nehru, India's first prime minister, was perceptive when he wrote in his jail diary on 7 August 1941, after hearing of Tagore's death:

> Gandhi and Tagore. Two types entirely different from each other, and yet both of them typical of India, both in the long line of India's great men. . . . Judged as types of men, I have felt for long that they were the outstanding examples in the world today. There are many of course who may be abler than them or greater geniuses in their own line. Einstein is great. There may be greater poets than Tagore, greater writers. . . . It is not so much because of any single virtue but because of the *tout ensemble*, that I felt that among the world's great men today Gandhi and Tagore were supreme as human beings. What good fortune for me to have come into close contact with them.

Since that time, while Gandhi's reputation has increased since his death, Tagore's, except in Bengal (where he is an icon), has fallen low and has only recently begun to revive. There were many reasons for the decay, but perhaps the most significant was that Tagore's best work, with the exception of his paintings, was accessible only in Bengali, a language known to very few westerners and of low economic and political prestige, internationally speaking.

Translations of course existed, many of them by Tagore himself; and they included, as well as poetry, plays, short stories, novels, essays and other works. It was Tagore's own manuscript translation, *Gitanjali*, that in 1912 captured the mind of first

William Rothenstein, and then, in quick succession, W. B. Yeats, Ezra Pound, André Gide and the members of the Swedish Academy. But even the best of the translations were not great literature, the vast majority of them were unworthy of the original, and many were absolutely feeble. By about 1930, few serious readers of literature were still reading Tagore in translation.

And yet his personal reputation had never been higher. In 1930, the *New York Times* published a conversation recorded in Germany between Einstein and Tagore on the nature of reality, headlined 'Einstein and Tagore plumb the truth'. When Tagore returned to the USA later that year, many thousands came to Carnegie Hall to hear him speak and he had a private audience with the president. A few years later, there was a press rumour that he was to play the Buddha in a film, which he had to deny. In 1937, having publicly supported the republican side in the Spanish civil war, he was denounced at the Nazi Party's biggest-ever rally at Nuremberg as part of 'world liberalism' in a speech by Joseph Goebbels (who as a student had read the German translation of Tagore's love songs, *The Gardener*, with delight). In 1938, *Life* magazine ran a captivating full-page photograph of Tagore being lip-read by Helen Keller. And in 1939, the BBC's journal, the *Listener*, began a review of a new biography of Tagore with the comment that he 'is the most famous of living poets; his renown is worldwide'.

His fame rested partly on his charisma – a word that might have been invented for Tagore – which was experienced at first hand in many countries during Tagore's extensive travels after 1912. (Many people were even reminded of Christ.) But more important than this relatively ephemeral phenomenon was the fact that Tagore's basic ideas, expressed in lectures before the world's greatest universities and through his many books in European languages, survived both translation and, frequently, the severest scrutiny.

'More than any other thinker of his time, Tagore had a clear conception of civil society, as something distinct from and of stronger and more personal texture than political or economic structures,' wrote E. P. Thompson in 1991, introducing a new edition of Tagore's *Nationalism* (1917). Thompson commented:

It would be folly to accuse Tagore of sentimental alarmism. *Nationalism* is a prescient, even prophetic, work whose foresight has been confirmed by sufficient evidence – two world wars, the nuclear arms race, environmental disasters, technologies too clever to be controlled. If its assertive denunciations of the Nation sometimes appear to be repetitious and tedious, this is in part because the indictment has become overfamiliar since Tagore drew it up.

Tagore was not an analytical thinker, always an intuitive one who preferred a poetic analogy to a prosaic argument. Sometimes his thinking was inchoate, on occasions he could be chauvinistic (especially around the turn of the century), but without exception he was courageous. In 1916, speaking in Japan and across the USA to large gatherings, he eloquently warned each nation about the dangers of militaristic nationalism, unbridled commercialism, and love of the machine for its own sake; lectures which formed the basis of *Nationalism*. In 1919, by repudiating his knighthood, Tagore became the first Indian to make a public gesture against the massacre at Amritsar. And in the 1920s, he stood up to Gandhi and the non-cooperation movement with pungent rationality: it was these criticisms that earned him Gandhi's somewhat grudging sobriquet, the 'Great Sentinel'.

When Rabindranath was born in 1861, notions of racial inferiority and superiority were engrained in educated minds eastern and western. By the time he died in 1941, such ideas were no longer respectable in democratic societies. Tagore was among the pioneers of that global sea change in attitudes.

The school and university he founded at Shantiniketan (the

'Abode of Peace'), in a poor rural area about a hundred miles north-west of Calcutta, his birthplace, was part of this effort to change minds. 'I merely started with this one simple idea that education should never be dissociated from life,' he wrote in 1922, after living at Shantiniketan for over twenty years. Though Shantiniketan had many faults, under Tagore it was a unique international meeting place for distinguished scholars, a magnet for foreigners seriously interested in Indian culture, and an important centre for music, painting and the study of oriental languages, besides training workers in rural development and educating some remarkable individuals, such as Satyajit Ray and Indira Nehru (later Indira Gandhi). In 1951, it was taken over by the central government of independent India, which continues to run it as a school and university; both Jawaharlal Nehru and his daughter became supportive chancellors of the university.

In foreseeing the need to apply western scientific expertise in what we would now call 'Third World development', Tagore was perhaps at the very head of the field. His earliest efforts date back to the turn of the century and took place on the Tagore estates in East Bengal (now Bangladesh). In 1921, with money from the American heiress Dorothy Whitney Straight and unstinting effort by a young British agricultural economist, Leonard Elmhirst (who later married Straight), Tagore started a farm adjacent to Shantiniketan, which became the nucleus of his 'institute for rural reconstruction', later named Shriniketan (the 'Abode of Plenty'). Although the institute had limited success, it influenced many in the government of independent India; it inspired the Elmhirsts to buy Dartington Hall in Britain and to found the Dartington Trust; and it left a legacy that became the orthodoxy in successful development aid half a century later. In Tagore's scheme of development, the developer must strive to be in sympathy with the developing – imposed solutions and imported technology do not last. 'It was not the Kingdom of the Expert in the midst of the inept and ignorant which we wanted to establish – although the experts' advice [is] valuable,' Tagore chided Elmhirst in 1932. 'The villages are waiting for the living touch of creative faith and not for the cold aloofness of science which uses efficient machinery for extracting statistics.'

Tagore insisted that science, which he studied and wrote about from an early age, must, in its application to society, serve society, and *not* vice versa. This was a conviction with a philosophical basis. In 1930, talking to Einstein, Tagore told him: 'This world is a human world – the scientific view of it is also that of the scientific man.' Though Einstein did not agree, some distinguished scientists now see Tagore's point. One of them, Ilya Prigogine, a Nobel laureate in chemistry, claimed in 1984: 'Curiously enough, the present evolution of science is running in the direction stated by the great Indian poet.'

Tagore's faith in the unity of man and nature informed everything he did. Dwelling on Shakespeare's plays in an essay, he commented that despite Shakespeare's 'great power as a dramatic poet', there was in him 'a gulf between Nature and human nature owing to the tradition of his race and time. It cannot be said that beauty of nature is ignored in his writings; only that he fails to recognize in them the truth of the inter-penetration of human life with the cosmic life of the world.' A fascinating letter Rabindranath wrote in 1892 from the family estates to his niece Indira goes further:

I feel that once upon a time I was at one with the rest of the earth, that grass grew green upon me, that the autumn sun fell on me and under its rays the warm scent of youth wafted from every pore of my far-flung evergreen body. As my waters and mountains lay spread out through every land, dumbly soaking up the radiance of a cloudless sky, an elixir of life and joy was inarticulately secreted from the immensity of my being. So it is that my feelings seem to be those of our ancient planet, ever germinant and efflorescent, shuddering with sun-kissed delight. The current of my consciousness streams through each blade of grass, each sucking root, each sappy vein, and breaks out in the waving fields of corn and in the rustling leaves of the palms.

I am impelled to give vent to this sense of having authentic ties of blood and affection with the earth. But I know that most people will not understand me and think my idea distinctly queer.

*

The young man who could write such a startling passage, and go on to inspirit the world with his joyful instinct – for this is what gave *Gitanjali* its unfamiliar power for westerners – is today revered in Bengal as the greatest of Bengalis. But he was not, of course, the first Bengali to demonstrate striking sophistication of intelligence and imagination (nor the last). That distinction belongs to Raja Ram Mohan Roy (1772–1833), who was in turn revered by Rabindranath. Best known today for his stand against *sati*, widow-burning, Ram Mohan was colonial India's first reformer, who used his phenomenal command of languages to examine the world's great religious texts, including the Hindu scriptures, and to apply what he found to be their essence to contemporary Hinduism, in order to rid it of inauthentic traditions. After years of debate with Christian missionaries in Calcutta, he founded, around 1830, the Brahmo Sabha, a Hindu movement opposed to the prevailing idolatry and caste practices that took its beliefs from Ram Mohan's interpretation of the *Vedas*, Hinduism's earliest scriptures. Within a few decades, this movement became the Brahmo Samaj, the most influential movement of religious and social reform in nineteenth-century India. One of its pillars was the Tagore family.

Dwarkanath Tagore (1794–1846), Rabindranath's grandfather, was among Ram Mohan Roy's greatest admirers. He was also one of the wealthiest men of his day. His combination of idealism and worldliness made for a life of exceptional interest and lasting significance, despite his being almost forgotten today.

Dwarkanath's money came from business, the firm Carr, Tagore and Company he had founded. It covered indigo factories, coal mines, tea picking and sugar production and owned a fleet of cargo boats that plied as far as Britain, a bank that for two decades was the keystone of the commercial structure of Calcutta, and extensive agricultural estates in East Bengal and Orissa – estates that would be managed by Rabindranath Tagore in the 1890s.

But if Dwarkanath was businesslike, he was philanthropic too, and on a scale that had few equals. British and Indian alike, the celebrated and the unknown, practical works, charitable activities and religious institutions were all beneficiaries of his largesse. He also threw the most spectacular parties in Calcutta, attended by the British elite of the 'City of Palaces'. When he travelled to Europe in 1842 (in his own steamer), his reputation for munificence increased still further, and he became known as 'Prince' Dwarkanath Tagore, 'the Oriental Croesus' (according to Dickens), friend of both Queen Victoria and King Louis-Philippe. At the end of one party in Paris, the 'Prince' draped a fine Indian shawl over the shoulders of every lady present as she left the room.

He had a vision of an industrialized India as a partner in Empire, with Indians collaborating on equal terms with Europeans, who would settle in India as they had settled in America, Australia and South Africa. Had he lived, he might have brought some of this to pass by sheer determination and energy. But the British rejected his vision in favour of short-term material gain, and his family rejected it in favour of spiritual and artistic gains. Astonishing as it is to record, Rabindranath Tagore refers only once, in the most passing manner, to his pioneering grandfather in his memoirs, *My Reminiscences*. In his forties he is said to have burned most of Dwarkanath's correspondence. It is almost as if he felt the memory contaminated him.

Perhaps he inherited this feeling from his austere father

Debendranath (1817–1905), known for the last half-century of his life as the Maharshi, 'Great Sage'. To the dismay of Dwarkanath, his eldest son largely lost interest in the family firm in 1838 at the age of twenty-one. Inspired by the example of Dwarkanath's late friend Ram Mohan Roy, Debendranath took to religion, reviving the Brahmo Samaj and beginning a search for true Hinduism all over northern India: he was especially drawn to the profoundly intellectual *Upanishads*. Upon Dwarkanath's death (in London in 1846), his son scandalized the family by refusing to perform the usual idolatrous funeral rituals. For many years he made it a point to abandon the family mansion at Jorasanko in north Calcutta at festival time, to avoid witnessing the orthodox Hindu rites of his domestic circle. When Carr, Tagore and Co. crashed, he insisted on giving whatever the family owned to pay the creditors, regardless of his legal obligations. So impressed were they by his probity, that the Tagores were permitted to continue the administration of the firm and to receive an allowance for the maintenance of the family. Within ten years most of the debts had been paid off.

None of Debendranath's eight surviving sons (or his four daughters) inherited a head for business, but three of them, Dwijendranath, Satyendranath and Jyotirindranath, were remarkable men, even when compared with Rabindranath, who was the youngest. Between them they performed with distinction in almost every branch of the arts and humanities. They also helped to create the national movement that in 1885 gave rise to the Indian National Congress; and Satyendranath, ironically, became the first Indian to enter the Indian Civil Service (ICS). Their examples, combined with those of other gifted Tagores living in Jorasanko and the cream of the city's artists and intelligentsia attracted to the house, infused Rabindranath's childhood and youth (and the pages of his two memoirs of that time) with a variety, vivacity and celebration of eccentricity virtually bound to nourish any seeds of talent.

The three or four decades following Tagore's birth in 1861 were the zenith of what is generally termed the Bengal Renaissance. They were also the high noon of the British Empire. Though the precise relationship between these two facts is controversial, there can be little doubt that they are connected. Tagore is the most dazzling instance of the benefits of this cultural collision; while others described by him in his writings, especially in his brilliantly ironic short stories, adumbrate the damage that more typically resulted and has persisted in Bengali society ever since.

In his celebrated minute written in Calcutta in 1835, Thomas Babington Macaulay defined the aim of colonial education as the creation of 'a class of persons, Indian in blood and colour, but English in taste, in opinions, in morals and in intellect'. Many young Bengalis of the time embraced Macaulay's idea with passion. 'I can speak in English, write in English, think in English, and shall be supremely happy when I can dream in English,' quipped one of them, the Bengali poet Michael Madhushudan Dutta, who tried to become a poet in English before reverting to his own language.

Those Bengalis who by contrast accepted internal colonization formed a class, the Bengali *babu*, that was a subject of ridicule both to other Bengalis, that is the vast majority of orthodox Hindus, and to the British in Calcutta, as pinpointed by Rudyard Kipling. The most extreme examples were dubbed *ingabangas*, 'anglomaniacs', by Tagore's elder brother. The teenage Rabindranath came across them in London on his first visit in 1878–80 and wrote home: 'If you happen to use the wrong knife to eat fish, an Englishman would not think much of it; he would put it down to your being a foreigner. But if an *ingabanga* Bengali saw you, he would probably have to take smelling salts.'

Rabindranath was drawn neither to religious orthodoxy nor crass anglicism. Even as a teenager he began intuitively to borrow what he liked from English literature to enrich his Bengali writing. Other Bengali writers were doing the same, with varying degrees of imitation, but Tagore was the most creative. He absorbed not the details but the spirit behind the foreign work. In his memoirs, he tells of how Chatterton, the eighteenth-century boy poet, inspired him when he was sixteen to write his first worthwhile verse. Chatterton had passed off his own poems as the work of a fifteenth-century monk, been ostracized when the deception was revealed, and committed suicide. What Chatterton's poetry was like Tagore had no idea, but the 'melodramatic element' in the story fired his imagination: 'Leaving aside suicide, I girded my loins to emulate young Chatterton.' He pretended to discover the work of an old Bengali poet while rummaging in the Brahmo Samaj library. The first friend who read it was ecstatic and declared that it must be published. When Tagore revealed the truth, his friend's face fell and he muttered, 'Yes, yes, they're not half bad.' In due course, when the poems appeared in the family magazine *Bharati*, it was under the pseudonym Bhanu Singh (Bhanu meaning 'Sun', as does Rabi). A Bengali then in Germany included Bhanu Singh in his thesis on the lyric poetry of Bengal, giving him a 'place of honour as one of the old poets, such as no modern writer could have aspired to'. And was then awarded his PhD – as Tagore informs us in his memoirs with wry amusement.

He lets us know what he himself thought of the poems – not much – but does not bother to spell out his point: we are left to make of it what we will, as with most of the anecdotes in *My Reminiscences*. Still, it is clear that Tagore regarded the whole episode as typical of the 'multicultural' confusion of the time: the Bengali critic fell for the bogus because he did not know Bengal and Bengali properly; and his German supervisors, not knowing Bengal and Bengali at all, lacked the means to detect the mistake. Only hard-won knowledge and sincere empathy will do when attempting to analyse one's own culture to determine what is wheat and what is chaff, Tagore implies. Furthermore, they form the only sound basis on which to hope to judge other cultures – whether one is a Bengali *babu* or a European Orientalist.

Maharshi Debendranath, and before him Ram Mohan Roy, tried to treat Hinduism in this way, in order to purge it of excrescences like *sati* and, in his eyes, idolatry. But Debendranath was not prepared to go as far as his youngest son; he remained, in some ways, highly conservative. He arranged for Rabindranath to be invested with the Brahmin's sacred thread, for example, and he insisted on his marrying a wife he had never met, an almost illiterate ten-year-old of the right Pirali Brahmin caste. Such was the custom then, even among the enlightened Tagores. If Rabindranath objected, he did not reveal it in writing, dutiful son that he was.

In other important ways, however, Debendranath was liberal. In 1878, he sent Rabi to Britain, intending that he should train as a barrister like many – too many – of his contemporaries. When his son showed no inclination towards the law, his father made no attempt to force him.

Tagore writes of his fifteen months in the heart of the Empire with sympathy and self-mocking humour, sometimes tinged with disgust. His letters of the time, which he later regretted publishing, show that much of his stay was an uneasy experience. He spent happy days with his elder brother Satyendranath's family in Brighton and Devon, and as a lodger with an English doctor in London, who treated him as one of the family and whose young daughter taught him many English and Irish songs that he later adapted for his 'operas'. Otherwise, he felt mostly dismay or indignation.

Unsurprisingly, perhaps, he hated the lack of light and space compared to what he knew of Bengal and the rest of India. As for human relationships and art, he felt there to be a dearth of intimacy and a preoccupation with the superficial at the cost of the essential. The very aspects of English society that seem to have appealed to his fêted grandfather in 1840s London (so far as one can tell from surviving letters and reports) repelled Rabindranath, not that he ever made the comparison. It is as if he sensed in the soul of mid-Victorian London a cold-hearted despair of the kind that had driven Robert Clive to suicide a century before. As a boy, this story of Clive had shaken Rabi. 'How could there be such brilliant success on the outside and such dismal failure within?'

However, Tagore was too subtle an artist and judge of human beings ever to tar a whole nation or race; in fact, he specifically stated that 'human nature is everywhere the same', after observing in London the devotion of the doctor's wife to her husband, an attitude he admitted earlier believing to be the unique prerogative of the Indian wife. Tempting though it was to generalize about the ruler or the ruled (and sometimes he succumbed), Tagore always knew that it was the individual, in all his or her lonely mystery, who mattered most. He was deeply shocked when his favourite sister-in-law Kadambari, wife of Jyotirindranath, killed herself when he was twenty-two, four months after his marriage. Her motive is no clearer to us than Clive's. It would be easy to conclude from Tagore's memoirs, and especially from his paintings and his moving novella *The Broken Nest* (filmed by Satyajit Ray as *Charulata*), that Kadambari was in love with Rabindranath and he with her, but we can never know the full cause of the tragedy.

Tagore eventually overcame it and found himself strengthened. Much less easy for him to accept was his lack of genuine appreciation by Bengalis. The applause for Bhanu Singh's poetry, despite its artificial sentiments, is symptomatic of Tagore's lifelong reception in Bengal. Whenever he departed from convention in his work or in his life, which was almost always, he was attacked – often scathingly. A section of the press kept him under constant fire, frequently descending into mud-slinging; one newspaper even alleged that Rabindranath had syphilis. 'Few writers have been more scurrilously abused [than Tagore],' wrote Nirad C. Chaudhuri, the leading critic of modern Bengal.

The strongest attacks were provoked by his ventures into politics. In 1905, he was a leader of the Swadeshi Movement, a Bengali equivalent of Ireland's Sinn Fein ('Swadesh' means 'Our Country' in Bengali). Had he wanted, at that time he could have become the political leader of Bengal; but after less than two years he suddenly withdrew, disgusted by the bombing and killing and the compromises of politics: his novel *The Home and the World*, written some years later, was his response to that troubled time. Both his withdrawal and his novel were heavily criticized by Bengalis. And again, in the 1920s, when Tagore resolutely refused to become a non-cooperator and expressed his reasons in both essays and stories, he was the subject of regular vilification by nationalists.

All this hurt him, but, being Tagore, he refused to bend. For as he once told his daughter, after failing to raise funds for his university from wealthy Americans because he would not fall in with their demands, 'I have always been attacked by political groups, religious groups, literary groups, social groups and so on. If I belonged to the opposition camp, each group would have forgiven me. That I do not belong to any group makes them all angry. No one will be able to put a chain on my feet.'

★

This book contains examples of all the genres in which Tagore worked, letters, short stories, poetry, and so on, each genre being separately introduced. It opens with his little play *The Post Office*, because this seems to distil the thoughts and feelings that mattered most of all to its author into a vessel of timeless and universal appeal. After that, in line with our view that Tagore's life is important in understanding his fictional works, there follow extracts from his memoirs and his letters, which were written to his family and to famous people like Yeats, Rolland and Gandhi, and also to not-so-famous people. Then come his ideas, in the form of essays, statements and conversations, ranging from East–West relations to art and music. Finally, there are the short stories, which are perhaps his greatest fictional achievement for the non-Bengali, an extract from *The Home and the World*, some poetry from almost all periods of his poetic career, and a few songs, to give a hint of what is unquestionably his best-loved achievement in his native Bengal.

Oxford University, in giving Tagore a doctorate at a special convocation in Shantiniketan in 1940, called him 'the myriad-minded poet', 'most dear to all the muses'. We, in our biography of Tagore, called him the 'myriad-minded man'. Here, in this *Anthology*, we hope both the artist and the man will come alive. But we know, as Tagore knew, that his is a personality remarkably resistant to being captured and caged on the printed page.

> I leave no trace of wings in the air,
> but I am glad I had my flight.

# Note on the Translations

About a third of the pieces in this book – the essays, statements, conversations and letters – were written in English, two-thirds in Bengali. We ourselves have translated *The Post Office*, two extracts from *Letters from an Exile in Europe*, the letters to Tagore's wife and niece and to Mahalanobis, all the short stories except *The Parrot's Training* (which is very brief), and more than half the poems. The rest of the pieces were originally translated either by Tagore, or by various Bengalis, including his nephew and niece, or in two cases (*My Boyhood Days* and 'The Flower Says', a song) by English translators. These translations seemed to us basically satisfactory, with the added advantage that Tagore himself had approved most of them. However, we have revised them against their Bengali originals, in a few cases extensively. The significant exception is the translation of *The Home and the World*, which is untouched; here we have selected passages that do not suffer from the stiltedness that affects much of the original translation.

In selecting and revising the travel writings, we have not hesitated to omit passages and paragraphs that are either repetitious or dull, but the rest of the prose extracts are presented complete, except for the conversation with Einstein on music, which has been slightly edited for clarity. Omissions in the travel writings are indicated by three dots.

As for the use of Bengali/Indian words, *pan*, *luchi*, *puja*, for example, we have been sparing, and tried to introduce them in such a way that the non-Indian reader may half guess their meaning from the context. It would be wrong to omit them altogether as Tagore himself tended to do, equally wrong to overload the text with them as more academically minded translators do: a balance is required, as in the use of colloquialisms in dialogue; and the acceptable line has surely shifted appreciably in recent years through the spread of Indian food, clothes, films and customs abroad, and through the polyglot writings of Salman Rushdie and others. A glossary of Indian/Bengali words is provided (most plant names have been excluded from this).

The transliteration of Bengali names and words in English is a tricky and unsatisfactory business. Rabindranath is pronounced 'Robindronath', for example, Satyajit as 'Shottojeet'; Tagore is an anglicized form of Thakur, Chatterji of Chattopadhyay. Many names and places mentioned here have no widely agreed spelling, for example Shantiniketan/Santiniketan (Tagore used both spellings), and some were spelt differently in Tagore's lifetime from their modern spelling, for instance Dacca/Dhaka, Benares/Varanasi. We have adopted a spelling that it is commonly used or reasonably consistent and, if possible, not too off-putting for a non-Bengali reader. All Bengali words we have spelt without cumbersome diacritical marks, and have tried instead to use a spelling that reproduces the sound not the orthography of Bengali. This means that, rather than employing the conventional but confusing 's' and 'sh' to represent the three Bengali letters for *s*, we have transliterated all three letters as 'sh', hence *shandesh* not *sandesh* for Bengali sweets, except where there is an established spelling, as in the words sari and sahib, or the name of Tagore's elder brother Satyendranath and his Calcutta house, Jorasanko.

### Acknowledgements

We thank Robert Weil, senior editor of St Martin's Press, New York, for suggesting to us that we should translate *Dak Ghar* (*The Post Office*).

# DRAMA

Of all Tagore's many plays, *The Post Office* continues to occupy a special place in his reputation, both within Bengal and in the wider world. According to Anita Desai, 'In appearance the play is as modest as a dewdrop; in effect it is as profound as the ocean.'

When Mahatma Gandhi saw the play in Calcutta in 1917, he wrote to a friend: 'I was enraptured to witness *The Post Office* performed by the Poet and his company. Even as I dictate this, I seem to hear the exquisitely sweet voice of the Poet and the equally exquisite acting on the part of the sick boy. . . . I did not have enough of it, but what I did have had a most soothing effect upon my nerves which are otherwise always on trial.' W. B. Yeats, who first had the play produced in English and also wrote a preface to it, thought it a masterpiece and said: 'On the stage the little play shows it is very perfectly constructed, and conveys to the right audience an emotion of gentleness and peace.'

Tagore wrote it in Bengal in 1911, not long after losing his youngest son, his daughter, and his wife to disease. In the middle of the night, while lying beneath the stars on the roof of his house in Shantiniketan, he had a strange experience. 'My mind took wing. Fly! Fly – I felt an anguish. . . . There was a call to go somewhere and a premonition of death, together with intense emotion – this feeling of restlessness I expressed in writing *Dak Ghar* [*The Post Office*].' Soon afterwards, Tagore's worldwide odyssey began.

Ten years on, having watched a German performance in Berlin (with the young Elisabeth Bergner playing the boy Amal), Tagore explained the play's intended meaning to an English friend, C. F. Andrews:

Amal represents the man whose soul has received the call of the open road. . . . But there is the post office in front of his window, and Amal waits for the King's letter to come to him direct from the King, bringing him the message of emancipation. At last the closed gate is opened by the King's own physician, and that which is 'death' to the world of hoarded wealth and certified creeds brings him awakening in the world of spiritual freedom.

The only thing that accompanies him in his awakening is the flower of love given to him by Shudha.

Such was its universal appeal, *The Post Office* was translated into many European languages. Each artist coming to it has made it speak afresh to his own place and time in his own idiom. Its Spanish translator, the celebrated poet Juan Ramón Jiménez, wrote of 'my hand that helped to give our Spanish form to the rhythm of Tagore's immense heart'. In 1940, the evening before Paris fell to the Nazis, André Gide's French translation was read over the radio. And in 1942, in the Warsaw ghetto, a Polish version was the last play performed in the orphanage of Janusz Korczak. When after the performance Korczak was asked why he chose the play, he answered that 'eventually one had to learn to accept serenely the angel of death'. Within a month, he and his children were taken away and gassed.

Tagore's insight into death is perhaps at its deepest in this play. Discussing it with an Italian nobleman, who felt that the play was about death 'as a kind of revelation of the divine', Tagore made this beautiful response, later read at the funeral of his American admirer Dorothy Whitney Elmhirst:

I have had so many experiences of loved ones who have died that I think I have come to know something about death, something perhaps of its deeper meaning. Every moment that I have spent at the death bed of some dear friend, I have known this, yet it is very difficult to describe how for me that great ocean of truth to which all life returns, can never suffer diminution by death. . . . I see how the individual life comes back to the bosom of this ocean at the moment of death, I have felt too how great and fathomless this ocean is, yet how full it is of personality. For personality is ever flowing into it. . . . It becomes instilled with personality. Yet this ocean seems as nothing, as neither light nor darkness, but as one great extension of the universe, an eternity of peace and life.

Science recognizes atoms, all of which can be weighed and measured, but never recognizes personality, the one thing that lies at the basis of reality. All creation is that, for apart from personality, there is no meaning in creation. Water is water to me, because I am I. And so I have felt that in this great infinite, in this ocean of personality, from which my own little personal self has sprung, lies the completion of the cycle, like those jets of water from a fountain which rise and fall and come back home again.

# The Post Office

........................................................................................................

*Dramatis Personae*

Madhav Dutta

Amal, a small boy and
Madhav's adopted child

Doctor

Curdseller

Watchman

{ Thakurda, a wanderer }

{ Fakir }

Village headman, a bully

Shudha, a flower girl

Village boys

Raja's (King's) herald

Raja's (King's) physician

........................................................................................................

## 1

[*Madhav's house*]

MADHAV DUTTA  What a mess I'm in. Before he came, he meant nothing to me – I had no worries. Then he came here out of nowhere and filled my entire home; if he leaves me now this house will no longer seem like my home. Doctor, do you think he will—

DOCTOR  If the child is fated for long life, then he shall have it, but it is written in the *Ayurveda* that—

MADHAV  What? Please tell me!

DOCTOR  The scriptures say, 'Bile and fever, palsy and phlegm all—'

MADHAV  Stop, stop, please don't recite those *slokas*; they just make me more anxious. Tell me instead what must be done.

DOCTOR  [*taking snuff*]  Great care must be observed.

MADHAV  That I know, but what kind of care? You must tell me.

DOCTOR  I have told you before: on no account should he be allowed out of doors.

MADHAV  But he's so young! To keep him inside all day is really cruel.

DOCTOR  What choice do you have? The autumn sun and wind are both like venom to the boy, for as the scriptures say, 'In epilepsy, fever or wheezing fit, in jaundice or in swelling—'

MADHAV  Enough, that's enough scripture. So we have to shut him indoors – is there really no other cure?

DOCTOR  None at all, for in the wind and the sun—

MADHAV  Oh cease with your 'this, that and the other'. Please, stop it – just tell me what I have to do. Your remedies are so harsh. The poor boy is already putting up with a lot without complaining – but it breaks my heart to see how your prescription makes him suffer further.

DOCTOR  The greater the suffering, the happier the outcome.

As the great sage Chyabana says, 'In medication as in good counsel, the bitterest brings the speediest results.' Well, I must be going, Mr Dutta.

[*He goes. Thakurda enters*]

MADHAV Oh no, Thakurda's back! Looks like trouble.

THAKURDA Why? Why should a fellow like me scare you?

MADHAV Because you make children run wild.

THAKURDA You are not a boy, you have no child in your house, and you are past the age for running away – why do you worry?

MADHAV Because I have brought a child to the house.

THAKURDA Indeed!

MADHAV My wife wanted to adopt a boy.

THAKURDA I've known that for a long time, but I thought you didn't want to.

MADHAV You know I was making a lot of money by hard work, and I used to think how terrible it would be if some boy turned up and wasted all my money without any effort. But this one has somehow charmed me so much that—

THAKURDA —that no wealth is too much for him. And you now feel that the more you spend, the merrier your money's fate.

MADHAV Before, I was addicted to making money – I couldn't help myself. But now my reward is the knowledge that whatever I earn will be his.

THAKURDA And where did you find him?

MADHAV He's a sort of nephew of my wife through some village connection. He lost his mother very early, poor boy. And just recently, he lost his father, too.

THAKURDA How sad! Maybe I could be of some help to him.

MADHAV The doctor says that he is so sick with fever that there isn't much hope. Now the only cure is somehow to keep him inside, away from the autumn sunshine and breezes.

But you always come along and gaily lead children outside – that's why you scare me.

THAKURDA  Yes, I admit it, I have become a free spirit, like the autumn sun and wind. But I also know how to play games indoors. Let me finish a few errands of mine, then I will make friends with this boy of yours.

[*He goes. Amal enters*]

AMAL  Uncle!

MADHAV  What is it, Amal?

AMAL  Can't I even go out into the courtyard?

MADHAV  No, Amal.

AMAL  Look, over there, where Auntie is grinding lentils, there's a squirrel, balancing on its tail and munching the broken bits between its paws – can't I please go and see?

MADHAV  No, my son.

AMAL  I wish I could be a squirrel – Uncle, why can't I go out?

MADHAV  The doctor says that if you go out you will get ill.

AMAL  How does the doctor know that?

MADHAV  What do you mean, Amal! Of course he knows! He has read so many huge old books.

AMAL  Does reading make you know everything?

MADHAV  Of course! Don't you know?

AMAL  [*with a sigh*]  I have not read a single book, so I guess I don't know anything.

MADHAV  But you are just like the greatest of pundits – you know, they never leave their houses.

AMAL  Don't they?

MADHAV  No, they don't, how can they? They only sit and read books, and never glance in any other direction. Amal, young fellow, you too will become a pundit – you will sit and read all those books, and everyone will gaze at you in wonder.

AMAL  No! Uncle, please no, I beg you, I don't want to be a pundit, I don't want to be one, Uncle.

MADHAV Why not, Amal! If I could have been a pundit, my life would have been totally different.

AMAL I want to see everything – everything there is to see.

MADHAV What are you talking about? See what?

AMAL Those faraway hills, for instance, which I can see from my window – I would so love to cross over them.

MADHAV What a crazy idea! Just like that, for nothing, on a whim, you want to cross those hills? You are not talking sense. Those hills stand up so tall because they are forbidding you to go beyond them – otherwise, why would stone have been piled upon stone to form such a huge heap?

AMAL Uncle, are you sure they are really forbidding us? To me, it looks like the earth is mute, and so she is raising up her hands towards the sky and calling us. Distant people sitting beside their windows in the heat of midday are also hearing the call. Don't the pundits hear it?

MADHAV They are not mad like you – they don't want to listen.

AMAL Yesterday I met someone as mad as me.

MADHAV Really? Tell me.

AMAL There was a bamboo pole across one of his shoulders. At the top of it was tied a small bundle. He held a small brass pot in his left hand. There was an old pair of curly-toed slippers on his feet, and he walked along the path through the fields towards the hills. I called out, 'Where are you going?' He said, 'I don't know – wherever I happen to go.' So I asked him, 'Why are you going?' And he replied, 'I'm seeking work.' Uncle, does everyone have to seek work?

MADHAV Of course. People are always looking for work.

AMAL All right, I'll be like them and go searching for work, too.

MADHAV What if you seek and don't find?

AMAL I will keep on searching. When the man with the slippers walked away, I watched him from the doorway. Not far off, where the stream flows past the fig tree, he put his pole down and gently washed his feet. Then he opened his sack, took out some maize flour, kneaded it with water and ate *chhatu*. When he was finished, he picked up the sack again and put it on his shoulder, hitched up his clothes, waded into the stream and made his way across. I said to Auntie that I'm going to go to the stream some time and eat *chhatu*.

MADHAV  What did she say?

AMAL  She said, 'Get well first, then I myself will take you to the stream and feed you with *chhatu*.' When will I get better?

MADHAV  It won't be much longer, young fellow.

AMAL  Not long? You know, as soon as I get well I must be off.

MADHAV  Where to?

AMAL  There are so many winding streams I want to dip my feet in. And at noontime, when everyone is resting behind shuttered doors, I want to walk and walk in search of work, further and further.

MADHAV  All right, but first get better, then you—

AMAL  You won't tell me to become a pundit, Uncle, will you?

MADHAV  What will you become then?

AMAL  I can't think of anything yet – I will tell you when I've thought.

MADHAV  But you shouldn't talk to strangers like that.

AMAL  I like strangers very much.

MADHAV  What if one were to snatch you away?

AMAL  That would be fun. But no one ever takes me away; everyone wants me to sit right here.

MADHAV  I have some work to do, so I must go. But son, don't wander outside, all right?

AMAL  I won't. But Uncle, you must let me sit here in this room next to the road.

[*Madhav goes*]

★

## 2

CURDSELLER *Dai – dai –* good *dai!*

AMAL Daiwallah, Daiwallah, oh Daiwallah!

CURDSELLER What do you want? To buy *dai?*

AMAL How can I? I have no money.

CURDSELLER What kind of a child are you? If you're not buying, why are you wasting my time?

AMAL I just want to walk with you.

CURDSELLER With me?

AMAL When I hear your cry in the distance, it makes me so restless.

CURDSELLER [*taking off his yoke*] Young fellow, what are you doing sitting there like that?

AMAL The doctor's forbidden me to go outdoors, so I must sit here all day every day.

CURDSELLER You poor child. What's wrong?

AMAL I don't know. I haven't read any books, so I can't know what is the matter with me. Daiwallah, where do you come from?

CURDSELLER I come from our village.

AMAL Your village? Is it far away?

CURDSELLER Our village is at the foot of the Panchmura hills, beside the Shamli River.

AMAL Panchmura Hills, Shamli River – I think I've seen your village, although I don't remember when.

CURDSELLER You have been there? Have you been to the foot of the hills?

AMAL No, I've never been there. But I feel as if I have. Doesn't your village lie beneath some ancient sprawling trees, next to a red road?

CURDSELLER You are right, son.

AMAL And there are cows grazing on the hillside.

CURDSELLER Right again! In our village, cows do graze, yes indeed.

AMAL And women come to fetch water from the river and carry it in pitchers on their heads – and they wear red saris.

CURDSELLER Yes, yes, that's it. All of our dairywomen come to the river for their water. But not all of them wear red saris. You must have visited the place sometime.

AMAL No, I assure you, I have never been there. As soon as the doctor lets me go out, will you take me to your village?

CURDSELLER Of course I will, with pleasure.

AMAL Teach me how to sell *dai* as you do – walking all those far-off roads with your harness across your shoulder.

CURDSELLER But my son, why sell *dai*? You should read books and become a pundit.

AMAL No, no, I will never become a pundit. I will take some *dai* from your village beneath the old banyan tree beside the red road and I will sell it in distant villages. How does your call go? '*Dai* – *dai* – good *dai*!' Teach me the tune, won't you, please?

CURDSELLER Heavens! Is such a tune worth teaching?

AMAL Don't say that, I like it. You know when you hear a hawk shrieking high up in the sky, the cry gives you a strange feeling? Well, your distant call – which seems to float through the trees from some far bend in the road – has the same effect on me.

CURDSELLER Son, please have a pot of my *dai*.

AMAL But I have no money.

CURDSELLER It doesn't matter, don't mention money. I would be ever so pleased if you ate some of my *dai*.

AMAL Have I delayed you much?

CURDSELLER No, not at all, son, it's no loss at all. For you have shown me the joy in selling *dai*.

[*He goes*]

AMAL [*chanting*] *Dai, dai, good dai! Dai* from the dairies beside the Shamli River in the Panchmura Hills. *Dai – dai!* Every dawn the dairywomen milk the cows under the trees, and every evening they set the *dai* – and what *dai* it is! *Dai, dai, dai-i*, delicious *dai*! Ah, look, there's the watchman doing his rounds. Watchman, oh Watchman, won't you come and listen to me for just a minute?

[*Watchman enters*]

WATCHMAN  What's all this shouting for? Aren't you afraid of me?

AMAL  Why should I be afraid of you?

WATCHMAN  What if I arrest you, take you away?

AMAL  Where will you take me? Far away, over the hills?

WATCHMAN  I might take you straight to the Raja!

AMAL  To the Raja! Would you really? But the doctor has forbidden me to go out. No one can take me anywhere. I must just sit here all day and night.

WATCHMAN  Doctor's orders? Ah, I can see your face is quite pale. There are dark rings under your eyes. The veins are sticking out in both of your arms.

AMAL  Are you going to sound your gong?

WATCHMAN  The time is not yet right.

AMAL  Some people say, 'time flies', while others say that 'time is not yet ripe'. But if you strike your gong, won't the time be right?

WATCHMAN  How so? I sound the gong only when the time is right.

AMAL  I do like your gong. I love listening to it, especially at noon after everyone's eaten and my uncle has gone out somewhere to work and Auntie dozes off reading the *Ramayana*, and our small dog curls up into its tail in some shadow of the courtyard – then I hear your gong strike *dhong dhong, dhong dhong dhong*! But why do you strike it?

WATCHMAN  It tells everyone that time does not stand still, that time always moves onwards.

AMAL  Where is time going? To what land?

WATCHMAN Nobody knows that.

AMAL You mean nobody's been there? I would love to run away with time to this land that nobody knows.

WATCHMAN All of us will go there one day, young man.

AMAL Me too?

WATCHMAN Of course.

AMAL But the doctor has forbidden me to go out.

WATCHMAN Some day perhaps the doctor will hold your hand and take you there.

AMAL No, you don't know him, all he does is keep me locked up here.

WATCHMAN But there is a greater doctor than he, a doctor who can set you free.

AMAL When will this Great Doctor come for me? I'm so tired of staying here.

WATCHMAN Shouldn't say such things, son.

AMAL But I have to sit here all the time never going out, doing as I am told, and when your gong goes *dhong dhong dhong*, I feel so frustrated. Watchman—?

WATCHMAN What is it?

AMAL Tell me, over there across the road, that big house with a flag on top, with lots of people going in and out of it – what is it?

WATCHMAN It's the new post office.

AMAL Post office? Whose post office?

WATCHMAN The Raja's, of course – who else could have a post office? [*Aside*] He's a strange boy.

AMAL Do letters come to the post office from the Raja himself?

WATCHMAN Yes, of course. Some day there may even be a letter addressed to you.

AMAL A letter with my name on it? But I am only a child.

WATCHMAN The Raja sends his littlest letters to children.

AMAL Really? When will I get my letter? And how do you know that he's going to write to me?

WATCHMAN  Why else would he bother to set up a post office with a splendid golden flag outside your open window? [*Aside*] But I rather like the boy.

AMAL  When the Raja's letter comes, who will give it to me?

WATCHMAN  The Raja has many messengers – surely you have seen them running about with gold badges pinned to their chests.

AMAL  Where do they go?

WATCHMAN  From door to door, country to country. [*Aside*] The boy's questions really are amusing.

AMAL  When I grow up, I want to be a Raja's messenger.

WATCHMAN  Ha ha ha! A Raja's messenger! Now there's a responsible job. Come rain, come shine, among rich, among poor, wherever you are you must deliver your letters – it's a tremendous job!

AMAL  Why are you smiling that way? It's the best job there could be. Oh, I don't mean that your job isn't good too – you strike your gong during the heat of noon, *dhong dhong dhong*, and also in the dead of night – sometimes I suddenly wake up and find that the lamp has gone out and I hear a deep, dark, *dhong dhong dhong*!

WATCHMAN  Uh-oh, here comes the big boss – time to run. If he catches me chatting with you, he's sure to cause trouble.

AMAL  Where's the boss, which one is he?

WATCHMAN  Over there, way down the road. Don't you see his big umbrella – the one made of palm leaves – bobbing up and down?

AMAL  Has the boss been appointed by the Raja?

WATCHMAN  Oh no – he's been appointed by himself. But if you don't obey him, he'll cause endless difficulties – that's why people are afraid of him. Our Headman's entire job seems to be trouble-making, for everyone. So that's enough talk for today, time to leave. I'll be back tomorrow morning to bring you the news of the town.

*[He goes]*

AMAL  If I receive a letter every day from the Raja, that would be wonderful. I'll sit here by the window and read them. Oh, but I don't know how to read. I wonder who can read them for me? Auntie reads *Ramayana*. Maybe she can read the Raja's writing? If nobody can read the letters, I'll keep them and read them all later, when I grow up. But what if the Raja's messengers don't know about me? Mr Headman, oh dear Mr Headman, could I talk to you for a minute?

HEADMAN  Who's this? Bellowing at me in the road! Who's this monkey?

AMAL  You are the Headman. I hear that everyone pays attention to you.

HEADMAN  *[flattered]*  Yes, yes, they do. They do, or else.

AMAL  Do the Raja's messengers listen to you, too?

HEADMAN  Of course! Would they dare to ignore me?

AMAL  Will you tell the messengers that my name is Amal, and that I am always here, sitting by the window?

HEADMAN  Why should I do that?

AMAL  In case there is a letter addressed to me.

HEADMAN  A letter for you! Who would write *you* a letter?

AMAL  If the Raja writes to me then—

HEADMAN  Well now, aren't you a mighty fellow! Ho ho ho! So the Raja will write to you, will he? Of course he will, for you are his dear friend. In fact, he's getting sadder by the day because he's not seen you lately, so I hear. Well, your waiting's almost over; I bet that your letter will come any day now.

AMAL  Mr Headman, why is your voice so harsh? Are you angry with me?

HEADMAN  Goodness me. Why should I be angry with you? Could I be so bold? After all, you are a correspondent of the Raja. *[Aside]* I can see that Madhav Dutta thinks he can drop the names of rajas and maharajas, just because he has made a little money. We'll soon see that he gets his comeuppance.

[*To Amal*] Yes my lad, you'll soon get a royal letter at your house, I shall see to it myself.

AMAL  No no, please, you don't have to go to any trouble for me.

HEADMAN  And why not? I will tell our Raja about you, and I am sure he will not keep you waiting long. In fact, I bet he will send a footman at once to hear your news. [*Aside*] Really, Madhav Dutta's arrogance is too much. Just as soon as this reaches the ears of the Raja, there'll be trouble, that's for sure.

[*He goes*]

AMAL  Who is that, with her jingling anklets? Please stop awhile.

[*A girl enters*]

GIRL  How can I stop? The day's already passing.

AMAL  You don't want to stop, even for a moment – and I don't want to sit here a moment longer.

GIRL  To look at you reminds me of the fading morning star. What's the matter with you, tell me?

AMAL  I don't know, but the doctor has forbidden me to go out.

GIRL  Then don't go out, obey Doctor's words – if you don't, people will say you are naughty. I can see that just looking outside makes you restless. Let me close this window a bit.

AMAL  No no, don't close it! Everything is closed to me except this window. Tell me who you are, I don't seem to know you.

GIRL  I am Shudha.

AMAL  Shudha?

SHUDHA  Don't you know? I am the daughter of the local flower seller.

AMAL  And what do you do?

SHUDHA  I fill a wicker basket with plucked flowers and make garlands. Just now I'm off to pick some.

AMAL You're going to pick flowers? Is that why your feet are
so lively, and your anklets go jingle-jangle with each step? If I
could go with you, I would pick flowers for you from the
highest branches, beyond your sight.

SHUDHA Would you now?! So you know where the flowers
are better than I do?

AMAL Yes, I know a lot. For example, I know all about the
seven *champak*-flower brothers. If I were well I would go
deep into the forest where there is no path to be seen. There
I would blossom as a *champak* flower on the tallest tip of the
thinnest twig, where the hummingbird gets drunk on honey.
Will you be Parul, my *champak*-flower sister?

SHUDHA How silly! How could I be your Parul *didi*? I am
Shudha, daughter of Shashi, the flower seller. Every day I
have to string many flower garlands. If I could spend the day
sitting like you, then I would be very happy.

AMAL What would you do if you had all day?

SHUDHA First, I would play with my *bene-bou* doll and marry
her off, and then there's my pussycat Meni. I would love to –
but it's getting late, and there won't be any flowers left if I
dawdle here.

AMAL Please talk to me a little longer, I'm enjoying it.

SHUDHA All right, if you are a good boy and stay here quietly,
on my way back with the flowers I'll stop for another chat.

AMAL Will you bring me a flower?

SHUDHA How can I? Can you pay?

AMAL I'll pay you when I grow up, when I've gone out
seeking work beyond the stream over there – then I'll repay
you.

SHUDHA I accept.

AMAL So you will return after picking flowers?

SHUDHA I will return.

AMAL Promise?

SHUDHA I promise.

AMAL You won't forget me? My name is Amal. Will you remember it?

SHUDHA No, I won't forget. You will be remembered.

[*She goes. Some boys enter*]

AMAL Brothers, where are you going? Stop for a while.

BOYS We're off to play.

AMAL What game are you going to play?

BOYS The ploughman's game.

FIRST BOY [*waving a stick*] This is our ploughshare.

SECOND BOY And we two will be the oxen.

AMAL Will you play all day?

BOYS Yes, the entire day.

AMAL After that, will you come back home along the path by the river?

A BOY Yes we will, when it's evening.

AMAL Please drop by here, in front of my house.

A BOY You can come with us now, come and play.

AMAL Doctor's ordered me not to go out.

A BOY Doctor! Why do you listen to him? Come on, let's go, it's getting late.

AMAL Please, friends, won't you play in the road outside my window, just for a little while?

A BOY But there's nothing here to play with.

AMAL All my toys are lying right here, take them all. It's no fun playing indoors all alone – the toys are just lying here, doing nothing, scattered in the dust.

BOYS Oh, what wonderful toys! Look at this ship! And this one with the matted hair is the old witch, Jatai. And here's a terrific sepoy to play soldiers with. Are you really giving us these? Won't you miss them?

AMAL No, I won't miss them, you can have them all.

A BOY So we don't have to give them back?

AMAL No, you don't need to.

A BOY Nobody will scold you?

AMAL  No, nobody will. But promise me that you will come
and play with them outside my house for a while each
morning. When they get worn out, I'll get you some new
ones.

A BOY  All right, friend, we'll come and play here every day.
Now let's take the sepoys and have a battle. Where can we
get muskets? Over there, there's a large piece of reed —
that'll do if we cut it up into pieces. But friend, you are
dozing off!

AMAL  Yes, I'm very sleepy. Why I feel sleepy so often, I don't
know. But I've been sitting up a long time and I can't sit any
longer; my back is aching.

A BOY  It's only the beginning of the day — why are you sleepy
already? Listen, there goes the gong.

AMAL  Yes — *dhong dhong dhong*; it lulls me to sleep.

BOYS  We're going now, but we'll be back in the morning.

AMAL  Before you go, let me ask you something. You go about
a lot. Do you know the Raja's messengers?

BOYS  Yes we do, quite well.

AMAL  Who are they? What are their names?

BOYS  One's called Badal, another's called Sharat, and there are
others.

AMAL  Well, if a letter comes for me, will they know who I
am?

A BOY  Why not? If your name is on the letter, they will
certainly find you.

AMAL  When you come back in the morning, please ask one of
them to stop by and meet me, will you?

BOYS  Yes, we will.

★

[*Amal in bed*]

AMAL Uncle, can't I even sit near the window today? Doctor really forbids it?

MADHAV Yes, he does. He says that sitting there every day is making your illness worse.

AMAL But Uncle, that's not right – I don't know about my illness, but I know I feel better when I sit there.

MADHAV Sitting there you have become friends with half the town – young and old alike. The area outside my door looks like a fairground. How will you stand the strain? Look at your face today – so wan!

AMAL If my friend the fakir comes by my window, he will miss me and go away again.

MADHAV Who is this fakir?

AMAL Every day he drops in and tells me tales of lands far and wide; he's so much fun to listen to.

MADHAV I don't know of any fakir.

AMAL He usually comes along about now. Uncle, I beg you, please ask him to come and sit with me.

[*Thakurda enters, dressed as a fakir*]

AMAL There you are, Fakir. Come and sit on my bed.

MADHAV What! Is that your—

THAKURDA [*winking*] I am the fakir.

MADHAV Of course you are.

AMAL Where have you been this time, Fakir?

FAKIR To the Island of Parrots. I just got back.

MADHAV Parrot Island, eh?

FAKIR Why so sceptical? Am I like you? When I travel, there are no expenses. I can go wherever I please.

AMAL [*clapping in delight*] You have so much fun. When I get well, you promised I could be your disciple, remember?

THAKURDA Of course. I will initiate you in my travel mantras, so that neither ocean nor mountain nor forest will bar your way.

MADHAV What is all this crazy talk?

THAKURDA Dearest Amal, there is nothing in mountain or ocean that frightens me – but if the doctor and your uncle get together, my mantras will be powerless.

AMAL You won't tell Doctor about all of this, will you Uncle? Now I promise I will lie here, sleep and do nothing. But the day I get well I will swear by Fakir's mantras, and then I shall cross the rivers, mountains and oceans.

MADHAV Hush, son, don't keep on talking about leaving – just to hear you makes me feel so sad.

AMAL Tell me, Fakir, what is Parrot Island like?

THAKURDA It is a rather weird place, a land of birds without any human beings. The birds do not speak or come to land, they only sing and fly around.

AMAL How fantastic! And is there ocean all around?

THAKURDA Yes, of course.

AMAL And are there green hills?

THAKURDA Yes, in the hills, the birds make their nests. In the evening, as the rays of the setting sun make the green hillsides glow, the parrots flock to their nests in a green swarm – and then the hills and the parrots become one single mass of green. It's indescribable.

AMAL And what about streams and waterfalls?

THAKURDA Absolutely! How could there not be?! They flow like molten diamonds, and how the drops dance! The small pebbles in the streams hum and murmur as the waters gush over them, until finally they plunge into the ocean. No one, not even a doctor, can restrain them for even a single second. I tell you, if the birds did not ostracize me as a mere man, I would make myself a small hut among the thousands of nests beside some waterfall and pass my days watching the waters and the ocean waves below.

AMAL  If I were a bird then—

THAKURDA  Then there would be a problem. I hear you have
already arranged with the *daiwallah* to sell *dai* when you grow
up. I don't think your business would do too well among
parrots. Who knows, you might even take a loss.

MADHAV  I can't take this nonsense any longer! You two will
drive me mad. I am going.

AMAL  Uncle, has my Daiwallah come and gone yet?

MADHAV  Of course he has. He won't make ends meet by
carrying things for you and your fancy fakir friend, or by
flitting around Parrot Island, will he? But he left a pot of *dai*
for you, and he said to tell you that his youngest niece is
getting married in his village – so he's rather busy, because he
has to go and book the flute players from Kalmipara.

AMAL  But he promised that his youngest niece would marry
me.

THAKURDA  Now we *are* in trouble.

AMAL  He said she would be a delicious bride, with a nose ring
and a red-striped sari. With her own hands she would milk a
black cow in the mornings and bring me an earthenware bowl
full of frothy, fresh milk. And at evening time, after taking a
lamp to the cowshed, she would settle down with me and tell
me tales of the seven *champak*-flower brothers.

THAKURDA  Well, she sounds like a wonderful bride. Even a
fakir like me feels tempted. But don't lose heart, my child, let
him marry off this niece. I give you my word that when your
time comes, there will be no shortage of nieces in his family.

MADHAV  Be off with you! This time you really have gone too
far.

[*Madhav goes*]

AMAL  Fakir, now that Uncle's gone, tell me secretly – has the
Raja sent a letter in my name to the post office?

THAKURDA  I hear that his letter has been despatched -- it is on
its way.

AMAL On its way? Which way? Is it coming by that path through the dense forest that you see when the sky clears after rain?

THAKURDA Yes. You seem to know it.

AMAL I know a lot, Fakir.

THAKURDA So I see – but how?

AMAL I can't say. I can see everything before my eyes, as if I have really seen it many times, but long ago – how long ago I cannot recall. Shall I describe it to you? I can see the Raja's messenger coming down the hillside alone, a lantern in his left hand and on his back a bag of letters, descending for days and nights; and then at the foot of the hills, where the waterfall becomes a winding stream, he follows the footpath along the bank and walks on through the corn; then comes the sugar cane field and he disappears into the narrow lane that cuts through the tall stems of sugar canes; and then he reaches the open meadow where the cricket chirps and where there is no one to be seen, only the snipe wagging their tails and poking at the mud with their beaks. I can picture it all. And the nearer he gets, the gladder I feel.

THAKURDA Though I do not have your fresh vision, still I see it.

AMAL Tell me Fakir, do you know the Raja?

THAKURDA I certainly do. I often go to his court to seek alms.

AMAL I see! When I get better I will go with you and seek alms from him. Can I go with you?

THAKURDA Son, you do not need to seek – he will give without your asking.

AMAL But I would rather seek. I'll go to the road outside his palace chanting 'Victory to the Raja!' and begging alms – maybe I will also dance with a cymbal. What do you think?

THAKURDA It sounds good; and if I accompany you, I will receive gifts, too. What will you ask him for?

AMAL  I will ask him to make me a Raja's messenger, who will go all over the land with a lantern in his hand delivering messages from door to door. You know, Fakir, someone has told me that as soon as I am well, he will teach me how to beg. I will go out begging with him wherever I please.

THAKURDA  And who is this person?

AMAL  Chidam.

THAKURDA  Which Chidam?

AMAL  Blind and lame Chidam. Every day he comes to my window. A boy just like me pushes him around in a cart with wheels. I've often told Chidam that when I'm better, I will push him around, too.

THAKURDA  That would be interesting, I can see.

AMAL  He is going to teach me all about begging. I tell Uncle that we should give Chidam something, but Uncle says that he's not really blind or lame. Perhaps he is not totally blind, but I know he does not see very well – I am sure of that.

THAKURDA  You are right. Whether you call him blind or not, it is true that he does not see well. But if he gets no alms from you, why does he like to sit with you?

AMAL  Because he hears all about different places from me. The poor fellow cannot see, but he listens when I tell him about all the lands that you tell me about. The other day you told me of the Land of No Weight, where everything weighs nothing and even a tiny hop will send you sailing over a hill. He really liked hearing about that place. Fakir, how do you reach that land?

THAKURDA  There's an inner road, but it's hard to find.

AMAL  Since the poor man is blind, he will never see any place, and will have to go on begging alms. Sometimes he moans to me about it, and I tell him that at least he visits a lot of places as a beggar – not everyone can do that.

THAKURDA  Son, why do you feel so sad to stay at home?

AMAL  Not sad, not now. Until now, my days did drag

endlessly – but I have seen the Raja's post office and I am happier, I even like sitting indoors. I know my letter will come, and the thought keeps me company, so I wait quite happily. But I have no idea what the Raja will write in his letter.

THAKURDA You do not need to know. As long as your name is there, that is enough.

[*Madhav enters*]

MADHAV Do you two realize what trouble you have got us into?

THAKURDA Why, what's up?

MADHAV Rumour has it that you are saying that the Raja has established his post office only to correspond with you.

THAKURDA So?

MADHAV And so the Headman has sent an anonymous letter about this to the Raja.

THAKURDA We all know that most things reach the Raja's ears.

MADHAV Then why didn't you watch yourself! Why did you take the names of rajas and maharajas in vain? You'll pull me in, too.

AMAL Fakir, will the Raja be angry?

THAKURDA Who says so? Why should he be? How can he rule his kingdom with majesty if he becomes mad at a child like you and a fakir like me?

AMAL You know, Fakir, since this morning there has been a kind of darkness in my mind; sometimes things look as if in a dream. I feel like being totally silent. I don't want to talk any more. Won't the Raja's letter ever come? Just now, this room seemed to vanish, as if everything – as if all—

THAKURDA [*fanning Amal*] It will come, my dear, the letter will come today.

[*Doctor enters*]

DOCTOR So how do you feel today?

AMAL Doctor, I am now feeling comfortable, all my pain seems to be going away.

DOCTOR [*aside to Madhav*] I don't like the look of that smile very much. When he says he feels better there is danger in store. As the great Chakradhar Dutta says—

MADHAV *Please*, Doctor, spare me Chakradhar Dutta. Just tell me what is the matter?

DOCTOR It looks as if we cannot hold on to him much longer. I recommended certain precautions, but he seems to have been exposed to the outside air.

MADHAV No, Doctor, I have done my utmost to keep him from such exposure. He has been kept indoors, and most of the time the place was kept shut.

DOCTOR The air has turned rather strange today, and I notice a severe draught blowing through your door. That is not at all good. You must shut the door at once. Try not to have any visitors for a few days. If people drop in, they can come through the back door. And you should get rid of this glare that comes through the window when the sun sets – it disturbs the patient's mind.

MADHAV Amal's eyes are closed. I think he's asleep. When I look at his face, it's as if – oh Doctor! this child who is not my own but whom I have loved as my own, will he be taken from me?

DOCTOR Who's coming now? It's the Headman, coming here. Drat! I must go, my friend. Go inside and shut your door tight. When I get home, I'll send over a strong dose – give it to the boy. If he can resist its power, he may yet pull through.

[*Doctor and Madhav go. Headman enters*]

HEADMAN Hey, boy!

THAKURDA [*suddenly standing up*] Ssh ssh . . . be quiet!

AMAL No, Fakir, you thought I was sleeping, but I wasn't. I heard everything. And I also heard faraway talk; my parents were talking beside my bed.

*[Madhav enters]*

HEADMAN  So, Madhav Dutta, these days you are rubbing shoulders with people in high places!

MADHAV  What do you mean, Headman? Don't make fun of us. We are very humble folk.

HEADMAN  But isn't your boy awaiting a letter from the Raja?

MADHAV  Here's a mere child, and sick and confused at that. Why do you listen to him?

HEADMAN  On the contrary. Where else could our Raja find a worthier correspondent than your boy? That must be why he has built his new royal post office outside your window. Hey little fellow, there is a letter from the Raja addressed to you.

AMAL  *[startled]* Really?

HEADMAN  And why not? – with your royal friendship! *[Hands him a blank sheet]* Ha ha ha, here's your letter.

AMAL  Are you teasing? Fakir, Fakir, tell me, is it really the letter?

THAKURDA  Yes, my boy, you have your Fakir's word, it is indeed the letter.

AMAL  But my eyes can't see anything – everything looks blank to me! Headman, sir, tell me what's in the letter.

HEADMAN  His Majesty writes, 'I will be visiting your home shortly. Prepare me a meal of puffed rice and parched paddy with molasses. I don't like to stay in the palace for one minute more than I have to.' Ha ha ha!

MADHAV  *[with folded hands]* I beg you, sir, I implore you, do not ridicule us.

THAKURDA  Ridicule! What ridicule? Who would dare to ridicule!

MADHAV  What! Thakurda, are you out of your mind?

THAKURDA  Maybe I am. But I also see letters on this blank sheet. The Raja writes that he will personally visit Amal, and that his royal physician will accompany him.

AMAL  Fakir – it is true! I hear his herald! Can you hear the call?

HEADMAN Ha ha ha! Let him become a bit more demented, then he'll hear it.

AMAL Headman, sir, I thought that you were angry with me, that you disliked me. I never imagined that you would bring me the Raja's letter – it never occurred to me. I must wash the dust from your feet.

HEADMAN Well, I'll say this much, the boy certainly has good manners. Not too bright, but he has a good heart.

AMAL The day is nearly over, I can feel it. There goes the evening gong – *dhong dhong dhong, dhong dhong dhong*. Has the evening star appeared yet, Fakir? Why don't I see it?

THAKURDA They have shut all your windows. I will open them.

[*A banging at the outside door*]

MADHAV What's that! Who's there? What an annoyance!

[*from outside*] Open the door.

MADHAV Who are you?

[*from outside*] Open the door.

MADHAV Headman, could it be robbers?

HEADMAN Who's there? Panchanan Morhal, Headman, speaking. Aren't you scared? [*To Madhav*] Listen! The banging has stopped. Even the toughest thieves know to fear Panchanan's voice!

MADHAV [*looking out of the window*] Look! They have smashed the door, that's why the banging has ceased.

[*Raja's Herald enters*]

RAJA'S HERALD His Majesty will arrive tonight.

HEADMAN Disaster!

AMAL When in the night, Herald? At what hour?

HERALD In the dead of night.

AMAL When my friend the watchman strikes his gong at the town's Lion Gate, *dhong dhong dhong, dhong dhong dhong* – at that hour?

HERALD Yes, at that hour. In the meantime, the Raja has sent his finest physician to attend to his little friend.

[*Raja's Physician enters*]

RAJA'S PHYSICIAN What's this! All closed up?! Open up, open up, open all the doors and windows. [*He feels Amal's body*] How are you feeling, young fellow?

AMAL Quite well, very well, Doctor. My illness is gone, my pain is gone. Now everything is open – I can see all the stars, shining on the far side of darkness.

PHYSICIAN When the Raja comes in the dead of night, will you rise and go forth with him?

AMAL I will, I have the will. I long to go forth. I will ask the Raja to show me the Pole Star in the heavens. Perhaps I have seen it many times, but have not recognized it.

PHYSICIAN The Raja will show you all things. [*To Madhav*] Please make the room clean and decorate it with flowers to greet our Raja. [*Pointing to the Headman*] That man should not be permitted here.

AMAL Oh no, Doctor, he is my friend. Before you came, he brought me the Raja's letter.

PHYSICIAN All right, my boy, since he is your friend, he may remain.

MADHAV [*whispering in Amal's ear*] My son, the Raja loves you, and he is coming here in person. Please entreat him to give us something. You know our condition – we are not well off.

AMAL Uncle, I have already thought about it – do not worry.

MADHAV What will you request?

AMAL I will beg him to make me a royal messenger in his post office. I will deliver his messages to homes everywhere.

MADHAV [*striking his forehead*] Alas, such is my fate!

AMAL Uncle, when the Raja comes, what shall we offer him?

HERALD The Raja has commanded a meal of puffed rice and parched paddy with molasses.

AMAL  Headman, those were your very words! You knew everything about the Raja, and we knew nothing!

HEADMAN  If you would send someone to my house, we will endeavour to provide His Majesty with good—

PHYSICIAN  No need for it. Now you must all be calm. It is coming, coming, his sleep is coming. I will sit beside his pillow as he drifts off. Blow out the lamp; let the starlight come in; his sleep has arrived.

MADHAV  [to Thakurda] Thakurda, why so hushed, with your palms pressed together like a statue? I feel a kind of dread. These do not seem like good omens. Why has the room been darkened? What use is starlight?

THAKURDA  Be quiet, unbeliever! Do not speak.

[Shudha enters]

SHUDHA  Amal?

PHYSICIAN  He has fallen asleep.

SHUDHA  I have brought flowers for him. Can I put them in his hand?

PHYSICIAN  Yes, you may give him your flowers.

SHUDHA  When will he awake?

PHYSICIAN  Directly the Raja comes and calls him.

SHUDHA  Will you whisper a word in his ear for me?

PHYSICIAN  What shall I say?

SHUDHA  Tell him, 'Shudha has not forgotten you.'

# MEMOIRS

There are two books of memoirs by Tagore, both concerned with his early life up to his mid-twenties. *Jiban Smriti* (*My Reminiscences*) was written in 1911, when he was fifty; *Chhelebela* (*My Boyhood Days*), a slimmer book, appeared in 1940, when he was almost eighty.

Both books, especially the first, are among Tagore's most enchanting writings. W. B. Yeats thought *My Reminiscences* 'a most valuable and rich work', and urged Tagore to write about his adult life too. Reading *My Reminiscences* after *Gitanjali*, the prose poems that had so greatly stirred him, Yeats must suddenly have comprehended the complexity of the culture that had given birth to such simplicity.

Through anecdotes, seamlessly interlinked not so much by chronology but by the alchemy of memory, Tagore reveals the interplay of two great civilizations at the height of the Bengal Renaissance. He and his gifted brothers were able to borrow at will from both Indian and European literature, music and thought in an atmosphere that was gloriously open and creative.

Being anecdotes, however, they are coloured by Tagore's recollected emotions and emphases. He claims to have been virtually a complete dunce at school, for instance – which is unlikely – and he paints a picture of a harsh regime at home under servant rule, in which he was forbidden to wear socks and shoes until he was ten. But according to the Tagore family cash book, two dozen pairs of socks were bought for Rabi in one month alone, when he was not yet four!

It is likely that, rather than clothes, affection was what was lacking, and this lack of love was transformed into a lack of clothes in Rabi's fertile imagination. Certainly, he never enjoyed a close relationship with either his mother or his father, whose austere and independent personality stands out from his son's account of their joint trip to the Himalayas in 1873. But at the same time, even at the age of eleven, Rabi was already so determined to be a free spirit that one feels he would have rebelled against any great display of affection by his parents.

Freedom is the keynote of Tagore's memoirs. Freedom from orthodox education, freedom from artistic conventions, freedom from conventional beliefs of all kinds. At the end of *My Reminiscences*, he writes:

> In other parts of the world there is no end to the movement, clamour and revelry of life. We, like beggar-maids, stand outside and look longingly on. When have we had the wherewithal to deck ourselves and join in? Only in a land where an animus of divisiveness reigns supreme, and innumerable petty barriers separate one from another, must this longing to express a larger life in one's own remain unsatisfied. I strained to reach humanity in my youth, as in my childhood I yearned for the outside world from within the chalk ring drawn around me by the servants: how unique, unattainable and remote it seemed! And yet if we cannot get in touch with it, if no breeze can blow from it, no current flow out of it, no path be open to the free passage of travellers, then the dead things accumulating around us will never be removed but continue to mount up until they smother all vestige of life.

This was written in mid-1911. Within a year, Tagore set off for the West, so as to get in direct touch with the 'movement, clamour and revelry of life'.

# FROM *My Reminiscences*

I do not know who has painted the pictures of my life imprinted on my memory. But whoever he is, he is an artist. He does not take up his brush simply to copy everything that happens; he retains or omits things just as he fancies; he makes many a big thing small and small thing big; he does not hesitate to exchange things in the foreground with things in the background. In short, his task is to paint pictures, not to write history. The flow of events forms our external life, while within us a series of pictures is painted. The two correspond, but are not identical.

We do not make time for a proper look at this inner canvas. Now and then we catch glimpses of a fragment of it, but the bulk remains dark, invisible to us. Why the painter ceaselessly paints, when he will complete his work, and what gallery is destined to hang his paintings, who can say?

Some years ago, someone questioned me on the events of my past and I had occasion to explore this picture-chamber. I had imagined I would stop after selecting a few items from my life story. But as I opened the door I discovered that memories are not history but original creations by the unseen artist. The diverse colours scattered about are not reflections of the outside world but belong to the painter himself, and come passion-tinged from his heart – thereby making the record on the canvas unfit for use as evidence in a court of law.

But though the attempt to gather a precise and logical story from memory's storehouse may be fruitless, it is fascinating to shuffle the pictures. This enchantment took hold of me.

As long as we are journeying, stopping only to rest at various shelters by the wayside, we do not see these pictures – things seem merely useful, too concrete for remembrance. It is when the traveller no longer needs them and has reached his destination that pictures start to come. All the cities, meadows, rivers and hills that he passed through in the morning of his life float into his mind as he relaxes at the close of day. Thus did I look leisurely backwards, and was engrossed by what I saw.

Was this interest aroused solely by natural affection for my past? Some personal attachment there must have been, of course, but the pictures had a value independent of this. There is no event in my reminiscences worthy of being preserved for all time. Literary value does not depend on the importance of a subject, however. Whatever one has truly felt, if it can be made sensible to others, will always be respected. If pictures which have taken shape in memory can be expressed in words, they will be worthy of a place in literature.

So it is as literary material that I offer my memory pictures. To regard them as an attempt at autobiography would be a mistake. In such a light they would appear both redundant and incomplete.

*

## Within and Without

Luxury was a thing almost unknown in my early childhood. The standard of living was then much plainer than it is now, as a whole. But it meant at least that the children of our household were entirely free from the fuss of being too much looked after. The fact is that for guardians the looking after of children may be an occasional treat; but for children being looked after is always an unmitigated nuisance.

We lived under the rule of the servants. To save themselves trouble they virtually suppressed our right of free movement. This was hard to bear — but the neglect was also a kind of independence. It left our minds free, unpampered and unburdened by all the usual bother over food and dress.

What we ate had nothing to do with delicacies. Our clothing, were I to itemize it, would invite a modern boy's scorn. On no pretext might we wear socks or shoes until we had passed our tenth year. In the cold weather a second cotton shirt over our first one was deemed sufficient. It never entered our heads to consider ourselves ill clad. Only when old Niyamat, the tailor, forgot to put a pocket into a shirt would we complain – for the boy has yet to be born who is so poor that he cannot stuff his pockets; by a merciful dispensation of providence, there is not much difference in wealth between boys whose parents are rich and poor. We used to own a pair of slippers each, but not always where we put our feet. The slippers were generally several moves ahead of us, propelled there by the following feet, their *raison d'être* thrown into doubt with every step we took.

Our elders in every way kept a great distance from us, in their dress and eating, coming and going, work, conversation and amusement. We caught glimpses of all these activities, but they were beyond our reach. Elders have become cheap to modern children, too readily accessible; and so have all objects of desire. Nothing ever came so easily to us. Many trivial things were rarities, and we lived mostly in the hope of attaining, when we were old enough, the things that the distant future held in trust for us. The result was that what little we did get we enjoyed to the utmost; from skin to core nothing was thrown away. The modern child of a well-to-do family nibbles at only half the things he gets; the greater part of his world is wasted on him.

Our days were spent in the servants' quarters in the south-east corner of the outer apartments. One of our servants was Shyam, a dark chubby boy with curly locks, hailing from the district of Khulna. He would place me in a selected spot, trace a chalk line around me, and warn me with solemn face and uplifted finger of the perils of transgressing this circle. Whether the danger was physical or mental I never fully understood, but fear certainly possessed me. I had read in the *Ramayana* of the tribulations of Sita after she left the ring drawn by Lakshman, so I never for a minute doubted my ring's potency.

Just below the window of this room was a tank with a bathing ghat; on its west bank, along the garden wall, stood an immense banyan tree; and to the south was a fringe of coconut palms. Like a prisoner in a cell, I would spend the whole day peering through the closed Venetian shutters, gazing out at this scene as on a picture in a book. From early morning our neighbours would drop in one by one to take their baths. I knew the time of each one's arrival. I was familiar with the oddities of each one's toilet. One would stop his ears with his fingers while taking his regulation number of dips, and then depart. Another would not risk complete immersion but be content to squeeze a wet towel repeatedly over his head. A third would carefully flick the surface impurities away from him with a rapid strokes of his arms, and then suddenly plunge in. Another would jump in from the top steps without any preliminaries at all. Yet another would lower himself slowly in, step by step, while muttering his morning prayers. Then there was one who was always in a hurry, hastening home as soon as his dip was over, and a second who was in no sort of hurry at all, following a leisurely bath with a good rub-down, changing from wet bathing clothes into clean dry ones with a careful adjustment of the folds of his waist-cloth, then ending with a turn or two in the outer garden and the gathering of flowers, after which he would finally saunter homewards, radiating cool comfort as he went. All this would go on till past noon. Then the bathing place would become deserted and silent. Only the ducks would remain, paddling about and diving after water snails or frantically preening their feathers, for the rest of the day.

When solitude thus reigned over the water, my whole attention would focus on the shadows beneath the banyan tree. Some of its aerial roots, creeping down its trunk, had formed a dark complication of coils at its base. It was as if by some sorcery this obscure corner of the world had escaped the regime of natural laws, as if some improbable dreamworld, unobserved by the Creator, had lingered on into the light of modern times. Whom I saw there, and what those beings did, I am unable to express in intelligible language. It was of this banyan tree that I later wrote:

> Day and night you stand like an ascetic with matted hair.
> Do you ever think of the boy whose fancy played with your
> shadows?

That majestic banyan tree is no more, alas, and neither is the tank that served as her mirror. Many of those who once bathed in it have departed too, merging with the shade of the great tree. And the boy, grown older, has put down roots far and wide and now contemplates the pattern of shadow and sunlight, sorrow and cheer, cast by the tangled skein.

To leave the house was forbidden to us, in fact we did not even have the run of the interior. We had to get our glimpses of nature from behind barriers. Beyond my reach stretched this limitless thing called the Outside, flashes, sounds and scents of which used momentarily to come and touch me through interstices. It seemed to want to beckon me through the shutters with a variety of gestures. But it was free and I was bound – there was no way of our meeting. So its attraction was all the stronger. Today the chalk line has been wiped away but the confining circle is still there. The horizon is just as far away; what lies beyond it is still out of reach, and I am reminded of the poem I wrote when I was older:

> The tame bird was in a cage, the free bird was in the forest,
> They met when the time came, it was a decree of fate.
> The free bird cries, 'O my love, let us fly to the wood.'
> The cage bird whispers, 'Come hither, let us both live in the
> cage.'

Says the free bird, 'Among bars, where is the room to spread
    one's wings?'
'Alas,' cries the cage bird, 'I should not know where to sit
    perched in the sky.'

The parapets of our terraced roofs were higher than my head. When I had grown taller and when the tyranny of the servants had relaxed, when, with the coming of a newly married bride into the house, I had achieved some recognition as a companion of her leisure, I would sometimes climb to the terrace in the middle of the day. By that time everybody in the house would have finished their meal and there would be an interlude in the business of the household; over the inner apartments would settle the quiet of a siesta, with wet bathing clothes hanging over the parapets to dry, the crows picking at the leavings on a refuse heap in the corner of the yard; and in the solitude, the cage bird and the free bird would commune with each other, beak to beak.

I loved to stand and look. My gaze fell first on the row of coconut trees at the far edge of our inner garden. Through these I could see the Singhi's Garden with its cluster of huts and its tank, and at the edge of the tank the dairy of our milkwoman, Tara; and beyond that, mixed up with the treetops, the various shapes and different levels of the terraced roofs of Calcutta flashing under the whiteness of the midday sun, stretching away and merging with the greyish blue of the eastern horizon. And some of these far-distant dwellings, from which jutted out a covered stairway leading to the roof, seemed like upraised fingers signalling to me, with a wink, that there were mysteries below. The beggar at the palace door imagines impossible treasures in its strong-rooms. I can hardly describe the spirit of fun and freedom which these unknown dwellings seemed to me to suggest. In the farthest recesses of a sky full of burning sunshine I would just be able to detect the thin shrill cry of a kite; and from the lane adjoining the Singhi's Garden, past the houses dormant in noonday slumber, would float the singsong of the bangle-seller – 'chai churi chai' – at such times my whole being would float away too.

My father was constantly on the move, hardly ever at home. His rooms on the third storey remained shut up. I would pass my hands through the Venetian shutters, open the latch of the door and spend the afternoon lying motionless on his sofa at the south end. In the first place, a closed room is always fascinating; then there was the lure of stolen entry, with its savour of mystery; finally, there was the deserted terrace outside with the sun's rays beating upon it, which would set me dreaming.

And there was yet another attraction. The waterworks had just started up in Calcutta, and in the first flush of triumphant entry it did not stint its supply even to the Indian quarters. In that golden age, piped water used to flow even to my father's third-storey rooms. Turning on his shower-tap I would take an untimely bath to my heart's content – not so much for the feel of the water, as to indulge my desire to do just as I fancied. The simultaneous joy of liberty and fear of being caught made that shower of municipal water seem like arrows of delight.

Perhaps because the possibility of contact with the outside was so remote, the excitement of it came to me much more readily. When things surround us at every hand, the mind becomes lazy, commissions others, and forgets that the joy of a feast depends more on nourishment by imagination than on external things. This is the chief lesson which infancy has to teach a human being. Then his possessions are few and trivial, yet he needs no more to be happy. For the unfortunate youngster who has an unlimited number of playthings, the world of play is spoilt.

To call our inner garden a garden is to go too far. It consisted of a citron tree, a couple of plum trees of different varieties, and a row of coconut trees. In the centre was a paved circle, cracked and invaded by grasses and weeds waving their victorious standards. Only those flowering plants which refused to die of gardener's neglect continued to perform their duties. In the northern corner was a rice-husking shed, where when need arose the occupants of the inner apartments would congregate. This last vestige of rural life in Calcutta has since owned defeat and slunk silently away.

None the less I have an idea that the Garden of Eden was no grander than this garden of ours, for Adam and his paradise were alike naked: they needed no embellishment with material things. Only since he tasted the fruit of the tree of knowledge, and until such time as he can fully digest it, has man's need for external trappings come to dominate him. Our inner garden was my paradise; it was enough for me. I clearly remember how in the early autumn dawn I would run there as soon as I was awake. A whiff of dewy grass and foliage would rush to meet me, and the morning, with cool fresh light, would peep at me over the top of the eastern garden wall from below the trembling tassels of the coconut palms.

Another piece of vacant land to the north of the house to this day we call the *golabari*. The name shows that in some remote past this must have been the barn where the year's store of grain was kept. In those days town and country visibly resembled each other, like brother and sister in childhood. Now the family likeness can hardly be traced. This *golabari* would be my holiday haunt when I got the chance. I did not really go there to play – it was the place itself that drew me. Why, it is difficult to tell. Perhaps its being a deserted bit of waste land lying in an out-of-the-way corner gave it charm. Entirely outside the living quarters, it bore no stamp of functionality; what's more, it was as unadorned as it was useless, for no one had ever planted anything there. It was a desert spot. No doubt that is why it offered free rein to a boy's imagination. Whenever I saw a loophole in my warders' vigilance and could contrive to reach the *golabari*, I felt I had a real holiday.

Yet another region existed in our house and this I have still not succeeded in finding. A little girl playmate of the same age as I called it the 'King's palace'. 'I have just been there,' she would sometimes tell me. But somehow the right moment for her to take me never turned up. It was said to be a wonderful place, with playthings as fabulous as the games that were played there. It seemed to me it had to be somewhere very near – perhaps in the first or second storey – but I never seemed able to reach it. How often did I say to my friend, 'Just tell me, is it really inside the house or outside?' And she would always reply, 'No, no, it's right here in this house.' I would sit and wonder: 'Where? Where? Don't I know all the rooms in the house?' I never cared to enquire who the King was; his palace remains undiscovered to this day; only this much is clear – it lay within our house.

Looking back at my childhood I feel the thought that recurred most often was that I was surrounded by mystery. Something undreamt of was lurking everywhere, and every day the uppermost question was: when, oh! when, would we come across it? It was as if Nature held something cupped in her hands and was asking us with a smile 'What d'you think I have?' We had no idea there might be any limit to the answer.

I vividly remember a custard apple seed which I planted and kept in a corner of the south veranda, and used to water every day. The idea that the seed might actually grow into a tree kept me in a state of fluttering anticipation. Custard apple seeds today still have a habit of sprouting, but no longer to the accompaniment of that feeling of wonder. The fault lies not in the custard apple but in my mind.

Once we stole some rocks from an elder cousin's rockery and started a little rockery of our own. The plants we sowed in its crevices we cared for so excessively that only the stoicism of vegetables can account for their survival. Words cannot express the excitement this miniature mountain top held for us. We were never in any doubt that our creation would be a wonderful thing to our elders too. The day that we tried to put this to proof, however, our hillock, with all its rocks and all its vegetation vanished from the corner of our room. The knowledge that the schoolroom floor was not a proper base for mountain-building was imparted so rudely, and with such abruptness, that it gave us quite a shock. A weight equivalent to that of the stone lifted from the floor settled on our minds as we realized the gulf between our fancies and the will of our elders.

How intensely did life throb for us! Earth, water, foliage and sky all spoke to us and would not be disregarded. How often were we struck by poignant regret that we could see only the upper storey of the earth and knew nothing of its inner storey! All our plans were aimed at prying beneath its dust-coloured cover. If we could drive in bamboo after bamboo, one over the other, we might somehow get in touch with its inmost depths.

During the Magh festival a series of wooden pillars used to be planted round the outer courtyard to support chandeliers. The digging of holes for these would begin on the first of Magh. Preparations for a festival interest children everywhere, but this digging had a special attraction for me. Though I had watched it done year after year – and seen a hole grow deeper and deeper till the digger had completely disappeared inside – nothing extraordinary, nothing worthy of the quest of a prince or knight, had ever appeared; yet every time I had the feeling that a lid was about to be lifted off a treasure chest. A little bit more digging would surely do it. Year after year that little bit more never got done. The mysterious veil was tweaked but not drawn. Why did the elders, who could do whatever they pleased, rest content with such shallow delving? If we younger generation had been in charge, the inmost enigma of the earth would not have been allowed to remain covered for very long.

The thought that behind every portion of the blue vault of the sky there reposed the secrets of the heavens also spurred our imaginations. When our pundit, wishing to illustrate some lesson in our Bengali science primer, told us that the sky was not a finite blue sphere, we were thunderstruck! 'Put ladder upon ladder,' he said, 'and go on mounting, but you will never bump your head.' He must be mean with his ladders, I thought, and aloud said in a tone of rising indignation, 'And what if we put more ladders, and more and more?' When I grasped that to multiply ladders was fruitless I was dumbfounded. Surely, I concluded after much pondering, such an astounding fact must be part of the secret knowledge of schoolmasters, known to them and to no one else.

*

## My Father

Shortly after my birth my father took to constant travel. So it is no exaggeration to say that in my early childhood I hardly knew him. He would now and then come back home all of a sudden, and with him came outsiders as servants with whom I felt extremely eager to make friends. Once he brought a young Punjabi servant named Lenu. The cordiality of the reception we gave him would have been worthy of Maharaja Ranjit Singh himself. Not only was he a foreigner, but a Punjabi too – this really stole our hearts away. We had the same reverence for the whole Punjabi nation as we did for Bhima and Arjuna of the *Mahabharata*. They were warriors, and if they had sometimes lost the fight, that was clearly the enemy's fault. It was glorious to have Lenu of the Punjab in our very home.

My sister-in-law had a model warship under a glass case which, when wound up, rocked on blue-painted silken waves to the tinkling of a musical box. I would beg hard for the loan of this to display its marvels to the admiring Lenu.

Caged in the house as we were, anything savouring of foreign parts had a peculiar charm for me. It was one of the reasons why

I made so much of Lenu. It was also why Gabriel, the Jew, with his embroidered gaberdine, who came to sell attar and scented oils, stirred me so; and why the huge Kabulis, with their dusty, baggy trousers and knapsacks and bundles, worked my young mind into a fearful fascination.

So, when my father came, we would be content with wandering among his entourage and keeping the company of his servants. We did not reach his actual presence.

Once, while my father was away in the Himalayas, that old bogey of the British Government, a Russian invasion, became a subject of agitated conversation among the people. Some well-meaning lady friend had enlarged on the impending danger to my mother with all the fancy of a prolific imagination. How could anybody tell from which of the Tibetan passes the Russian host might suddenly flash forth like a baleful comet?

My mother was seriously alarmed. The other members of the family possibly did not share her misgivings so, despairing of grown-up sympathy, she sought my boyish support. 'Won't you write to your father about the Russians?' she asked.

My letter, bearing the tidings of my mother's anxieties, was the first I wrote to my father. I did not know how to begin or end a letter, or anything at all about it. I went to Mahananda, the estate *munshi*. My resulting form of address was doubtless correct enough, but the sentiments could not have escaped the musty flavour inseparable from correspondence emanating from an estate office.

I had a reply. My father asked me not to be afraid; if the Russians came he would drive them away himself. This confident assurance did not seem to have the effect of relieving my mother's fears, but it served to free me from all timidity as regards my father. After that I wanted to write to him every day, and pestered Mahananda accordingly. Unable to withstand my importunity he would make out drafts for me to copy. But I did not know that there was postage to be paid for. I had an idea that letters placed in Mahananda's hands got to their destination without any need for further worry. It is hardly necessary to add that Mahananda was old enough to ensure that these letters never reached the Himalayan hilltops.

After his long absences, when my father came home even for a few days, the whole house seemed filled with the gravity of his presence. We would see our elders at certain hours, formally robed in their *chogas*, passing to his rooms with restrained gait and sober mien, casting away any *pan* they might have been chewing. Everyone seemed on the alert. To make sure that nothing went wrong, my mother would superintend the cooking herself. The old retainer Kinu, with his white livery and crested turban, on guard at my father's door, would warn us not to be boisterous in the veranda in front of his rooms during his midday siesta. We had to walk past quietly, talking in whispers, and dared not even take a peep inside.

On one occasion my father came home to invest the three of us with the sacred thread. With the help of Pandit Vedantavagish he had collected the old Vedic rites for the purpose. For days at a time we were taught to chant in correct accents the selections from the *Upanishads*, arranged under the name of *Brahma Dharma*, by my father seated in the prayer hall with Becharam Babu. Finally, with shaven heads and gold rings in our ears, we three budding Brahmins went into a three-days' retreat in a portion of the third storey.

It was great fun. The earrings gave us a good handle to pull each other's ears with. We found a little drum lying in one of the rooms; taking this we would stand out in the veranda, and when we caught sight of any servant passing along in the storey below, we rapped a tattoo on it. This would make the man look up, only to avert his eyes and beat a hasty retreat at the next moment. We certainly cannot claim that we passed these days of our retirement in ascetic meditation.

I am convinced that boys like us must have been common in

the hermitages of old. If some ancient document has it that the ten- or twelve-year-old Saradwata or Sarngarava spent the whole of his boyhood offering oblations and chanting mantras, we are not compelled to put unquestioning faith in the statement; because the book of Boy Nature is even older and is also more authentic.

After we had attained full Brahminhood I became very keen on repeating the *gayatri*. I would meditate on it with great concentration. It is hardly a text of which the full meaning may be grasped at that age. I distinctly remember what efforts I made to extend the range of my consciousness with the help of the initial invocation of 'Earth, firmament and heaven'. How I felt or thought it is difficult to express clearly, but this much is certain: that to be clear about the meaning of words is not the most important part of the process of human understanding.

The main object of teaching is not to give explanations, but to knock at the doors of the mind. If any boy is asked to give an account of what is awakened in him by such knocking, he will probably say something silly. For what happens within is much bigger than what comes out in words. Those who pin their faith on university examinations as the test of education take no account of this.

I can recollect many things which I did not understand, but which stirred me deeply. Once, on the roof terrace of our riverside villa, at the sudden gathering of clouds my eldest brother repeated aloud some stanzas from *The Cloud Messenger* by Kalidasa. I could not understand a word of the Sanskrit, neither did I need to. His ecstatic declamation and the sonorous rhythm were enough for me.

Then, again, before I could properly understand English, a profusely illustrated edition of *The Old Curiosity Shop* fell into my hands. I went through the whole of it, though at least nine-tenths of the words were unknown to me. Yet, with the vague ideas conjured up by the rest, I spun out a variously coloured thread on which to string the illustrations. Any university examiner would have given me zero, but for me the reading of the book had not proved quite so empty.

Another time I had accompanied my father for a trip on the Ganges in his houseboat. Among the books he had with him was an old Fort William edition of Jayadeva's *Gita Govinda*, printed in Bengali script. The verses were not in separate lines, but ran on like prose. I did not know any Sanskrit then, yet because of my knowledge of Bengali many of the words were familiar. How often I read that *Gita Govinda* I cannot say. I particularly remember this line:

> The night extinguished in solitary forest exile.

It roused a feeling of beauty in my mind. That one Sanskrit word *nibhrita-nikunja-griham*, meaning 'solitary forest exile', was quite enough for me.

I had to work out for myself the intricate metre of Jayadeva's poetry, because its divisions were lost in the clumsy prose form of the book. And this discovery gave me very great delight. Of course I did not fully comprehend Jayadeva's meaning. One could not even truthfully say that I grasped it partly. But the sound of the words and the lilt of the metre filled my mind with pictures of such grace that I was impelled to copy out the whole book for my own use.

The same thing happened, when I was a little older, with a verse from Kalidasa's *Birth of the War-God*. The verse really moved me, though the only words of which I gathered the sense, were 'the zephyr wafting the spray from the falling waters of the sacred Mandakini and trembling the deodar leaves'. They left me pining to taste the whole. When a pundit later explained to me that in the next two lines the breeze 'split the feathers of the peacock plume on the head of the eager deer-hunter', the thinness of the conceit disappointed me. I was much better off when I had relied only upon my imagination to complete the verse.

Whoever goes back to his early childhood will agree that his greatest gains were not in proportion to the completeness of his understanding. Our *kathakas* know this very well: when they give public recitals, their narratives always have a good proportion of ear-filling Sanskrit words and abstruse remarks calculated not to be fully understood by their simple hearers, but only to be suggestive.

The value of such suggestion is by no means to be despised by those who measure education in terms of material gains and losses. They insist on trying to tot up the account and find out exactly how much of a lesson can be rendered up. But children, and those who are not over-educated, dwell in that primal paradise where humans can obtain knowledge without wholly comprehending each step. Only when that paradise is lost comes the evil day when everything has to be understood. The road that leads to knowledge without going through the dreary process of understanding is the royal road. If that be barred, even though commerce may continue, the open sea and the mountain top cease to be possible of access.

So, as I was saying, though at that age I could not realize the full meaning of the *gayatri*, something in me could do without a complete understanding. I am reminded of a day when, as I was seated on the cement floor in a corner of our schoolroom meditating on the text, my eyes overflowed with tears. Why they came I do not know; to a strict cross-questioner I would probably have given some explanation having nothing to do with the *gayatri*. The fact is that what goes on in the inner recesses of consciousness is not always known to the surface dweller.

★

# A Journey with my Father

My shaven head after the sacred thread ceremony caused me one great anxiety. However partial Eurasian lads may be to the sacred Cow, their reverence for the Brahmin is definitely minimal. I expected that at school, apart from other missiles, our shaven heads were sure to be pelted with jeers. While I kept worrying over this possibility I was summoned upstairs to my father. How would I like to go with him to the Himalayas? Away from the Bengal Academy and off to the Himalayas! How would I like it? Oh, I would have needed to rend the skies with a shout to give some idea of How!

The day we left home my father, as was his habit, assembled the whole family in the prayer hall for divine service. After I had taken the dust of my elders' feet I got into the carriage with my father. This was the first time in my life that I had a full suit of clothes made for me. My father had selected the pattern and colour himself. A gold-embroidered velvet cap completed my costume. This I carried in my hand, assailed as I was with misgivings about its impact atop my hairless head. As I got into the carriage my father insisted on my wearing it, so I had to put it on. Every time he looked away I took it off. Every time I caught his eye it had to resume its proper place.

My father was very particular in all his arrangements. He disliked leaving things vague or undetermined, and never allowed slovenliness or make-do. He had a well-defined code to regulate his relations with others and theirs with him. In this he was different from the generality of his countrymen. Among the rest of us a little laxity this way or that did not signify; in our dealings with him we therefore had to be anxiously careful. The size and significance of a task did not concern him so much as failure to maintain its required standard.

My father also had a way of picturing to himself every detail of what he wanted done. On the occasion of any ceremonial gathering at which he could not be present, he would think out and assign a place for each thing, a duty for each member of the family, a seat for each guest; nothing would escape him. After everything was over he would ask each one for a separate account and gain a complete impression of the whole for himself. So while I was with him on his travels, though nothing would induce him to interfere in how I amused myself, no loophole was left in the strict rules of conduct prescribed for me in other respects.

Our first halt was to be at Bolpur for a few days. Satya had been there a short time before with his parents. No self-respecting nineteenth-century boy would have credited the account of his travels which he gave us on his return. But I was different, and had had no opportunity of learning to determine the line between the possible and the impossible. Our *Mahabharata* and *Ramayana* gave us no clue to it. Nor had we then any illustrated books to guide us. All the hard-and-fast rules that govern the world we learnt by knocking ourselves against them.

Satya had told us that, unless one was exceedingly expert, getting into a railway carriage was a terribly dangerous affair – the least slip, and it was all up. Once aboard, a fellow had to hold on to his seat with all his might, otherwise the tremendous jolt on starting might throw him off – there was no telling where to.

When we got to the railway station I was all aquiver. So easily did we enter our compartment that I felt sure the worst was yet to come. And when, at length, we made an absurdly smooth start without any hint of adventure, I felt woefully disappointed.

The train sped on; the broad fields bordered by blue-green trees and the villages nestling in their shade flew past in a stream of pictures that melted away like a flood of mirages. It was evening when we reached Bolpur. As I got into the palanquin I closed my eyes. I wanted to preserve the whole of the wonderful vision to be unfolded before my waking eyes in the morning light. The freshness of the experience would be spoilt, I feared, by incomplete glimpses caught in the vagueness of twilight.

When I woke at dawn I was tremulously excited as I stepped outside. My predecessor had told me that Bolpur had one feature which was to be found nowhere else in the world. This was a path leading from the main buildings to the servants' quarters, which, though not covered over in any way, did not allow a ray of sun or a drop of rain to touch anybody passing along it. I started to hunt for this wonderful path, but the reader will perhaps not wonder at my failure to find it to this day.

Town boy that I was, I had never seen a rice field and had a charming portrait of the cowherd boy, of whom we had read, pictured on the canvas of my imagination. I had heard from Satya that the Bolpur house was surrounded by fields of ripening rice, and that playing in these with cowherd boys was an everyday affair, of which the plucking, cooking and eating of the rice was the crowning feature. I eagerly looked about me. Where was the rice field on all that barren heath? Cowherd boys might have been somewhere about, but how to distinguish them from any other boys was the question!

What I could not see did not take me long to get over – what I did see was quite enough. There was no servant rule, and the only ring which encircled me was the blue of the horizon, drawn around these solitudes by their presiding goddess. Within this I was free to move about as I chose.

Though I was still a mere child my father did not place any restriction on my wanderings. In the hollows of the sandy soil the rain water had ploughed deep furrows, carving out miniature mountain ranges full of red gravel and pebbles of various shapes through which ran tiny streams, revealing the geography of Lilliput. From this region I would gather in the lap of my tunic many curious pieces of stone and take the collection to my father. He never made light of my labours. On the contrary he was enthusiastic.

'Splendid!' he exclaimed, 'Wherever did you get all these?'

'There are many many more, thousands and thousands!' I burst out. 'I could bring as many every day.'

'That *would* be nice!' he replied. 'Why not decorate my little hill with them?'

An attempt had been made to dig a tank in the garden but, the water table proving too low, the digging had been abandoned with the excavated earth left piled up in a hillock. On top of this my father used to sit for his morning prayer, and as he did so the sun would rise at the edge of the undulating expanse which stretched away to the eastern horizon in front of him. It was this hill he asked me to decorate.

I was very troubled, on leaving Bolpur, that I could not carry away my store of stones. I had not yet understood the encumbrance entailed and that I had no absolute claim on a thing merely because I had collected it. If fate had granted me my prayer, as I had dearly desired, and determined that I should carry this load of stones about with me forever, today this story would be no laughing matter.

In one of the ravines I came upon a hollow full of spring water which overflowed as a little rivulet, where tiny fish played and battled their way up the current.

'I've found such a lovely spring,' I told my father. 'Couldn't we get our bathing- and drinking-water from there?'

'Perfect,' he agreed, sharing my rapture, and gave orders for our water supply to be drawn from that spring.

I was never tired of roaming these miniature valleys and plateaus in hopes of alighting on something never before discovered. I was the Livingstone of this land which looked as if seen through the wrong end of a telescope. Everything there, the dwarf date palms, the scrubby wild plums and the stunted *jambolans*, was in keeping with the miniature mountain ranges, the rivulet and the tiny fish.

Probably to teach me to be careful my father placed some

small change in my charge and required me to keep an account of it. He also entrusted me with the winding of his valuable gold watch. He overlooked the risk of damage in his desire to train me to a sense of duty. When we went out together for our morning walk he asked me to give alms to any beggars we came across. I could never render him a proper account at the end. One day my balance was larger than the account warranted.

'I really must make you my cashier,' observed my father. 'Money seems to have a way of growing in your hands!'

His watch I wound with such indefatigable zeal that very soon it had to be sent to the watchmaker's in Calcutta.

I am reminded of the occasions in later life when I used to tender the estate accounts to my father, who was then living in Park Street. I would do this on the second or third of every month. He was by then unable to read them himself. I had first to read out the totals under each heading, and if he had any doubts on any point he would ask for the details. If I made any attempt to slur over or conceal any item I feared he would not like, it was sure to come out. These first few days of the month were very anxious ones for me.

As I have said, my father had the habit of keeping everything clearly before his mind – whether figures of accounts, or ceremonial arrangements, or additions or alterations to property. He had never seen the new prayer hall at Bolpur, and yet he was familiar with every detail of it from questioning those who came to see him after a visit there. He had an extraordinary memory, and when once he got hold of a fact it never escaped him.

My father had marked his favourite verses in his copy of the *Bhagavad Gita*. He asked me to copy these out for him, with their translation. At home I had been a boy of no account, but here, when these important functions were entrusted to me, I felt the glory of the situation.

By this time I was rid of my blue manuscript book and had got hold of a bound volume, one of Letts' diaries. I saw to it now that my poetizing should not be lacking in outward dignity. It was not just writing poems, but holding a picture of myself as a poet before my imagination. When I wrote poetry at Bolpur I loved to do it sprawling under a coconut palm. This seemed to me the true manner. Thus resting on the hard unturfed gravel in the burning heat of the day, I composed a martial ballad on the 'Defeat of King Prithvi'. In spite of its superabundance of martial spirit, it could not escape early death. That bound volume of Letts' diary followed the way of its elder sister, the blue manuscript book, leaving no forwarding address.

We left Bolpur and, making short halts on the way at Sahibganj, Dinapur, Allahabad and Kanpur, we stopped at last at Amritsar.

An incident en route remains engraved on my memory. The train had stopped at some big station. The ticket collector came and punched our tickets. He looked at me curiously as if he had some doubt that he did not care to express. He went off and came back with a companion. Both of them fidgeted about for a time near the door of our compartment and then again retired. At last the station master himself came. He looked at my half-ticket and then asked: 'Is not the boy over twelve?'

'No,' said my father.

I was then only eleven, but looked older than my age.

'You must pay the full fare for him,' said the station master.

My father's eyes flashed as, without a word, he took out a currency note from his box and handed it to the station master. When they brought the change my father flung it disdainfully back at them, while the station master stood abashed at this exposure of the meanness of his doubt.

The Golden Temple of Amritsar comes back to me like a dream. On many a morning I accompanied my father to this *gurudarbar* of the Sikhs in the middle of the lake. There the sacred chanting continually resounds. My father, seated amidst the throng of worshippers, would sometimes add his voice to the hymn of praise and, finding a stranger joining in their devotions they would welcome him most cordially, and we would return loaded with the sanctified offerings of sugar crystals and other sweets.

One day my father invited one of the chanting choir to our place and had him sing some of their sacred songs. The man went away probably more than satisfied with the reward he received. Soon we had to take stern measures in self-defence, such was the insistent army of singers that invaded us. When they found our house impregnable, the musicians began to waylay us in the streets. As we went out for our walk in the morning, from time to time would appear a *tanpura*, slung over a shoulder; it made us feel like game birds that had spotted the muzzle of a hunter's gun. So wary did we become that the twang of a *tanpura*, even in the distance, would scare us away and fail utterly to bag us.

When evening fell, my father would sit out on the veranda facing the garden. He would summon me to sing to him. I can see the moon risen; its beams, passing through the trees, falling on the veranda floor; and I am singing in raga Behag: 'O companion in the darkest passage of life . . .'

My father with bowed head and clasped hands listens intently. I recall the evening scene quite clearly.

I have already told of my father's amusement on hearing from a family friend of my maiden attempt at a devotional poem. I remember how, later, I had my recompense. On the occasion of one of our Magh festivals several of the hymns were of my composition. One of them was: 'The eye sees thee not, who art the pupil of every eye.' My father was then bed-ridden at Chunchura. He sent for me and my brother Jyoti. He asked my brother to accompany me on the harmonium, and me to sing all my hymns one after the other, some of them twice over. When I had finished he said: 'If the king of the country had known the language and could appreciate its literature, he would doubtless have rewarded the poet. Since that is not so, I suppose I must do it.' With which he handed me a cheque.

My father had brought with him some volumes of the Peter Parley series from which to teach me. He selected *The Life of Benjamin Franklin* to begin with. He thought it would read like a story book and be both entertaining and instructive. But he found out his mistake soon after we began. Benjamin Franklin was much too businesslike a person. The narrowness of his calculated morality disgusted my father. Sometimes he would become so impatient at Franklin's worldly prudence that he could not help using strong words of denunciation.

Until now I had had nothing to do with Sanskrit beyond learning some rules of grammar by rote. My father started me on the second Sanskrit reader at one bound, leaving me to learn the declensions as we went on. The advance I had made in Bengali stood me in good stead. My father also encouraged me to try Sanskrit composition from the very outset. With the vocabulary acquired from my Sanskrit reader I built up grandiose compound words with a profuse sprinkling of sonorous m's and n's, that made a most diabolical medley out of the language of the gods. But my father never scoffed at my temerity.

Then there were the readings from Proctor's *Popular Astronomy*, which my father explained to me in easy language and which I then rendered into Bengali.

Among the books which my father had brought for his own use, I often found myself gazing at a ten- or twelve-volume edition of Gibbon's *Rome*. They looked remarkably dry. I am only a helpless boy, I thought, I read many books because I have to. But why should a grown-up person, who doesn't have to read unless he pleases, give himself such bother?

*

# In the Himalayas

We stayed about a month at Amritsar, and, towards the middle of April, started for the Dalhousie hills. The last few days in Amritsar seemed as if they would never pass, the Himalayas were calling me so strongly.

The terraced hillsides, as we went up in a *jhampan*, were aflame with flowering spring crops. Every morning we made a start after bread and milk, and before sunset took shelter in the next staging bungalow. My eyes had no rest the entire day, so much did I fear missing something. Wherever the great forest trees clustered together at a bend of the road into a gorge, a waterfall trickled out from beneath their shade, like a little daughter playing at the feet of hoary sages rapt in meditation and babbling over the black moss-covered rocks; there the *jhampan* bearers would put down their burden, and take a rest. Why had we ever to leave such spots, cried my thirsting heart. Why could we not stay on for good?

That is the great advantage of a first vision: the mind is not aware that there are many more to come. When this fact penetrates that calculating organ it promptly tries to make a saving in its expenditure of attention. Only when it believes something to be rare does the mind cease to be miserly. In the streets of Calcutta I sometimes imagine myself a foreigner, and only then do I discover how much is to be seen. The hunger to see properly is what drives people to travel in strange places.

My father left his little cash box in my charge. He had no reason to imagine that I was the fittest custodian of the considerable sums he kept in it for use on the way. He would certainly have felt safer with it in the hands of Kishori, his attendant. So I can only suppose he wanted to instil in me the idea of responsibility. One day we reached the staging bungalow, I forgot to make it over to him and left it lying on a table. This brought me a reprimand.

Every time we got down at the end of a stage, my father had chairs placed for us outside the bungalow and there we sat. As dusk came on the stars blazed wonderfully through the clear mountain atmosphere, and my father showed me the constellations or treated me to an astronomical discourse.

The house we had taken at Bakrota was on the highest hilltop. Though May had almost come it was still bitterly cold there, so much so that on the shady side of the hill the winter frosts had not yet melted.

My father was not at all nervous about my wandering freely even here. Some way below our house stretched a spur thickly wooded with deodars. I would go alone into this wilderness with my iron-tipped staff. What lordly trees, towering above me like giants! What vast shadows! What immense lives they had lived over the centuries! And yet this boy, born only the other day, crawled around between their trunks unchallenged. I seemed to feel a presence the moment I stepped into their shade like that of some ancient saurian whose cool, firm and scaly body was made of checkered light and shade on the leaf mould of the forest floor.

My room was at one end of the house. Lying on my bed I could see, through the uncurtained windows, the distant snow peaks shimmering dimly in the starlight. Sometimes, half-awake, at what hour I could not make out, I saw my father, wrapped in a red shawl, with a lighted lamp in his hand, softly passing by to the glazed veranda where he sat at his devotions. After dozing off, I would find him at my bedside, rousing me with a push before the darkness had yet passed from the night. This was the hour appointed for memorizing Sanskrit declensions. What an excruciatingly wintry awakening from the caressing warmth of my blankets!

By the time the sun rose, my father, after finishing his prayers, joined me for our morning milk, and then stood with me, once more to hold communion with God by chanting the *Upanishads*.

Then we would go out for a walk. But how could I keep pace with him? Many adults could not! After a while, I would give up and scramble back home by some short cut over the mountainside.

Upon my father's return I had an hour of English lessons. At ten o'clock came a bath in ice-cold water. It was no use asking the servants to temper it with even a jugful of hot water without permission. To give me courage my father would tell of the unbearably freezing baths he had himself endured in his younger days.

Another penance was milk-drinking. My father was very fond of milk and could take quantities. But my appetite for it was grievously lacking, whether because I had failed to inherit it or because of my unfavourable early experiences with milk, I do not know. Unfortunately we used to have our milk together so I had to throw myself on the mercy of the servants, and to their human kindness (or frailty) I was indebted for my goblet being more than half full of foam.

After our midday meal lessons began again. This was more than flesh and blood could stand. My outraged morning sleep *would* have its revenge and I would be toppling over with uncontrollable drowsiness. But no sooner did my father take pity on my plight and let me off than my sleepiness was off likewise: the Lord of the Mountains was calling!

Staff in hand I would often wander away from one peak to another, but my father did not object. To the end of his life, I have observed, he never stood in the way of our independence. Frequently I have said or done things repugnant to his taste and his judgement alike; with a word he could have stopped me but he preferred to wait until the prompting to refrain came from within. A passive acceptance of the correct and the proper did not satisfy him: he wanted us to love truth with our whole hearts; mere acquiescence without love he knew to be empty. He also knew that truth, if strayed from, can be found again, but a forced or blind adherence effectively bars access to it.

In my early youth I had conceived a fancy to travel the Grand Trunk Road, right up to Peshawar, in a bullock cart. No one else supported the scheme, and doubtless there was much to be urged against it as a practical proposition. But when I discoursed on it to my father he was sure it was a splendid idea – travelling by railway was not worth the name! And he forthwith proceeded to recount his own adventures on foot and horseback. Of any chance of discomfort or peril he had not a word to say.

Another time, when I had just been appointed secretary of the Adi Brahmo Samaj, I went over to my father at his Park Street residence and informed him that I did not approve of the practice of having only Brahmins conducting divine service to the exclusion of the other castes. He unhesitatingly gave me permission to correct this if I could. Armed with the authorization I found I lacked the power. I was able to discover imperfections but could not create perfection! Where were the men? Where was the strength in me to attract the right man? Had I the means to build in place of what I might break? Until the right man arrives, any form is better than none – this, I felt, must have been my father's view. But not for a moment did he try to discourage me by pointing out these difficulties.

Just as he allowed me to wander the mountains at will, so he left me free to select my path in the quest for truth. He was not deterred by the risk of my making mistakes, neither alarmed at the prospect of my encountering sorrow. He held up a standard, not a disciplinary rod.

I would often talk to him of home. Whenever I got a letter from anyone there I immediately showed it to him. I believe I permitted him many a glimpse he could have had from no one else. My father also let me read letters to him from my elder brothers. It was his way of teaching me how I ought to write to him; for he by no means undervalued outward forms and ceremonial.

I remember how in one letter my second brother complained

of being worked to death, tied by the neck to his post, expressing himself in somewhat Sanskritized language. My father asked me to explain briefly what was meant. I did so in my way, but he thought a different explanation better. In my overweening conceit I stuck to my guns and argued the point at length. Another person would have stopped me with a snub, but my father patiently heard me out and took pains to justify his view to me.

Sometimes he would tell me funny stories. He had many anecdotes of the gilded youth of his time. There were some exquisites for whose delicate skins the embroidered border of even Dacca muslins proved too coarse; among them, for a while, it was the tiptop thing to wear one's muslins with the borders torn off.

I was also highly amused to hear, first from my father, the story of the milkman suspected of watering his milk. The more men one of his customers detailed to supervise his milking the bluer the fluid became, until at last, when the customer himself interviewed the milkman and asked for an explanation, the man bluntly stated that if any more superintendents had to be satisfied the milk would be fit only to breed fish!

After I had spent a few months with him, my father sent me back home with his attendant Kishori.

# FROM *My Boyhood Days*

And so began a new chapter of my lonely Bedouin life on the roof, and human company and friendship entered it. Across the roof kingdom a new wind blew, and a new season began there. My brother Jyoti *Dada* played a large part in this change. At that time my father finally left our home at Jorasanko. Jyoti *Dada* settled himself into that outside third-storey room, and I claimed a little corner of it for my own.

No purdah was observed in my sister-in-law's apartments. That will strike no one as strange today, but then it sounded an unimaginable depth of novelty. A long time even before that, when I was a baby, my second brother had returned from England to enter the civil service. When he went to Bombay to take up his first post he astonished the neighbourhood by taking off his wife with him before their very eyes. And as if it was not enough to take her away to a distant province instead of leaving her in the family home, he made no provision for proper privacy on the journey. That was a terrible breach of propriety. Even the relatives felt as if the sky had fallen on their heads.

A style of dress suitable for going out was still not in vogue among women. It was this sister-in-law who first introduced the manner of wearing the sari and the blouse which is now customary. Little girls had not then begun to wear frocks or let their hair hang in plaits – at least not in our family. The little ones used to wear the tight Rajput pyjamas instead of the traditional sari. When the Bethune School was first opened my eldest sister was quite young. She was one of the pioneers who made the road to education easy for girls. She was very fair, uniquely so for this country. I have heard that once when she was going to school in her palanquin the police detained her, thinking her in her Rajput dress to be an English girl who had been kidnapped.

I said before that in those days there was no bridge of intimacy between adults and children. Into the tangle of these old customs Jyoti *Dada* brought a vigorously original mind. I was twelve years younger than he, and that I should come to his notice in spite of such a difference in age is in itself surprising. What was more surprising is that in all my talks with him he never called me impudent or snubbed me. Thanks to this, I never lacked courage to think for myself. Today I live with children, I try all kinds of subjects of conversation, but I find them dumb. They seem to me to belong to those old times when the grown-ups talked and the children remained silent. The self-confidence that doubts and questions is the mark of the children of the new age; those of the former age are known for their meek and docile acceptance of what they are told.

A piano appeared in the terrace room. There came also modern varnished furniture from Bowbazar. My breast swelled with pride as the cheap grandeur of modern times was displayed before eyes inured to poverty. At this time the fountain of my song was unloosed. Jyoti *Dada*'s hands would stray about the piano as he composed and rattled off tunes in various new styles, and he would keep me by his side as he did so. It was my work to fix the tunes which he composed so rapidly by setting words to them then and there.

At the end of the day a mat and a pillow were spread on the terrace. Nearby was a thick garland of *bel* flowers on a silver plate, in a wet handkerchief, a glass of iced water on a saucer, and some *chhanchi pan* in a bowl. My sister-in-law would bathe, dress her hair and come and sit with us. Jyoti *Dada* would come out with a silk chadar thrown over his shoulder, and draw the bow across his violin, and I would sing in my clear treble voice. For providence had not yet taken away the gift of voice it had given me, and under the sunset sky my song rang out across the house-tops. The south wind came in great gusts from the distant sea, the sky filled with stars.

My sister-in-law turned the whole roof into a garden. She arranged rows of tall palms in barrels and beside and around them *chameli*, *gandharaj*, *rajanigandha*, *karabi* and *dolan-champa*. She considered not at all the possible damage to the roof – we were all alike unpractical visionaries.

A friend used to come almost every day. He himself knew he had no voice, and other people knew it even better. In spite of that nothing could stop the flow of his song. His special favourite was the Behag mode. He sang with his eyes shut, so he did not see the expression on the faces of his hearers. As soon as anything capable of making a noise came to hand, he took it and turned it into a drum, beating it in happy absorption, biting his lips with his teeth in his earnestness. Even a book with a stiff binding would do very well. He was by nature a dreamy kind of man; one could see no difference between his working days and his holidays.

The evening party would break up – but I was a boy of nocturnal habits. Everyone went to lie down, I alone would wander about all night with the demons. The whole district was steeped in silence. On moonlit nights the shadows of the lines of palm trees on the terrace lay in dream patterns on the floor. Beyond the terrace the top of the *shishu* tree swayed and tossed in the breeze, and its leaves gleamed as they caught the light. But, for some reason, what caught my eye more than anything was a squat room with a sloping roof built over the staircase of the sleeping house on the opposite side of the lane. It stood like a finger pointing for ever towards I know not what.

It may have been one or two in the morning, when from the main street in front a wailing funeral chant arose – 'Balo-Hari Hari-bol'.

★

When I was seventeen I had to leave the editorial board of *Bharati*, the family magazine, for it was even then decided that I should go to England. Further it was considered that before sailing I should live with my second brother, *Meja Dada*, for a time, to get some grounding in English manners. He was then a judge in Ahmedabad, and his wife and her children were in England, waiting for *Meja Dada* to get a furlough and join them.

I was torn up by the roots and transplanted from one soil to another, and had to get acclimatized to a new mental atmosphere. At first my shyness was a stumbling-block at every turn. I wondered how I should keep my self-respect among all these new acquaintances. It was not easy to habituate myself to strange surroundings, yet there was no means of escape from them: in such a situation a boy of my temperament was bound to find his path a rough one.

My fancy, free to wander, conjured up pictures of the history of Ahmedabad in the Mughal period. The judge's quarters were in Shahibagh, the former palace grounds of the Mughal kings. During the daytime *Meja Dada* was away at work, the vast house seemed one cavernous emptiness, and I wandered about all day like one possessed. In front was a wide terrace, which commanded a view of the Sabarmati River, whose knee-deep waters meandered through the sands. I felt as though the stone-built tanks, scattered here and there along the terrace, held locked in their masonry wonderful secrets of the luxurious hammams of the begums.

We are Calcutta people, and there history gives us no evidence of past grandeur. Our vision had been confined to the narrow boundaries of these stunted times. In Ahmedabad I felt for the first time that history had paused, and was standing with her face turned towards the aristocratic past. Her former glories lay buried in the earth like the treasure of the *yakshas*. My mind received the first suggestion of my story, 'The Hungry Stones'.

How many hundred years have passed since those times. Then,

from the *nahabat khana*, the musicians' gallery, music played day and night, with ragas appropriate to the eight divisions of the day. The rhythmic beat of horses' hooves echoed in the streets, and great parades were held of the mounted Turkish cavalry, the points of their spears glittering in the sun. In the court of the Badshah whispered conspiracies were ominously rife. Abyssinian eunuchs, with drawn swords, kept guard over the inner apartments. Rose-water fountains played in the hammams, bangles tinkled on begums' arms. Today Shahibagh stands silent, like a forgotten tale; all its colour has faded, and its varied sounds have died away; the splendours of the day-time are withered and the night-time has lost its savour.

Only the bare skeleton of those days remained, its head a naked skull missing its crown. It was like a mummy in a museum, but it would be too much to say that my mind was able fully to reclothe the dry bones with flesh and blood and restore the original form. Both the first rough model, and the background against which it stood, were largely a creation of fancy. Such patchwork is easy when little is known and most has been forgotten. After these eighty years even the picture of myself that comes before me does not correspond line for line with the reality, but is largely a product of my imagination.

After I had stayed there for some time *Meja Dada* decided that perhaps I should be less homesick if I could mix with women who could familiarize me with conditions abroad. This would also be an easy way to learn English. So for a while I lived with a Bombay family. One of the daughters of the house was a modern educated girl who had just returned with all the polish of a visit to England. My own attainments were only ordinary, and she could not have been blamed if she had ignored me. But she did not do so. Not having any store of book learning to offer her, I took the first opportunity to tell her that I could write poetry. This was the only capital I had with which to gain attention. When I told her of my poetical gift, she did not receive it in any carping or dubious spirit, but accepted it without question. She asked the poet to give her a special name, and I chose one for her which she thought very beautiful. I wanted that name to be entwined with the music of my verse, and I enshrined it in a poem which I made for her. She listened as I sang it in the Bhairavi mode of early dawn, and then said: 'Poet, I think that even if I were on my death-bed your songs would call me back to life.' This is an example of how well girls know how to show their appreciation by some pleasant exaggeration. They simply do it for the pleasure of pleasing. I remember that it was from her that I first heard praise of my personal appearance – praise that was often very delicately given.

For example, she asked me once very particularly to remember one thing: 'You must never wear a beard. Don't let anything hide the outline of your face.' Everyone knows that I have not followed that advice. But she herself did not live to see my disobedience proclaimed upon my face.

In certain years in Calcutta, birds strange to the city used to come and build in our banyan tree. They would be off again almost before I had learnt to recognize the dance of their wings, but they brought with them a strangely lovely music from their distant jungle homes. So, in the course of our life's journey, some angel from a strange and unexpected quarter may cross our path, speaking the language of our own soul, and enlarging the boundaries of the heart's possessions. She comes unbidden, and when at last we call for her she is no longer there. But as she goes, she leaves on the drab web of our lives a border of embroidered flowers, and our night and day are for ever enriched.

*

The Master workman, who made me, fashioned his first model from the native clay of Bengal. I have described this first model, which is what I call my boyhood, and in it there is little admixture of other elements. Most of its ingredients were gathered from within, though the atmosphere of the home and the home people counted for something too. Very often the work of moulding goes no further than this stage. Some others get hammered into shape in the book-learning factories, and these are considered in the market to be goods of a superior stamp.

It was my fortune to escape almost entirely the impress of these mills of learning. The masters and pundits who were charged with my education soon abandoned the thankless task. There was Jnana Chandra Bhattacharya, the son of Ananda Chandra Vedantavagish, who was a BA. He realized that this boy could never be driven along the beaten track of learning. The teachers of those days were not so strongly convinced that boys should all be poured into the mould of degree-holding respectability. There was then no demand that rich and poor alike should all be confined within the fenced-off regions of college studies. Our family had no wealth then, but it had a reputation, so the old traditions held good, which were indifferent to conventional academic success. From the lower classes of the Normal School we were transferred to De Cruz's Bengal Academy. It was the hope of my guardians that even if I got nothing else, I should get enough mastery of spoken English to save my face. In the Latin class I was deaf and dumb, and my exercise books of all kinds from beginning to end kept the unrelieved whiteness of a widow's cloth. Confronted by such unprecedented determination not to study my class teacher complained to Mr De Cruz, who explained that we were not born for study, but for the purpose of paying our monthly fees. Jnana Babu was of a similar opinion, but found means of keeping me occupied nevertheless. He gave me the whole of *The Birth of the War-God* in the original to learn by heart. He shut me in a room and gave me *Macbeth* to translate. Then Pundit Ramsarvasva read *Shakuntala* with me. By setting me free in this way from the fixed curriculum, they reaped some reward for their labours. These then were the materials that formed my boyish mind, together with what other Bengali books I picked up at random.

I landed in England, and foreign workmanship began to play a part in the fashioning of my life. The result is what is known in chemistry as a compound. How capricious is Fortune! – I went to England for a regular course of study, and a desultory start was made, but it came to nothing. My sister-in-law was there, and her children, and my own family circle absorbed nearly all my interest. I hung about the schoolroom, a master taught me at the house, but I did not give my mind to it.

However, gradually the atmosphere of England made its impression on my mind, and what little I brought back from that country was from the people I came in contact with. Mr Palit finally succeeded in getting me away from my own family. I went to live with a doctor's family, where they made me forget that I was in a foreign land. Mrs Scott lavished on me a genuine affection, and cared for me like a mother. I had then been admitted to London University, and Henry Morley was teaching English literature. His teaching was no dry-as-dust exposition of dead books. Literature came to life in his mind and in the sound of his voice, it reached to our inner beings where the soul seeks its nourishment, and nothing of its essential nature was lost. With his guidance, I found the study of the Clarendon Press books at home to be an easy matter and I took upon myself to be my own teacher. For no reason at all Mrs Scott would sometimes fancy that I did not look well, and would become very worried about me. She did not know that the portals of sickness had been barred against me from childhood. I used to bathe every morning in ice-cold water – in fact, in the opinion of the doctors, it was almost a sacrilege that I should survive such flagrant disregard of the accepted rules.

I was able to study in the university for three months only, but I obtained almost all my understanding of English culture from personal contacts. The Artist who fashions us takes every opportunity to mingle new elements in his creation. Three months of real intimacy with English hearts sufficed for this development. Mrs Scott made it my duty each evening till eleven o'clock to read aloud by turn from poetic drama and history. In this way I did a great deal of reading in a short space of time. It was not prescribed class study, and my understanding of human nature developed side by side with my knowledge of literature. I went to England but I did not become a barrister: I received no shock calculated to shatter the original framework of my life – rather East and West met in friendship in my own person. And thus it has been given me to realize in my own life the meaning of my name.[†]

† 'Rabi' in Bengali means 'the sun', which unites East and West.

# TRAVEL
# WRITINGS

Tagore was a restless man. From 1912 until 1932, he was away from India for long periods, nearly a year and a half in 1912–13. His travels took him to Europe, Russia, North and South America, the Middle East and the Far East. He also travelled extensively within India and visited Ceylon. With the exception of his visit to Persia in 1932 by aeroplane, he travelled everywhere by boat and rail.

But he was not a natural-born traveller. His motives were always mixed and contradictory; and after he won the Nobel prize in 1913 and became the world's most famous Indian, every visit inevitably acquired public as well as private significance. (In addition, his hosts were sometimes governments, as was the case in Russia and in Persia.) Curiosity for new experiences and friendships – intellectual, artistic and otherwise – was probably uppermost in his mind, followed by a wish to spread Indian culture, but there was also a strong element of wishing to escape his milieu in Bengal and, to a lesser extent, a desire for the adulation of foreign audiences, as well as his constant need (from 1920) to raise funds for his university and his periodic need for western medical treatment. Yet, once having arrived in a place, Tagore almost invariably began yearning to return to Bengal. His letters are full of this: to one English friend he spoke of his urge to travel as being 'like a homesickness for the far away', like a 'strange case of an oyster trying to run away from its own shell'; to another he remarked: 'It is not for me to travel about – to dissipate my attention – my mind sets forth on its true pilgrimage when it is at rest.'

As a writer about his travels, Tagore is never a tourist. With the exception of his sparky, ironic teenage letters from England written in 1878–80 – two of which are included here – which he later regretted 'for their want of . . . common courtesy', one finds none of the detached, concrete descriptions of places and peoples common in, say, Kipling or Twain. The adult Tagore was constitutionally incapable of writing about the surface of life in a foreign country, and so, when some encounter he had had provoked in him no urge to understand it more deeply, he simply ignored it in his writing.

Thus, visiting Burma on his way to Japan in 1916, he makes it clear that Rangoon, a basically European-built commercial city, is not worth his attention – but he gives a vivid description of visiting Rangoon's great Buddhist temple. But when he visits Java in 1927, besides being fascinated by Javanese dances based on the Hindu epics, as one would expect, he dwells too on the Dutch colonists' experience, having been deeply impressed by the devotion to ancient India of his Dutch scholar guides at the great temple of Borobudur.

His writings on Russia in 1930 are noteworthy for their mixture of optimism about Communist society – hardly an uncommon feature among foreign visitors to the Soviet Union at that time – tempered by a far-sighted and eloquent warning to the Communist leadership in his parting interview with *Izvestia*. Though published in the *Manchester Guardian* in 1930, the interview did not appear until 1988 in *Izvestia*, where it was read by Alexander Dubček, who wanted to quote it in a speech about Communist oppression in Czechoslovakia but then thought better of it.

Tagore himself, in his letter about Russia printed here, draws an explicit comparison with India; and such comparisons are to be found throughout this selection from his travel writings, all of which were written in Bengali in the form of letters to family and friends in Bengal. For a modern western reader, the authentically Indian viewpoint makes a piquant contrast with the more familiar viewpoint of western writers in the colonial period.

# from *Letters from an Exile in Europe*

## Torquay, Devon, 1879

Summertime. The sun is shining wonderfully. It is two o'clock in the afternoon. A sweet breeze is blowing, similar to the one that blows at noontime in winter in our country. Everything basks in the sunshine. How pleasant it feels and how languid it makes my mind, I just can't tell you.

We are now staying in a town called Torquay in Devonshire. It is beside the sea. Hills all around. Such a crystal-clear day – no clouds, no fog and no gloom; there are trees everywhere, birds chirping everywhere, flowers blooming everywhere. When I was in Tunbridge Wells, I used to think that if Madan[†] were to appear here he would have to grope his way through many thorny thickets and copses to find even a few wild flowers to decorate his bow. But here in Torquay, even if he invented a weapon like a Gatling gun which could fling a thousand flower arrows per minute and he kept this rate up twenty-four hours in a day, there would still be no likelihood of his bankrupting his flower stock, so much is here. Wherever you tread there are flowers. Every day we go for walks in the hills. Cows and sheep are grazing; in places the road slopes so much that climbing up or down is hard going. In other places the path is very narrow, the trees close in on both sides and cast dark shadows, there are rough steps for the benefit of climbers, and creepers and shrubs grow in the middle of the path. All around the sun shines mildly. The air is quite warm and reminds you of India. This warmth, though

† God of love, cf. Cupid.

little, seems to make the creatures more lethargic than those in London. Horses move rather slowly, people too do not rush around – everyone loiters.

The seaside here I like very much. When the tide comes in, the huge boulders on the shore are submerged, only their tops show. They look like small islands. There are many cliffs, large and small, rising above the water. The washing of the waves has formed caves beneath these cliffs; when the tide ebbs we sometimes go inside them and sit there. In the interiors pools of clear water collect, there are patches of lichen, the sea smell is invigorating and boulders are scattered in all directions. Some days we all try to shift these boulders by pushing and shoving, and we pick up various shells such as snail shells and cockles. Certain of the cliffs practically lean over the ocean; from time to time we clamber up them with a lot of effort and sit at the top watching the rise and fall of the waves below. A roaring sound reaches us, small boats float past with raised sails, the sun shines down, and with a parasol shading us we lie back, heads against the rocks, and chat. Where else shall I find such a fine place for idling? Once in a while I go up into the hills, look out for a secret spot enclosed by boulders and covered by vegetation, drop down into it with my book, and sit and read.

*

## London(?), 1879

By and by the ship arrives and docks at Southampton. The Bengali passengers have reached the shores of England. They set off for London. As they disembark from the train an English porter approaches them. Politely he enquires if he can be of service. As he takes down their luggage and ushers them into a carriage, the Bengali thinks to himself, How extraordinary! How polite the English are! That Englishmen could be so polite, he had no idea. He presses a whole shilling into the porter's hand. Never mind the cost, the newly arrived Bengali youth tells himself; the salaam of a white man was worth every penny of that shilling. . . .

Before the Bengalis arrive in England, their friends who are already here have arranged rooms for them. As the Bengali enters his room, he sees a carpet on the floor, pictures hanging on the walls, a large mirror in its proper place, a sofa, stools and chairs, one or two glass flower vases, and to one side a baby piano. Good heavens! The Bengalis summon their friends: 'We aren't here as rich men, you know! My dear fellows, we haven't much cash on us, we can't afford to stay in rooms like these.' Their friends are highly amused, having completely forgotten their own precisely similar behaviour when *they* first arrived. Treating the new arrivals as thoroughgoing rice-eating rustics they tell them in voices full of experience, 'All rooms are like this over here.' This reminds the newcoming Bengalis of the rooms in our own country: damp, with a wooden cot covered by a wicker mat, here and there people puffing on hookahs, others lounging around a board game, their bodies bare to the waist, their shoes cast casually aside, while a cow lies tethered in the courtyard that has walls plastered in cow-dung cakes, and wet washing hangs drying over a veranda. For the first few days the Bengalis find themselves terribly embarrassed to sit on a chair or stool, lie on a bed, eat off a table or walk about a carpet. They sit very awkwardly on the sofas, fearful lest they make them dirty or damage them in any way. They imagine that the sofas have been put there for decoration, the owners surely cannot have intended them to be spoilt by use. But if that is their first impression of their rooms, there follows another impression, almost as immediate and even more significant.

In some smaller types of accommodation in England the figure called the 'landlord' still exists; but most Bengali lodgers must deal with a 'landlady'. Settling the rent, sorting out various problems, arranging food, is all down to the landlady. When my Bengali friends first stepped into their rooms, she quickly appeared, an Englishwoman waiting to greet them with the politest of 'good morning's. Hurriedly they returned the greeting in the most proper manner, and then stood struck dumb. And when they saw their various England-worshipping friends strike up an easy conversation with the lady in question, their awkwardness turned to absolute awe. To think of it: they were talking to a real live memsahib, complete in shoes, hat and dress! Here was a sight to stir real respect in a Bengali heart. Would they ever acquire this courage shown by their England-worshipping friends? Surely it was beyond the bounds of possibility.

Afterwards, having installed the newcomers, the England-worshipping friends went off to their respective residences and spent the next few days making fun of Bengali ignorance – while the aforementioned landlady came each day to enquire, most politely, what my newly arrived friends liked to have, and what they did not like to have. My friends soon came to regard these occasions with real pleasure. One of them even told me that when he first ticked off this Englishwoman – ever so slightly – he felt thrilled with himself for the rest of the day. Notwithstanding, the sun did not rise in the West, mountains did not move and fire did not freeze that day. . . .

To know the *ingabanga* – the England-worshipping Bengali[†] – truly, one must observe him in three situations. One must see how he behaves with Englishmen; how he behaves with ordinary Bengalis; and how he behaves with fellow *ingabangas*. To see an *ingabanga* face to face with an Englishman is really a sight to gladden your eyes. The weight of courtesy in his words is like a

† Or anglomaniac.

burden making his shoulders droop; in debate he is the meekest and mildest of men; and if he is compelled to disagree, he will do so with an expression of extreme regret and with a thousand apologies. An *ingabanga* sitting with an Englishman, whether he be talking or listening, will appear in his every gesture and facial movement to be the acme of humility. But catch him with his own countrymen in his own sphere, and he will display genuine temper. One who has lived three years in England will regard himself as infinitely superior to one who has spent a mere one year here. Should the former type of resident happen to argue with the latter type, one may observe the 'three-year' man exert his prowess. Each word he utters, and each inflection he gives it, sounds like a dictum personally dictated to him by the lips of goddess Saraswati.[†] Anyone who dares to contradict him he will bluntly label 'mistaken', or even 'ignorant' — to his face. . . .

Had you seen for yourself the thorough research these people put into which way up a knife or fork should be held when dining, your respect would surely be still further increased. What the currently fashionable cut of a jacket is, whether today's gentleman wears his trousers tight or loose, whether one should dance the waltz, the polka or the mazurka, and whether meat should follow fish or vice versa — these people know all these things with unerring accuracy. Their preoccupation with trivia — what is and is not 'done' — is far greater than that of the natives of this country. If you happen to use the wrong knife to eat fish, an Englishman would not think much of it; he would put it down to your being a foreigner. But if an *ingabanga* Bengali saw you, he would probably have to take smelling salts. Were you to drink champagne out of a sherry glass, he would stare at you aghast, as if your ignorant blunder had totally upset the world's

† Goddess of learning.

tranquillity. And were you, God forbid, to wear a morning coat in the evening, had he a magistrate's power he would condemn you to solitary confinement. . . .

There is one other special feature of the *ingabanga* I must tell you about. The majority of those who come here do not confess if they are married – because married men naturally command less attention from unmarried ladies. By pretending to be bachelors they can mix much more freely in society and have much more fun, otherwise their unmarried companions would never permit such goings on. There is a lot to be gained by declaring oneself unattached.

No doubt there are many England-worshipping Bengalis who do not fit my description. I have written only of the general characteristics of the species as I have spotted them.

# FROM *On the Way to Japan*

## S.S. Tosha Maru, *May 1916*

We arrived in Rangoon on the afternoon of the 5th. . . .

I have sometimes been requested to take notes and give reports on a new place, but piecemeal impressions slip through my mental grasp and become scattered. I can only deal with visible facts where they reach the stage of re-expression, after they have become invisible in the green-room of my mind.

It is fruitless and fatiguing for me to rush here and there, trying to see things. So you will not get a nice traveller's tale from me. I can swear in a law-court that I visited a city called Rangoon; but in the court of last judgement, I am bound to say that I never saw Rangoon.

It may be that the city of Rangoon does not really exist, in the true sense of 'real'. Its streets are straight, broad and clean; its houses look spick and span; in the streets Madrasis, Punjabis and Gujaratis wander about, and when one suddenly comes across a Burman, man or woman, dressed in coloured silks, he or she strikes one as a foreigner. Like the bridge over the Ganges that, rather than belonging to the river, seems to be a halter around its neck, the city of Rangoon does not seem like a Burmese city but appears to run counter to the whole country.

What are one's initial impressions of Burma as one approaches the city along the River Irrawaddy? Along its banks one sees huge refineries of kerosene oil with tall chimneys sticking up into the sky as if lying flat on their backs and smoking Burma cheroots. Then, as one proceeds, crowds of ships come into view, flying flags of different nations. When one reaches the landing place, there is no sign at all of any riverside – the rows of piers seem to cling to Burma's body like so many hideous iron leeches. Then, passing by government offices, courthouses, shops and markets, we reached the house of my Bengali friends, without catching even a glimpse of the real Burma. It seemed to me as if Rangoon existed on the map, but not on the ground. In other words, the city has not sprung from the soil like a tree, but has come floating on the current of time like foam. It did not seem to matter where in the world it happened to be.

The vital point is that the cities that have become real cities derive from human affection for a particular place. Be it Delhi, Agra or Kashi,† they grow from the feeling of their inhabitants. The goddess of commerce is hard, and the lotus of beauty fed by human ideals does not bloom beneath her feet. She does not take account of men, only things – and the machine is her own special mount. When our boat was on the Ganges, signs of her shameless cruelty were evident on both banks of the river. It is because her heart knows no tenderness that she has been able so casually to deface the lovely banks of the Ganges in Bengal.

I consider it my inestimable privilege that I was born before the iron tide of ugliness hastened down both banks of the river at Calcutta, from Garden Reach to Hooghly. Before that, the landing places of the Ganges, like cool village arms, still held the river to their breast in a familiar embrace; and ferry-boats would pass from one landing stage to another, carrying each factory worker back home in the evening. There was as yet no hard and ugly barrier between the flowing of the country's heart on the one hand, and its river artery on the other.

In those days there was nothing to prevent anyone from seeing the true Bengal around Calcutta. Though Calcutta is a modern city, it had not then, like a young cuckoo, occupied all its foster-

† Varanasi (Benares).

mother's nest to the exclusion of everything else. But in due course, the face of the country gradually became hidden beneath the spread of commercial civilization. Now Calcutta is banishing the real Bengal from its outskirts; in the struggle between the place and the time, green loveliness has been defaced by fierce fashion, which has spread its iron nails and claws and belched forth its black breath.

Once upon a time men used to say that Lakshmi, the goddess of wealth and plenty, dwelt in trade. They visualized her not only as splendid but also as beautiful. For at that time man was not yet separated from trade, there was a communion between the weaver and his loom, the smith's hand and the smith's hammer, the artisan and his work of art. The heart of man used then to express itself through trade in varied forms of richness and beauty. How else could Lakshmi have acquired her lotus throne? . . .

This is why I say that though I saw Rangoon, in my seeing there was no knowing. I took away from the place recollections of my Bengali friends' hospitality, but did not succeed in receiving any gift from Burmese hands. Or perhaps I exaggerate somewhat. For one day, in the midst of this wall of modernism, I found a window on the country slightly open. One Monday morning my friends took me to the famous Buddhist temple of Rangoon. Here at last I really saw something. Until then I had been surrounded by an abstraction – it was a city, but not any particular city – but this place had a unique appearance. The whole of my mind was gladdened and responsive.

In modern Bengali homes I sometimes meet very fashionable young ladies, who walk quite stylishly and talk English quite fluently. But one misses something in them, one feels that the real Bengali girl has been lost sight of and fashion alone is being personified. If at the next moment you suddenly come across a simple and beautiful Bengali woman, unaffected and free from all the trappings of fashion, you at once realize that she is no mirage, that like a clear deep pool she holds within her a tremulous fullness that allays thirst, and is edged with lotus groves. The moment I entered this temple, I felt a similar joyful thrill; I thought, this is not hollow, it contains much more than meets the eye. The whole city of Rangoon seemed diminished by comparison – Burma, this great and ancient land of Brahma, stood revealed within the temple's precincts.

First, we stepped from the glare of the outside world into the ripe gloom of olden time. A broad flight of steps rose before us in tiers, covered with a canopy. To either side people were selling fruit, flowers, candles and sundry other offerings of worship, the sellers being chiefly Burmese women. The colours of the flowers mingled with the colours of their silk clothes making the shade inside the temple variegated like the sky at sunset. Buying and selling are not prohibited here, and Mohammedan shopkeepers were displaying miscellaneous foreign wares. Meat and fish are not excluded either, and domestic activities, including eating, were being carried on all around us. In other words, no line is drawn between the world and the temple; the two freely commingle. Only the commotion prevailing in a market was absent. There was no solitude, but there was privacy, no silence, but there was peace. In our party was a Burmese barrister who was asked why fish and flesh were permitted to be bought and sold and eaten on the temple steps. He replied, 'Buddha in his preaching tells us in which way man's salvation lies, and in which way lies his bondage; but he never wanted to achieve good by force; no good can be done by putting pressure on a person, salvation proceeds by one's own free will; and so there is no ritualistic tyranny in our temple or our society.'

The steps of this temple lead to an open space, over which various temples are scattered. There we saw no solemnity, rather a jostling crowd of carved images, like a lot of childish playthings. Such a strange medley is hardly to be met with anywhere else; it is like a nursery rhyme, whose metre is uniform but into which anything and everything enters at will and there is no necessity to keep a sequence of ideas. Here genuine old art lay cheek-by-jowl with the cheapest and flimsiest of trifles. The people seemed to be oblivious of the idea of irrelevance. This is on a par with the wedding processions of rich men's sons that flood the streets of Calcutta with all kinds of eccentric incongruities, the point of which is not adornment but display. Just as when a lot of children in the same room make a racket, and take delight in it, so the decorations, images and offerings of this temple are like a children's party, loud but signifying nothing. The gold- and brass-covered spires of the temple are Burmese shouts and laughter, rippling skywards. It is as if the Burmese have yet to attain the age of discretion and solemnity. Most of all, the gaily coloured women attract one's attention. They are like fragrant flowers blooming all over the branches and twigs of this land, catching the eye at every turn.

I am told that Burmese men are lazy and ease-loving, and that the work done by men in other lands is here nearly all done by women. At first this might seem a heavy burden imposed upon the womenfolk, but the reality proves the contrary – for the women seem to have blossomed in this stream of toil. Freedom of movement is not the only vital liberty; freedom of work is still more important. Nor is subjugation the greatest bondage; narrowness of opportunity is the worst cage of all.

FROM *Letters from Java*

........................................................................................................

## *August–September 1927*

In my last letter I wrote to you about the dancing here. I thought I had said all that was to be said about it. That very evening, however, a little before dinner, we were once more asked over to the dancing hall – the vast pavilion of which I told you – the marble floor and columns of which were now ablaze with electric light. The dance session began before dinner. This time it was a male dance, and the subject was Indrajit's battle with Hanuman. The raja's brother, a skilled dancer, had himself taken the part of Indrajit. It was all the more wonderful because he had learnt the art late in life. This kind of dancing requires to be practised early, while the limbs are supple, the bones not set too hard, the muscles under perfect control. But his natural talent had made it come easy to him.

The contrast between Indrajit, the cultured warrior, and Hanuman, the simple denizen of the forest, had to be skilfully brought out in the dance. The first thing to attract our notice was their get-up. In our rural *jatra* plays, the spectators are tickled by an exaggeration of Hanuman's monkey characteristics. Here, because his simian race was merely hinted at, Hanuman's human grandeur stood out vividly. It is extremely easy to have Hanuman indulge in monkey pranks, and thereby convulse the audience with loud guffaws. What is difficult is to invest him with nobility. From our *jatra* plays it is evident that the length of Hanuman's tail, the grimaces of his blackened face, in short his monkeyness, appeal more to the masses of Bengal than his gallantry, his self-abnegation, his single-minded devotion. The opposite is the case

........................................................................................................

in the Upper Provinces,[†] where parents do not hesitate to name a child after Hanuman – something unimaginable in Bengal. Here too, the greater side of Hanuman's nature is popularly appreciated.

In this dance, Hanuman's appearance was in every way human except for his tail, which was curved along his back up to his head. There was such dignity of attitude and gesture that no inclination to laugh could possibly be provoked. As for Indrajit, royally attired, he was the very picture of gracefulness, crown and all. Then came the battle dance. Its character was brought out by the tumult of gong and drum and cymbal, along with the bellicose shouts of the musicians that together gave it a note of grimness and passion. And yet the music was by no means harsh sounding, its tumultuousness being relieved by its melodiousness so as to form a wonderfully significant accompaniment. The dancing was extraordinarily skilful, in its combination of bravado and elegance. There was no wildness spoiling it, none of the cheap heroics of our stage braves. Every motion had an exquisite charm; the mace play, the spear thrusts, the wrestling, everything was faultlessly transformed. The female dancing that we had earlier seen and admired, paled before the force of this male rendering, just as in our music the sweetness of *tappa* seems insipid after a soul-stirring *dhrupad*.

This morning, at ten o'clock, our host arranged another performance. This time the girls played the men's parts. The story concerned a duel between Arjuna and Subal. It purported to be an episode from the *Mahabharata*, but I could not recollect the story in the original. Arjuna had hidden his weapons in some garden, from which they were stolen by Subal, who now sought Arjuna in order to kill him with their help. Arjuna was disguised as a gardener. After a short dialogue the two began to fight. One of Subal's weapons was the ploughshare of Balarama. Only when

† Now Uttar Pradesh.

Arjuna had wrested this from him, could Subal be overcome and slain.

It was abundantly obvious that the actors were women, indeed they had made no serious attempt to disguise the fact. For it was not the sex of the dancers that was on display, but the quality of the dance. The bodies were feminine, but the duel was fought in a masculine spirit. The very contrast between means and objective had the effect of highlighting the latter. Bravery was exhibited in a vessel of refined elegance. Imagine a battle, not between lions and tigers but between forest flowers. Stem rubs stem, leaves tear, petals scatter, meanwhile a *gamelan* storm rages: the wind whistles through the flutes, the thunder reverberates in the drums and the castanettes clash like the boughs of the trees striking against each other.

In the finale the raja's brother returned. He danced solo. This time he was Ghatotkacha, Bhima's son by his demon wife. Humour-loving Bengalis always hail the entrance of this type of character with laughter. But here he is an object of reverence, and consequently the *Mahabharata* text has had to be considerably embellished. Here they have given Ghatotkacha a wife named Bhargiva (Bhargavi?), who is a daughter of Arjuna, which shows that their custom with regard to first-cousin marriage resembles that of the Europeans. Bhargiva, according to them, bears Ghatotkacha a son named Shashi-kiran ('moonbeam'). This particular dance showed the grief of Ghatotkacha on being separated from his wife. He swoons, he raves at her image which he seems to see in the sky, and finally he flies away in search of her. They have not, for this purpose, endowed him with a pair of wings, such as angels in European art require; instead he manipulates his garment with dancing motions, to give the impression of flight. This reminded me of Kalidasa's stage-direction in *Shakuntala*: *Here play the speeding of the chariot.* Plainly it was not intended that a real chariot be brought on the stage.

Even during our short stay, what was more than evident was

how deeply the mind of the people of this country has been influenced by the stories of the *Ramayana* and *Mahabharata*. We have read in our geography books how, when fauna and flora migrate to a favourable soil, they multiply and spread more luxuriantly than in their original habitat. In the same way people's minds here have been overlaid by the epic stories. When such deep mental interpenetration takes place, it is driven to express itself in figurative art – an expression seen at its most joyful in the sculptures of Borobudur. And so even today, the people, through their bodies, are giving dance form to the lives of these epic characters, thrilled by the throb of life-blood coursing through the stories that are the never-ending subject of their plays. Although outwardly they appear to have been cut off from India for centuries, they have acquired a subtle refuge within India's soul through the epics. These islands are called the Dutch Indies; but in point of fact they are the Vyasa Indies.†

I have already remarked that Ghatotkacha's son has the name Shashi-kiran. Sanskrit names are still freely used here, sometimes somewhat strangely. For example, the raja's physician is designated Krida-nirmal ('whose play is to clean'). The Sanskrit word for play has here come to mean 'function', and 'to clean' means 'to heal'. Irrigation water is called *sindhu-amrita* ('the nectar of the sea'). *Sindhu*, the word for sea, is generally used for water, and it is here called nectar because it gives life to the fields. One of the sons of our host is named Sarosha ('the enraged one'!), but here *rosha* means courage, rather than rage. The raja's daughter is named Kusuma-vardhini ('she who causes flowers to bloom'). High-sounding Sanskrit names that are unknown even in our country are not uncommon here, as, for instance, Atma-suvijna ('who thoroughly knows himself'), Virya-suvrata ('who has taken

† Sage Vyasa is traditionally responsible for the writing down of the *Mahabharata*.

a vow of good courage'), Yaso-vidagdha ('on fire with the effulgence of fame') and a host of others.

I have not yet told you about the shadow pictures, which we saw at the house of Abhimanyu, the son of Raja Soesoe-hunan, to which we were recently invited. . . . They are a specialty of this country, remarkable in their way, which I have not seen anywhere else. A white screen was set up as background, in front of which stood a huge oil lampstand, the flame of which threw light on to the screen. Beside it lay scattered leather puppet cut-outs taken from the characters of the *Mahabharata*, with limbs attached in such a way that they can be moved by manipulating strings attached to long sticks. The text of the story is chanted by a narrator, and the puppets move to illustrate its incidents. A *gamelan* concert accompanies the show. If only our history lessons had been like this – the schoolmaster telling the story, a marionette show representing its main incidents, and a musical accompaniment voicing the emotions in various melodies and rhythms! . . .

When we first entered the part of the hall which was on the lighted side of the screen, the effect was somewhat disappointing. Then we were taken over to the dark side where the women were seated. Here the pictures themselves and their manipulators were no longer visible, we could see only the shadows dancing on the lighted screen, like the dance of Mahamaya on the prostrate body of Shiva. It is only when the Creator, who abides in the region of light, conceals himself, that we see his creation. He who knows that the Creator is in constant communion with created forms, knows the truth. He who views the process of creation as separate from the Creator, sees only *maya*. There are seekers of truth who would tear away the screen and go over to the lighted side – that is, they want to see the Creator separate from his creation – and nothing can be so empty as the *maya* of their illusion. That is what I felt as I looked at this show.

When we were coming away, our host gave me a present of great rarity – a piece of *batik* cloth made only for members of the raja's own family. I could never have purchased such a piece.

The chapter of our stay here is coming to an end. Tomorrow we go to Djokjakarta, where we shall be similarly entertained, but in a different, older style. From there we proceed to Borobudur which is quite near by, only an hour's run by motor. All this will take five or six days more, and after that I shall have earned a rest. . . .

From Djokjakarta we went over to Borobudur and stayed the night. But first we visited a small temple at a place called Mundung. It was falling to pieces, but the Government has set it up again. I liked the design. Inside were three immense figures of the Buddha in different attitudes. I stood and looked at them in awe.

Once, many men united to make these images and this shrine. What a turmoil of activity – conceiving, preparing and executing the plan – and what an exuberance of life arising! On the day these giant stones were raised into place on this hilltop, a vast human endeavour surged and swayed amid this verdant woodland, beneath this radiant, sun-lit sky. In those days, however, news did not circulate through the world – so this grand manifestation of human will-power occurring in this little island was not noised abroad, as happened when the Victoria Memorial was erected on the Calcutta Maidan.

The building of Borobudur must have taken an age, far exceeding the span of any individual life. The intense feeling of worship of which it was the outcome, must have been widespread and true over a prolonged period of time – the quotidian joys and sorrows of the people must have been permeated with praise, argument and gossip about the temple. Then, after it had been completed, every day there would have been the lighting of lamps, the bringing of offerings by successive groups of devotees, the thronging of men and women for special festivals – until eventually the cumulative dust of ages smothered both the original feeling and its expression.

What had been vitally true now lost its meaning. Today the temple is like the boulders of a watercourse left standing after the water has run dry. When the flow of life that played around them changed course, the stones still bore the impress of the old current, but they ceased to speak; with the cessation of life's movement, its message was lost. Then we came along in our motor car to see the temple. But where was the light to see it by? The vision behind this work of art had vanished.

I had often seen photographs of Borobudur, but had never been impressed by it as a whole. I had hoped it would be different when I stood before it, but I found myself no better pleased. It is so cut up into galleries, one above the other, and its pinnacle is so disproportionately small that in spite of its size, the whole lacks dignity. It looks like a mountain wearing a diminutive stone cap. Perhaps it was intended as a mere repository for stone figures – some hundreds of Buddhas and sculpted pictures representing the *Jataka* stories – like a huge basket of sculptures. For some of the sculptures are extraordinarily good. I especially liked the stone-carved *Jataka* pictures, with their crowds of figures depicting the multifarious intercourse of daily life in those times, and which are untainted by obscenity or vulgarity. I have seen images of gods and goddesses, or scenes from the sacred epics, in other Javanese temples; but here life is shown in its workaday aspect, whether it be the life of the king or the beggar. . . .

I remember having seen in my childhood a tender-eyed cow, coming up and licking a washerman's donkey tied to a peg – and how wonder-struck I was! The *Jataka* writer would have had no hesitation in asserting that the Buddha was such a cow in one of his births, and that the cow's loving kindness was but part of a series of such compassionate acts that end in liberation. In each of the small episodes with which the *Jatakas* are concerned, the artist has perceived the greatness of the ultimate consummation. The trivial has been transmuted into the sublime. That is how a simple and unaffected reverence has turned the vast space of these temple walls into a canvas of everyday life. Through Buddhism, the whole course of life on earth has been invested with glory, as the field in which dharma seeks self-expression.

Two Dutch savants had been deputed to expound the details to us. I was immensely pleased with the simplicity and warm-heartedness which permeated their scholarship. Most of all I was struck by their devotion, the way they have dedicated their lives to making these stone figures speak. They are not miserly in their scholarship, on the contrary they are exceedingly generous. We must accept them as our gurus if we want to understand India in her wholeness. It is love of knowledge for its own sake that fuels their doggedness; for though the history and culture of India are not matters that directly impinge on them, yet they have made study of India their life's work. I have seen other scholars like them, and I am drawn to their simple humility.

*

When, at the end of our Java chapter, we came to Batavia,† we thought we were at last in sight of the boat that would ferry us back to our homeland. But just as our minds had spread their wings ready to fly homewards, a telegram came to say that I was wanted at Bangkok, where hospitality was awaiting us. So again our course was changed. I felt like a hack horse whose driver suddenly takes a fresh turning when the stable is nearly reached, after a hard day's work. For I must confess that I am tired. I know people (I need not name them) who if the opportunity but

† Now Jakarta.

came would be ready to play the tourist to perfection all their lives, but whom fate has tied down to their household duties in a particular address in north Calcutta. And here am I, who find comfort in letting my mind range through the skies only when my body is at rest in its corner, doomed to flit from port to port. So I am off, not homewards, but Siamwards.

The government steamer in which we were to have proceeded to Singapore was overcrowded. So we have taken our passages in a smaller boat, which set off yesterday morning. Suniti and Dhiren remained behind for a day, as Suniti has to deliver a lecture on Indian civilization. He has made quite a reputation among the learned men here, for there is nothing spurious in his scholarship. He always knows what he talks about.

Our boat will go round by two other islands, so that the normal two-day journey will take three. When Visvakarma was engaged in creating the world, his bag of earth must have sprung a hole around these parts, and bits of it become scattered all over the sea. All these islands are now under Dutch rule. The one we are now anchored at is called Biliton.[†] It has few inhabitants but many tin mines, with their managers and miners. I am struck with wonder, as I sit and look on, to think how exhaustively these westerners are exploiting the earth. It is not so very long ago that different groups of them sallied forth by sailing ship into unknown waters. And, as they sailed around, they saw the earth, got to know it and took its measure. The history of these enterprises bristles with difficulties and dangers. I sometimes try to imagine the feelings of trepidation mixed with hopeful anticipation with which they must have furled their sails upon first sighting islands such as these in distant seas. The vegetation, the animals and the humans were all unknown to them: and yet today, how thoroughly studied and *possessed*.

We of the East have had to acknowledge defeat at their hands.

† Now Belitung.

Why? Chiefly because we are static and they are dynamic. We are variously bound to our social order, they are mobile, with individual liberty. A wandering life comes easily to them; and they have gathered knowledge and possessions through their wanderings. For the same reason, their desire to know and to acquire is keen – a desire that in us has become dull owing to the quietude of our settled lives. We neither know nor care about those who dwell, or the things that happen in our immediate neighbourhood, so thoroughly walled about by our homes are we. People who lack the urge to know are deficient in life force. The forcefulness that has enabled the Dutch people to make these islands their own in every way, also impels them to master its antiquities with the same thoroughness of disciplined endeavour, though both the islands and their antiquities are foreign to their own lives and culture. We are often indifferent to subjects and facts that intimately affect us; they, by contrast, have unbounded curiosity, even about things that remotely affect them.

Thus they are winning the world, outwardly and inwardly, not only by force of arms, but also by intellectual power. But we are wholly and solely householders, that is to say we have been reduced to mere appurtenances of our households, adhering to them beneath a thousand burdens. The burden of our livelihood has become intertwined with the burden of our social observances. So clogged and hampered are our lives by meaningless rites that more important duties become impossible of proper fulfilment. Our social rituals – from birth all the way through to death – exert their sway over both this world and the next, and leave us bereft of energy to take a forward step. Is it any wonder that children born and bred in this atmosphere are defeated by others at every turn?

We have begun to understand this, and perhaps for that reason some of our leaders have taken to preaching the ideal of renunciation. But in the same breath they ask us to hark back to our past culture as being the *sanatan dharma*, the sole and everlasting truth; they forget that our ancient dharma was based on the performance of our householder's duties, not on their renunciation. While those leaders who do not actively invoke the *sanatan dharma*, nevertheless see no harm in obeying it. If you destroy the old foundations, they say, how will you replace them? For every society has evolved its own traditions that help to keep its members on the right path, since few people are capable of reasoning out each step in their lives; and it is not simple to substitute one set of traditions for another: we may learn science from the West, but can we make her social system our own?

The owner of one of the tin mines was on our boat. He had been mining, he said, for sixteen years. Though there is nothing on Biliton except tin mines, he had made the place his home. In Batavia I met Sindhi shopkeepers. Their custom is to go home to Sind once in every two years. I asked them why they did not bring over their wives and children and set up house, and they said that would never do, for a wife is bound to family life, which would be disrupted if she were taken away. I hardly think such an argument would have been advanced in the India of the *Ramayana*! To return to the tin mine owner – he had spent his boyhood in a boarding-school, and when he came of age had set out to seek his fortune. Ever since he married, he had relied only on his own efforts, making no claim on his father's purse and having no yearning for uncles and aunts of various removes. It is because of such people that tin is being mined in this out-of-the-way place. They are homeless, and therefore they can make their homes anywhere. In the same spirit they keep their telescopes fixed on the planet Mars, night after night, year in year out, because their thirst for knowledge too is not home-bound. How can our *sanatan* home-dwellers hope to hold their own against these people? – for the very props of their homes have been undermined and are falling beneath this onrush, which cannot be stemmed.

So long as we were content to sit quiet, the cumulative burden of unmeaning things heaped mountain-high on our backs was not so unbearable – we could even use it as a cushion on which to recline. But when we attempt to get up and shoulder the burden, so as to advance, then our backbone bends under the strain. Mobile people must always be careful about what they will carry and what they will cast away, and this sharpens their powers of discrimination. But our *sanatan* householders, seated at their doorways, have not managed to get rid of any one of the three-hundred-and-sixty-five items of foolishness that encumber every page of the calendar they so religiously follow.

Filled to the brim and loaded to breaking point with all this rubbish, they hear the command from the platform of the Congress to keep in step and move at double-quick pace. They lack the language to articulate a reply, but their sore hearts within their crushed bodies burst with this unuttered plea: 'We are only too willing to march ahead at the bidding of our political leaders, if our social leaders will deign to relieve us of our burden.' Whereupon the social leaders stand aghast – 'What! Is that not your *sanatan* burden?'

# FROM *Letters from Russia*

## *Moscow, September 1930*

In Russia at last! Everything I see amazes me. This country is unlike any other. It is radically different. From top to bottom here they are rousing up everybody equally.

Through the ages, civilized communities have contained a body of common people. They form the majority – these beasts of burden, who have no time to become human beings. They grow up on the leftovers of a country's wealth, having the least food, the least clothes and the least education; and they serve the rest. They toil the most, yet receive the largest ration of indignity. At the least excuse they starve and are humiliated by their superiors. They are deprived of everything that makes life worth living. They are like a lampstand bearing the lamp of civilization on their heads: those above them receive light, while they are smeared with trickles of oil.

I had often thought about such people, but had come to the conclusion that there was no help for them. For if no one was down below, no one could be up above. People do not see beyond their immediate needs, unless they are above mere subsistence level. The earning of his livelihood cannot be the destiny of man. Human civilization consists of more than mere subsistence. The most cherished products of civilization have flourished in the field of leisure. Civilization must preserve a corner for leisure. So I used to think that for those fitted to labour at the bottom of the heap by their poor mental and physical constitution or by force of circumstances, the best that could be done was to make strenuous efforts to improve their education, health and comfort.

But the trouble is that nothing permanent can be built on charity; efforts to do good imposed from outside are vitiated at every step. Without equality, no real help can be rendered. I have not been able to think all this through satisfactorily – but whatever the case, the notion that the advance of civilization depends on keeping down the bulk of humanity and denying it its human rights, is a reproach to the human mind.

Consider how foodless India has fed England. Many English people think it natural that the fulfilment of India should lie eternally in the nourishing of England. To these people it is not wrong to keep a nation enslaved for ever, in order that England may become great and do great things for mankind – what does it matter if the nation has little to eat or wear? While other English people, out of sheer pity, sometimes feel they must help us to improve our conditions slightly. And yet, over the past hundred years we have acquired neither education nor health nor wealth.

At the level of the individual in all societies, the same truth applies: men cannot do good to those whom they do not respect. At the very least, one can say that whenever there is self-interest at stake, a clash ensues. Here in Russia they are seeking a root-and-branch solution to this problem. It is not yet time to consider the final results of the attempt, but for now I can say that whatever I see astonishes me. Education is the ideal path to solving all our problems. Everywhere the majority of people have been deprived of full opportunities for education – in India it is the vast majority. The extraordinary vigour with which education has taken hold of Russian society is amazing to witness. The measure is not merely the numbers being educated, but the thoroughness, the intensity of the education. What dedication and application to ensure that no one remains helpless or idle! Not only in European Russia, but among the semi-civilized races of Central Asia too, the floodgates of education have been opened. Tireless efforts are being made to bring the latest fruits of science to the people. The theatres and the fine opera houses are crowded, but those coming to them are peasants and workers. Nowhere are they humiliated. In the few institutions I have so far visited, I have seen the awakening of these people's spirit and the joy of their self-respect. The difference between them and the working class in England, leave alone our masses, is colossal. What we have been attempting to do at our Shriniketan, they are doing here at a superior level all over the land. How splendid it would be if our workers could come here for training. Every day I compare conditions here with those in India: what is, and what might have been! Doctor Harry Timbres, my American companion, is studying the health service of this country: its excellence is astonishing. But where does that leave diseased, hungry, hapless India! A few years ago, the condition of the Russian masses was fully comparable with that of the Indian masses. Over that short period things have rapidly changed here, whereas we Indians are still up to our necks in stagnation.

I do not say all is perfect here; there are grave defects, which will bring them trouble some day. Briefly, the problem is that they have made a mould for their education system – and human beings cannot endure being cast in a mould. If an educational theory does not correspond with the law of living minds, either the mould will shatter or the minds will be paralysed and men will become automata.

I notice that the boys here have been divided into groups and charged with different responsibilities. In running their dormitories, they have all sorts of duties: some look after health, others after the stores, over which they have sole control. They have only a single supervisor. I have long tried to do the same at our Shantiniketan, but little has happened beyond framing some rules. One reason is that the prime object of our school is seen as getting the boys through their examinations: everything else is considered secondary; in other words, if something extra can be achieved without bother, well and good, if not, let things be.

Our lazy minds are loath to tackle tasks that lie beyond what is compulsory. Moreover, from childhood we have been used to cramming books. But of what use are rules, unless the rule makers are sincere about them; otherwise, the rules are bound to be ignored. There is little happening here that goes beyond my own thinking on rural development and education – the difference is that here the ideas are backed by the power, enthusiasm and administrative ability of the authorities. Much of this derives from their greater physical strength: our malaria-struck, undernourished bodies do not work at full vigour. Progress here is easy because in a cold climate people have strong bones. The strength of our workers cannot be reckoned by counting heads; for they are not whole men.

*

## Interview with *Izvestia*

### *25 September 1930*

I wish to let you know how deeply I have been impressed by the amazing intensity of your energy in spreading education among the masses, the most intelligent direction which you have given to this noble work and also the variety of channels that have been opened out to train their minds and senses and limbs. I appreciate it all the more keenly because I belong to that country where millions of my fellow-countrymen are denied the light that education can bring to them. For human beings all other boons that are external, that are imposed from outside, are like paints and patches that never represent the bloom of health but only disguise the anaemic skin without enriching the blood. You have recognized the truth that in extirpating all social evils one has to go to the root, and not through police batons and military browbeating.

But I find here certain contradictions to the great mission which you have undertaken. Certain attitudes of mind are being cultivated which are contrary to your ideal.

I must ask you: are you doing your ideal a service by arousing in the minds of those under your training, anger, class hatred and revengefulness against those not sharing your ideal, against those whom you consider to be your enemies? True, you have to fight against obstacles, you have to overcome ignorance and lack of sympathy, even persistently virulent antagonism. But your mission is not restricted to your own nation or own party, it is for the betterment of humanity according to your light. But does not humanity include those who do not agree with your aim? Just as you try to help peasants who have other ideas than yours about religion, economics and social life, not by getting fatally angry with them, but by patiently teaching them and showing them where the evil lurks in secret, should you not have the same mission to those other people who have other ideals than your own? These you may consider to be mistaken ideals, but they have an historical origin and have become inevitable through a combination of circumstances. You may consider the men who hold them as misguided. But it should all the more be your mission to try to convert them by pity and love, realizing that they are as much a part of humanity as the peasants whom you serve.

If you dwell too much upon the evil elements in your opponents and assume that they are inherent in human nature meriting eternal damnation, you inspire an attitude of mind which with its content of hatred and revengefulness may some day react against your own ideal and destroy it. You are working in a great cause. Therefore you must be great in your mind, great in your mercy, your understanding and your patience. I feel profound admiration for the greatness of the things you are trying to do; therefore I cannot help expecting for it a motive force of love and an environment of charitable understanding.

There must be disagreement where minds are allowed to be free. It would not only be an uninteresting but a sterile world of mechanical regularity if all of our opinions were forcibly made alike. If you have a mission which includes all humanity, you must, for the sake of that living humanity, acknowledge the existence of differences of opinion. Opinions are constantly changed and re-changed only through the free circulation of intellectual forces and moral persuasion. Violence begets violence and blind stupidity. Freedom of mind is needed for the reception of truth; terror hopelessly kills it. The brute cannot subdue the brute. It is only the man who can do it.

Before leaving your country let me once again assure you that I am struck with admiration by all that you are doing to free those who once were in slavery, to raise up those who were lowly and oppressed, endeavouring to bring help to those who are utterly helpless all through the world, reminding them that the source of their salvation lies in a proper education and their power to combine their human resources. Therefore, for the sake of humanity I hope that you may never create a vicious force of violence which will go on weaving an interminable chain of violence and cruelty. Already you have inherited much of this legacy from the czarist regime. It is the worst legacy you could possibly have. You have tried to destroy many of the other evils of that regime. Why not try to destroy this one also? I have learnt much from you, how skilfully you evolve usefulness out of the helpfulness of the weak and ignorant. Your ideal is great and so I ask you for perfection in serving it, and a broad field of freedom for laying its permanent foundation.

# FROM *Journey to Persia*

........................................................................................................

## *Persia, 13 April 1932*

Yesterday we got up at three-thirty in the morning, and left at four o'clock. The aeroplane reached Bushire at half-past eight. The governor himself is acting as our host, and there is no end to his solicitude for our comfort.

Let me set down various thoughts on how I, this son of earth, first became intimate with the sky.

The thing about flying creatures that has struck me from my earliest years is the effortlessness of their motion. Their wings and the air have all the sweetness of friendship. How well I remember that at noontime, as I gazed endlessly from the top of the stairs to our roof at the kites soaring above us, it seemed to me they were flying for the sheer joy of unimpeded buoyancy, rather than to serve any purpose; a joy that was manifest not only in the grace of their movement but in the beauty of their physical form. Sails look beautiful because they are nicely adjusted to the wind. The wings of a bird, likewise, acquire their graceful proportions through being poised in harmony with the air currents, to say nothing of their play of colours. . . . Earthly motion always seems to require effort; gravity reigns supreme, and there is no getting rid of its burden. The aspect of the aerial regions that has long captivated me is the freedom they allow to the play of beauty, the freedom from weight.

Now comes an age in which man has lifted the burdens of earth into the air. His power is the aspect of himself he displays in flying. His progress is not in harmony with the wind, but in opposition to it, importing the spirit of conflict from the

........................................................................................................

mundane world into the empyrean. Its sound is not that of a bird singing, but of a raging beast: the earth, having conquered the air, bellows its victory. . . .

The herald of the modern age, the flying machine, is an unfeeling creature, which elbows aside whatever does not serve its purpose. Whether there is a rosy dawn suffusing the eastern sky or a pearly lustre of departing day lingering over the soft blue of the western horizon, this upstart machine drones on hideously, without shame, like a monstrous beetle.

As it goes higher and higher, it reduces the play of our senses to that of one sense alone – sight – and even that does not fully remain. The signs that tell us the earth is real are gradually obliterated, and a three-dimensional picture is flattened into two-dimensional lines. . . . Thus deprived of its substantiality, the earth's hold on our mind and heart is loosened. And it is borne in on me how such aloofness can become terrible, when man finds it expedient to rain destruction on the vagueness below. Who is the slayer and who the slain? Who is kin and who is stranger? This travesty of the teaching of the *Bhagavad Gita* is raised on high by the flying machine.

A British air force is stationed at Baghdad. Its Christian chaplain informs me that they are engaged in bombing operations on some Sheikh villages. The men, women and children done to death there meet their fate by a decree from the stratosphere of British imperialism – which finds it easy to shower death because of its distance from its individual victims. So dim and insignificant do those unskilled in the modern arts of killing appear to those who glory in such skill! Christ acknowledged all mankind to be the children of his Father; but for the modern Christian both Father and children have receded into shadows, unrecognizable from the elevation of his bombarding plane – for which reason these blows are dealt at the very heart of Christ himself.

The official priest of the Iraqi air force asked, on their behalf, for a message from me. I copy here what I gave them:

From the beginning of our days man has imagined the seat of divinity to be in the upper air, from which comes light, and blows the breath of life, for all the creatures on this earth. The peace of its dawn, the splendour of its sunset, the voice of eternity in its starry silence, have inspired countless generations of men with a sense of the ineffable presence of the infinite, urging their minds away from the sordid interests of daily life. Man is content with this dust-laden earth for his dwelling place, for the acting of the drama of his tangled life, ever waiting for a call to perfection from the boundless depth of purity in the translucent atmosphere surrounding him. If, in an evil moment, man's cruel history should spread its black wings to invade that realm of divine dreams with its cannibalistic greed and fratricidal ferocity, then God's curse will certainly descend upon us for such hideous desecration, and the curtain will finally be rung down upon the world of man, for whom God feels ashamed.

On the other hand, I should also mention the feeling of inferiority brought upon me by the aeroplane.... The air-chariot of old, of which we read, belonged to the realm of Lord Indra – mortals like King Dushyanta occasionally had a ride in it by special invitation. This was exactly my situation. The inventors of the aeroplane belong to a different race. Had this achievement of theirs been merely a matter of superior skill, it would not have so affected me, but it denotes superior force of character: indomitable perseverance, unflagging courage, things to be really proud of. For this I offer them my salutation.

Look at our four Dutch pilots – immensely built, the personification of energy. Their country of birth has not drained them of life, but kept them fresh. Their rude, overflowing health, bequeathed by generations brought up on nourishing food, does not permit them to remain tied down by dull routine. But the millions of India have not enough to eat and, moreover, they have been exhausted by the toll paid to internal and external enemies. Any worthwhile achievement depends on the collaboration of man's physical and mental forces. We may have the mind, but where is our vitality?

# LETTERS

The letters of Tagore run into many thousands, and that excludes those letters written on foreign visits later collected together and published as books of travel. They span over sixty years, from 1878 to the final months of Tagore's life in 1941. Almost all the significant ones written in Bengali have been published (though not translated) in the decades since his death, unlike those written in English, many of which remain virtually or wholly unknown. This is unfortunate, because Tagore's letters – Bengali and English together – are some of his most alert writings: they express his ideas in a more concise and vivid manner than many of his published writings and they show him struggling (and generally failing) against indifference and iniquity to give these ideas concrete expression; his unique sense of humour also shines out of the more intimate letters.

In Bengali, his finest letters were written during the 1890s to his niece Indira, a beautiful, sensitive and musically gifted person then in her late teens and twenties; she stayed either in Calcutta or in some other Indian city. At this period Uncle Rabi, in his thirties, was living away from Calcutta 'up-country', managing the family estates, the Tagore *zamindari*, in East Bengal (now Bangladesh), with time on his hands to write discursively. He enjoyed telling Indira about life on the estates, from the tragedies and comedies of his tenants' lives, his attempts to help them and his farcical attempts to play host to visiting British officials to the profoundly introspective states of his mind induced by being alone in such a quiet place, all permeated by the moods of nature in the Ganges delta which range from cyclonic storms that wreak dreadful havoc to moon-struck nights of mirror-like tranquillity. The rivers are a constant presence in these letters: often he wrote from on board his houseboat. Satyajit Ray described this time in Tagore's life thus, in his documentary film, *Rabindranath Tagore* (1961):

> With a worldly wisdom unusual in a poet but characteristic of the Tagores, Rabindranath in later life set about in a practical way to improve the lot of the poor peasants of his estates, and his varied work in this field is on record. But his own gain from this intimate contact with the fundamental aspects of life and Nature, and the influence of this contact on his life and work – are beyond measure. Living mostly in his boat and watching life through the window, a whole new world of sights and sounds and feelings opened up before him.

Nirad C. Chaudhuri has rightly called the estate letters to Indira 'great works of literature', which 'reveal [Tagore's] character and personality with unadorned truth'.

None of the letters in English reaches quite the same literary standard or level of intimacy. The compensation, apart from the greater familiarity of the material to a western reader, is in the quality of the thoughts and ideas. For example, when Tagore informs Mahatma Gandhi, who is fasting against Untouchability, 'You ask others actively to devote their energy to extirpate the evil which smothers our national life and enjoin only upon yourself an extreme form of sacrifice which is of a passive character.' Or when he writes to the poet Thomas Sturge Moore: 'I think it has been the good fortune of the West to have the opportunity of absorbing the spirit of the East through the medium of the Bible. . . . it has created a bifurcation in your mental system which is so needful for all life growth.'

The subject-matter of the English letters printed here ranges from the politics of the non-cooperation movement to the subtleties of literary translation. Many of the correspondents are famous, W. B. Yeats, Bertrand Russell, Jawaharlal Nehru, and so on, a few of them less well known, though all are remarkable in some way.

A brief introduction to a particular letter, whether Bengali or English, is occasionally provided, but the majority do not require any contextualization.

# TO Mrinalini Tagore, his wife

S.S. Siam
*Friday, 29 August 1890*

*Bhai Chhoto Bou*†

Today we will reach a place called Aden and touch land again after a long time. But we cannot disembark, in case we pick up some contagious disease. On arrival in Aden we have to change ship, which will be a big bother. I cannot tell you how seasick I have been this time – for three days, whatever I swallowed just came up again, my head felt dizzy and the rest of me was in turmoil – I even wondered whether I would pull through. On Sunday night I distinctly felt my self leave my body and go to Jorasanko. You were lying on one side of the big bed, Beli and Khoka beside you. I caressed you a little and said, 'Little wife, remember this Sunday night when I left my body and came to see you – when I return from Europe I shall ask you if you saw me.' Then I kissed Beli and Khoka and came back. When I was ill did you ever think of me? I became restless thinking of seeing you again. Nowadays I feel constantly that there is no place like home – this time when I get back I shall not stir out any more. Today I had my first bath for a week. But baths here are not a pleasure: the salt in the seawater makes the whole body sticky and my hair becomes matted and horribly glued together – it is an odd sensation. I think I shall avoid bathing until I leave the ship. It will be another week before we reach Europe – when we get there, I shall be glad to set foot on land. I have had enough of the ocean day and night. But at present the sea is

† My Dear Little Wife.

pretty calm, the ship hardly rolls, and I am no longer sick. All day I lie on deck in a long chair and either chat with Loken, ponder, or read a book. At night too, we make our beds on deck and avoid entering our cabins if possible. Going inside the cabin makes you feel queasy. Last night, though, it suddenly rained – we had to drag our bedding to a place where the rain could not get at us. Since then it has not stopped raining, after being fine and sunny yesterday. On board there are some little girls, whose mother has died and whose father is taking them to England. When I look at them I feel pity. Their father goes everywhere with them, but he does not know how to dress them properly or how to look after them. When they go out in the rain and he warns them not to, they tell him 'we like going out in the rain' – which makes him laugh a bit; seeing them happily playing in the rain he cannot bring himself to stop them. To look at them reminds me of my own babies. Last night I dreamt of Beli – she had come on board the steamer, and she looked lovelier than I can say. You must tell me what sort of thing I should bring them when I return home. If you answer this letter immediately, I might receive your reply while I am in England. Remember that Tuesday is the day for mailing to England. Give the children lots of kisses from me – and have some yourself too.

Shri Rabindranath Thakur

[signed in Bengali]

# TO Indira Tagore, his niece

*Shahzadpur, East Bengal*
*25 January 1890*

[Bibi]

And so at midday this zamindar babu placed his puggree on his head, picked up one of his visiting cards, climbed into his palanquin, and sallied forth. The magistrate was sitting in the veranda of his tent dispensing justice, flanked by constables. A crowd of supplicants waited nearby beneath the shade of a tree. My palanquin was set down under the sahib's nose and he received me cordially on his wooden cot. He was a young fellow with only the beginnings of a moustache. His hair was very fair with darker patches here and there, giving him an odd appearance – one could almost have mistaken him for a white-haired old man but for his extremely youthful face. Hospitability was required of me; I said, 'Do come and eat with me tomorrow night.' He said, 'I am due elsewhere to arrange for a pig sticking.' I (inwardly exultant) said, 'What a shame.' The sahib replied, 'I shall be back again on Monday.' I (now feeling despondent) said, 'Then please come and eat on Monday.' He instantly agreed. Never mind, I sighed to myself – Monday is a fair way off.

As I was returning to the house, terrific clouds rolled up and a tremendous storm began with torrents of rain. I had no desire to pick up a book, and writing was impossible, my mind was too disturbed for it – or to put my mood in more poetic language, I felt someone was missing, if only the person were here instead of being far away. So I took to wandering back and forth from room to room in a distracted frame of mind. It became quite dark. Thunder rumbled constantly, there was flash after flash of lightning, and every now and then gusts of wind got hold of the trunk of the big lychee tree outside the veranda and gave its shaggy top a thorough shaking. The dry pit in front of the house soon filled with water. . . . As I paced I was suddenly struck by the thought that I should offer shelter to the magistrate. I sent off a note, saying something like 'Sahib, to go out pig sticking in this weather will not work. Even though you are a strapping sahiblet, living in a watery tent can be trying for a land-based species – should you prefer dry land, my refuge awaits you.'

But having despatched the note, when I went to investigate the only spare room I found it a real sight. Two bamboo poles were hanging from the beams, over which were draped dirty old quilts and bolsters. Littering the floor were servants' belongings, tobacco pipes and two wooden chests containing a soiled quilt, a coverless oil-smeared pillow, a grimy mat, a bit of hessian variously stained and a layer of dirt. . . . besides sundry packing cases full of broken odds and ends such as a rusty kettle lid, an iron stove without a bottom, a discoloured old zinc teapot, some bottles and old glasses, bits of glass shade from an oil lamp, a sooty lampstand, a couple of filters, a meat safe, a soup plate caked in treacle and dust, some broken and unbroken plates and a pile of soggy and dirty dusters. In a corner was a tub for washing clothes, Gophur Mia's cook's uniform, soiled, and his old velvet skull cap. The furniture and fittings consisted of one rickety, worm-eaten dressing table bearing water stains, oil stains, milk stains, black, brown and white stains and all kinds of mixed stains, with damaged legs and detached mirror resting against a wall and drawers which were receptacles for dust, toothpicks, napkins, old locks, the bases of broken glasses, wires from soda bottles and bed casters, rods and stuffing; one wash-hand stand, with broken legs; and four walls, with smelly stains and nails poking out of them.

For a moment I was overwhelmed with dismay, then it was a case of send for everyone, the manager, the storekeeper, the cashier and all the servants, get hold of extra men, bring a broom, fetch water, put up ladders, unfasten ropes, pull down poles, take away bolsters, quilts and bedding, pick up broken glass bit by little bit, wrench nails from the wall one by one. Why are you people standing there staring? – grab hold of those and try not to break them. Bang, bang, crash! – there go three glass lamp holders – pick them up piece by piece. I myself whisk a wicker basket and mat encrusted with the filth of ages off the floor and out of the window, thereby dislodging a family of cockroaches that scatter in all directions, to whose business I have been unwitting host as they dined off my bread, my treacle and the polish on my shoes.

The magistrate's reply arrives: 'I'm on my way out of real trouble.' Hurry up everyone! You must hurry! Soon there's a shout: 'The sahib has arrived.' In a flurry I brush the dust off my hair, my beard, and the rest of my person, and try to look, as I receive my guest in the drawing room, like a gentleman who has been reposing there comfortably all afternoon. I shake the sahib's hand, converse and laugh without apparent concern; but inside I cannot stop thinking about his sleeping accommodation. When at last I showed him his room, I found it passable; he should have had a night's rest – if the homeless cockroaches did not tickle the soles of his feet. The sahib said, 'Tomorrow morning I shall go for a spot of shikar.' I refrained from making any comment. In the evening a routed footman from the sahib's camp turned up with the news that the storm had torn his sleeping tent to pieces; his office tent too was soaked and in a pretty bad state. And so the sahib had to put off hunting other animals and put up with this zamindar babu.

[Uncle Rabi]

# TO Indira Tagore, his niece

*Kaligram, East Bengal*
*19(?) January 1891*

[Bibi]

As I began to write to you, one of our clerks here came and chattered away about his sad state of poverty, the need for an increase in his wages and the necessity of a man getting married – he went on talking and I went on writing, until finally I paused and briefly tried to get him to understand the idea that when a sensible person grants someone's petition it is because the petition is reasonable, not because it has been repeated five times instead of once only. I had imagined that such a wise and wonderful remark would render the fellow speechless, but I saw that in fact it had the opposite effect. Instead of falling silent he asked me a question – if a child does not open its mind to its own parents, who will he talk to? This left me stumped for a satisfactory reply. So once again he started chattering and I for my part continued to write. To be nominated a parent out of the blue and for nothing is quite a trial.

Yesterday, while I was listening to the petitions of my tenants, five or six boys appeared and formed a disciplined line in front of me. Before I could open my mouth their spokesman launched into a high-flown speech: 'Sire! The grace of the Almighty and the good fortune of your benighted children have once more brought about your lordship's auspicious arrival in this locality.' He went on like this for nearly half an hour, pausing from time to time to stare at the sky when he forgot his lines, correct himself, and then continue. His subject was the shortage of school benches and stools. 'For want of these wooden supports,' as he put it, 'we know not where to seat ourselves, where to seat our revered teachers, or what to offer our most respected inspector when he pays a visit.' Such a torrent of eloquence from such a small boy made it hard for me to hide a smile. Particularly in a place like this, where the unlettered ryots[†] normally voice their humble needs and sorrows in the plain and direct vernacular. The talk is usually of floods, famines, cows, calves and ploughs – in other words the unavoidable facts of life – and even those words get twisted out of shape. So a speech about stools and benches in such refined language sounded really out of place! The clerks and ryots, however, were duly impressed by the boy's mastery of words – they seemed to be lamenting to themselves, 'Our parents failed to educate us properly, or we too could appear before the zamindar and make appeals in equally grand language.' One of them nudged another and said enviously, 'He must have been coached!'

In due course I interrupted and said, 'Well, boys, I shall arrange for the required benches and stools.' Undaunted, the boy took up where he had left off and, despite my having spoken, finished to the last word, bowed low in order to touch my feet with a *pranam*, and then took himself and the others home. He had lavished such pains over his learning by heart. Had I refused to supply the seats he probably would not have minded, but had I deprived him of his speech – that would have struck him as intolerable. Therefore, though it kept more important matters waiting, I gravely heard him out. If someone with the right sense of humour had been about, probably I would have jumped up and run next door to share the joke. But a zamindari is simply not the place for a humourmonger – here we display only solemnity and high learning.

[Uncle Rabi]

† Peasants.

# TO Indira Tagore, his niece

*Shahzadpur, East Bengal*
*June 1891*

[Bibi]

Last night I had an extraordinary dream. The whole of Calcutta was enveloped by some formidable but peculiar power, the houses rendered only dimly visible by a dense dark mist, through which strange doings could be glimpsed. I was on my way down Park Street in a hackney carriage, and as I passed St Xavier's College I found it to be growing rapidly with its top fast vanishing into darkness and fog. I came to know that a band of men had come to town who could, if properly paid, perform many such magical tricks. When I reached our house at Jorasanko, I found the magicians had got there too. They were ugly-looking fellows, Mongolian in features, with wispy moustaches and a few long hairs sticking out of their chins. They had the power to make people, as well as houses, grow. All the ladies in our house were keen to become taller, and the magicians sprinkled some powder on their heads and they promptly shot up. I could only mutter: 'This is most extraordinary – just like a dream!' Then someone proposed that our house should be made to expand. Our visitors agreed, and as preparation they quickly demolished some portions. Dismantling done, they demanded money, or else they would not go on. The cashier was aghast; how could payment be made before the job was completed? The magicians became wild. They twisted the building into a stupendous tangle, so that half of some occupants was set into the brickwork and the other half was left sticking out. It was a diabolical business. I said to my eldest brother: 'Just look at the mess we're in. We'd better start praying to God for help!' I went into the corridor and concentrated on praying. When I had finished I thought I would go and reprimand these creatures in the name of God – but though my heart was bursting, no words came out of my throat. Then I woke up – I am not sure when. A curious dream, wasn't it? Calcutta entirely under the control of Satan: everything in it inflating tremendously in size and prosperity with his help, while enveloped in an infernal fog. One aspect was rather funny: with the whole city to choose from, why single out the Jesuit college for special satanic attention?

The schoolmasters of the English school in Shahzadpur paid me a courtesy call yesterday. They showed no sign of leaving, even though I could not find a word to say. Every five minutes or so I managed a question, to which they offered the briefest of replies; and then I sat like a dunce, twirling my pen and scratching my head. At last I ventured a query about the crops, but being schoolmasters they knew nothing of this subject whatsoever. About their pupils I had already asked everything I could think of, so I had to start over again: 'How many boys had they in the school?' One said eighty, another a hundred and seventy-five. I hoped that this might provoke an argument, but no, they settled their difference. Why, an hour and a half later, they should have decided to take their leave, is hard to know. They might just as well have gone an hour earlier or, for that matter, twelve hours later. They seemed not to follow any rule but to rely on blind fate.

[Uncle Rabi]

# TO Indira Tagore, his niece

*Shelidah, East Bengal*
*4 January 1892*

[Bibi]

A few days ago the engineer sahib arrived from Pabna with his wife and children. You know, Bob, that looking after guests does not come easily to me – I become soft in the head – moreover I had no idea he would turn up with a couple of children. I had planned to be alone this time, so I was especially low on edibles. Somehow, by ignoring my creature comforts, I had been getting by on scraps. Now the memsahib likes tea, and I had none to give her; she has an aversion for dal formed in childhood, and I offered her dal for lack of any other food; she has not touched fish for years and years and I, little suspecting, gave her fish curry. Luckily she likes 'country sweets' and consumed an old and dried-up piece of *shandesh* with great determination by using a fork to break it. Last year's biscuit box, whatever might be the state of its contents, is going to come in handy.

I have committed another major blunder. I told the sahib that though his wife drinks tea, most regrettably I lack tea and have only cocoa. He replied, the lady loves cocoa even more than tea. Well, I've raided my cupboard – no cocoa! It's all been sent back to Calcutta. So now I have to tell him there's no tea and no cocoa either – Padma water only, and a teapot. I wonder how he will react.

The two children are really unruly and mischievous, I must say. The memsahib, with her cropped hair, is not as bad looking as I had thought – she is moderately pretty. Periodic rows break out between husband and wife which I can hear from my boat.

The combination of children squabbling, servants loudly chattering, and this couple bickering is bothersome. I can't see much writing getting done today. The memsahib has just shouted at her offspring: 'What a little pig you are!' What have I done to deserve this! What's more, this evening she wants to come ashore for a stroll and has asked me to keep her company – as though I haven't enough afflictions already. If you could see me now you would be itching to laugh – I myself, as I write these words, am having a sad laugh. I had never imagined I would go walking around my zamindari with a mem on my arm. My ryots will doubtless be astonished. If I can only bid them all farewell tomorrow morning, I will survive; but if they say they will be staying another day, I will be dead, Bob.

[Uncle Rabi]

# to Indira Tagore, his niece

Shelidah, East Bengal
12 June 1892

[Bibi]

I hate all the demands of good manners. Nowadays I keep repeating that line: 'Much rather would I be an Arab Bedouin!' Oh for a healthy, strong, unfettered barbarity! I want to quit this creeping senility of mind and body, constantly preoccupied with ancient quibbles over custom and convention, and feel the joy of a vigorous incautious life; to hold confident, carefree, generous ideas and aspirations – for better or for worse; to break free of this perpetual friction between custom and reason, reason and desire, desire and action. If I could only escape utterly the bonds of this restricted life, I would storm the four quarters with wave upon wave of excitement, grab a sturdy wild horse and tear away on it to the very heights of ecstasy.

But I am a Bengali, not a Bedouin! I sit in my corner, moping and worrying and arguing. My mind is like a fish being fried – first this way up, now the other – blistered by the boiling oil on one side, and then on the other. Enough of this. Since it is impracticable to be uncivilized, I had better try to be thoroughly civil – why foment a quarrel between the two?. . .

I am by nature unsocial – human intimacy is almost unbearable to me. Unless I have a lot of space around me in all directions I cannot unpack my mind, mentally stretch my arms and legs. Let the human race flourish with my blessings, but let its members not lean on me. . . . Let the general public leave me completely aside and most probably it will still find the good counsel it seeks. People will not lack for comfort and solace.

[Uncle Rabi]

# TO Indira Tagore, his niece

*Shahzadpur, East Bengal*
*5 September 1894*

[Bibi]

I love it when I move into the Shahzadpur house after living on the boat for a long period. The large doors and windows let in light and air on all sides without hindrance. And when I look out my eye falls on green branches and I hear constant birdsong – the moment I step into the south veranda every pore of my brain is saturated with the fragrance of *kamini* flowers. All of a sudden I realize how hungry for space I have become and so I take my fill of it. I am sole monarch of these four large rooms and so I throw open every door and window. I feel the mood and the will to write here as nowhere else. The living essence of the outside world floats in freely in verdurous waves of light and air and sound and scent that mingle with my bewitched mind and mould it into story after story after story. The intoxication is especially strong in the afternoons. Heat, hush, solitude, birdsong – especially the cawing of crows – and languid, limitless leisure remove me from reality. I believe, though I have no proof, that the *Arabian Nights* came into being upon such sun-baked afternoons in Damascus, Samarkand and Bokhara. I can see the bunches of grapes and the wild gardens of roses, hear the melody of *bulbuls*, taste the wines of Shiraz. In the desert there is only a file of camels, an itinerant horseman or a crystal spring beneath a date palm to be seen. But in the city, below bright canopies overhanging narrow alleys in the bazaar, there sit turbanned, loosely attired merchants selling melons and pomegranates, while not far away in a great palace perfumed with incense, on bolsters and kincob-covered divans within balconies, reclines Zobedia or Amina or Sufia, dressed in a gaily decorated jacket, flowing pyjamas and gold-embroidered slippers, her hubble-bubble pipe coiled at her feet and her person guarded by gorgeously liveried Abyssinians. Such a prodigiously grand and mysterious setting in such a faraway country was bound to lead to a thousand tales – credible and incredible – of the deepest hopes and fears of mankind.

Noontime in Shahzadpur is high noon for story writing. It was at this time, at this very table, I recall, that my story 'The Postmaster' took over my thoughts. The light, the breeze and the movement of leaves on all sides combined and entered my writing. There are few kinds of happiness in the world more filling than the happiness of creating something in which the mind is totally immersed in its surroundings. This morning I set about writing a piece on folk literature, and I became so caught up in it that I enjoyed myself greatly. These folk rhymes belong to an independent realm in which there are no rules and regulations, like cloud-cuckoo-land. Unfortunately, the mundane world with its rules and regulations always catches up and dominates this other world. And so all of a sudden, while I was writing away, officialdom irrupted in the form of my clerks, and blew away my fantasy kingdom. Sorting out the business matter took until lunchtime. It is an imbecile thing to eat a bellyful of food at midday, which stupefies one's imagination and other higher faculties. By overfilling themselves with food at midday, Bengalis fail to drink in the moody intensity of noontime – instead they close their doors, puff away at tobacco, chomp on betel and prepare themselves for a thoroughly torpid siesta. That is how they become glistening and corpulent. But how can anywhere compare with the way in which the exhausted solitude of noontime soundlessly pervades the monotonous fields of the limitless plain of Bengal? Noontime has fascinated me since my early boyhood. In those days the second floor of our house was empty and I used to lie down alone in one of the rooms on a curved couch and feel the hot blast from outside through the open door – I spent whole days there lost in my imagination amid who knows what inarticulate fancies.

[Uncle Rabi]

# TO Indira Tagore, his niece

_Shelidah, East Bengal_
_12 December 1895_

[Bibi]

The other evening an insignificant incident startled me. As I mentioned before, of late I have taken to lighting a lamp in the boat and sitting and reading till I feel sleepy. One should not seek to be alone always and everywhere, particularly in the evening, lest one falls prey to that old saw about wanting some aunt to die so that one can wallow in sorrow; and since, in the absence of a suitable aunt, one may be tempted to fall back on oneself, I prefer to take up a book. That evening I was reading a book of critical essays in English full of contorted disputation about poetry, art, beauty and so forth. As I plodded through these artificial discussions, my weary mind seemed to have strayed into a mirage, a land where things were constructed out of words. A deadening spirit seemed to dance before me like a mocking demon. The night was far advanced, so I shut the book with a snap and flung it on the table, intending to head for bed after blowing out the lamp. But the moment I extinguished the flame, moonlight burst through the open window and flooded the boat. It was like a shock to an infatuated man. The glare from a satanic little lamp had been mocking an infinite radiance. What on earth had I been hoping to find in the empty wordiness of that book? The heavens had been waiting for me soundlessly outside all the time. Had I chanced to miss them and gone off to bed in darkness, they would not have made the slightest protest. Had I never given them a glance during my mortal existence and remained unenlightened even on my death-bed, that lamp would have triumphed. But the moon would always have been there, silent and sweetly smiling, neither concealing nor advertising her presence.

Since then I have begun doing without the lamp in the evenings.

[Uncle Rabi]

# TO William Butler Yeats

........................................................................................................................................

*21 Cromwell Road, South Kensington, London*
*2 September 1912*

Dear Mr Yeats

It has been such a great joy to me to think that things that I wrote in a tongue not known to you should at last fall in your hands and that you should accept them with so much enjoyment and love. When, in spite of all obstacles, something seemed to impel me to come to this country I never dreamt that it was for this that I was taking my voyage. What my soul offered to my master in the solitude of an obscure corner of the world must be brought before the altar of man where hearts come together and tongues mingle like the right and the left palms of hands joined in the act of adoration. My heart fills with gratitude and I write to you this letter to say that appreciation from a man like you comes to me not only as a reward for my lifelong devotion to literature but as a token that my songs have been acceptable to Him, and He has led me over the sea to this country to speak to me His approval of my works through your precious friendship.

We intend to leave England in the beginning of November. I do hope I shall be able to see you before that, and, if possible, to have a sight of my translations published with your introduction.

I hope you will kindly accept from me a copy of the English translation of my father's *Autobiography* which I left with Mr Rothenstein to be sent to your address.

Very sincerely yours
Rabindranath Tagore

........................................................................................................................................

154 – RABINDRANATH TAGORE

# TO Bertrand Russell

.....................................................................................................................................

*37 Alfred Place W., South Kensington, London*
*13 October 1912*

Dear Mr Russell

Thanks for your kind letter. I will ask Dr Seal to pay you a visit at Cambridge, when you will have an opportunity to know him.

I read your article on the Essence of Religion in the last issue of the *Hibbert Journal* with very great interest. It reminded me of a verse in the *Upanishad* which runs thus—

> Yato veiche nivartante aprapya manasa saha
> Anandam Brahmano Vidvan na vibheti Kutushchama.

'From him words, as well as mind, come back baffled. Yet he who knows the joy of Brahman (the Infinite) is free from all fear.'

Through knowledge you cannot apprehend him; yet when you live the life of the Infinite and are not bound within the limits of the finite self you realize that great joy which is above all the pleasures and pains of our selfish life and so you are free from all fear.

This joy itself is the positive perception of Brahman. It is not a creed which authority imposes on us but an absolute realization of the Infinite which we can only attain by breaking through the bonds of the narrow self and setting our will and love free.

Yours sincerely
Rabindranath Tagore

.....................................................................................................................................

# to Ezra Pound

*508 W. High Street, Urbana, Illinois*
*5 January 1913*

Dear Mr Ezra Pound

I send you the recent translations that I made here. I am not at all strong in my English grammar – please do not hesitate to make corrections when necessary. Then again I do not know the exact value of your English words. Some of them may have their souls worn out by constant use and some others may not have acquired their souls yet. So in my use of words there must be lack of proportion and appropriateness perhaps, that also could be amended by friendly hands.

Yours sincerely
Rabindranath Tagore

156 – RABINDRANATH TAGORE

# то Ezra Pound

.................................................................

1000 Massachusetts Avenue, Cambridge, Massachusetts

*5 February 1913*

Dear Mr Ezra Pound

I am so glad that I sent you some of my later translations. When the meaning and music of [the] original haunts you it is difficult for you to know how much has been realized in the translation.

I had my misgivings about the narrative poems myself. But I must say they have not been purposely made moral, they are not to guide people to [the] right path. They merely express the enjoyment of some aspects of life which happen to be morally good. They give you some outlook upon life which has a vastness that transcends all ordinary purposes of life and stirs [the] imagination. I am sure in the original there is nothing that savours of [the] pulpit. Perhaps you miss that sense of enjoyment in the English rendering and bereft of their music and suggestiveness of language they appear as merely didactic. Of course I am not going to include in my next book anything that you think should be left out. I will send you all the translations that I have made lately and I should be thankful to you to have your advice about them. As for the possible sale of my book I should dismiss all thoughts of it altogether from my mind, which is not at all difficult for me to do as I never had any financial success from my books.

Very sincerely yours
Rabindranath Tagore

.................................................................

# TO William Rothenstein

*Shantiniketan, West Bengal*
*18 November 1913*

My dear friend

The very first moment I received the message of the great honour conferred on me by the award of the Nobel prize my heart turned towards you with love and gratitude. I felt certain that of all my friends none would be more glad at this news than you. Honour's crown of honour is to know that it will rejoice the hearts of those whom we hold the most dear. But, all the same, it is a very great trial for me. The perfect whirlwind of public excitement it has given rise to is frightful. It is almost as bad as tying a tin can to a dog's tail making it impossible for him to move without creating noise and collecting crowds all along. I am being smothered with telegrams and letters for the last few days and the people who have never had any friendly feelings towards me nor ever read a line of my works are loudest in their protestations of joy. I cannot tell you how tired I am of all this shouting, the stupendous amount of its unreality being something appalling. Really these people honour the honour in me and not myself. The only thing that compensates for this is the unfeigned joy and pride that the boys of my school feel at this occasion. They are having festivities and making the most of me.

I know how glad Mrs Rothenstein must have been at my great good fortune – please give her my kindest remembrances and love to the children.

Yours
Rabindranath Tagore

# TO William Rothenstein

.......................................................................................................................................

*Shelidah, East Bengal*
*10 December 1913*

My friend, my days are riddled all over with interruptions, they are becoming perfectly useless to me. I am worn out writing letters, distributing thanks by handfuls and receiving visitors. I cannot tell you how unsuitable this sudden eruption of honour is to a man of my temperament. The winter sun is sweet, the green is luxuriant all around me – I want to be gloriously idle and let my thoughts melt and mingle in the blue of the space. I am beginning to envy the birds that sing and gladly go without honour. I was watching a calf this morning, tired of browsing, basking in the sun on the grass, supinely happy and placid; it made my heart ache with the desire to be one with the great life that surrounds this earth and to be able to be peacefully joyous in the simple enjoyment of the wealth lavished everywhere without being asked. But my mind is invaded and my time is wasted with things that are of the least significance to the inner. Perhaps you will smile and think this mood of mine absurdly oriental – but still it has its truth which must not be overlooked.

With love I am

Ever yours

Rabindranath Tagore

# TO William Rothenstein

........................................................................................................................................

*16 December 1913*

My dear Friend,

My ordeal is not yet over. I still have dinners to attend to, and listen to speeches in praise of my genius, and to answer them in a becoming spirit of modesty. This has brought me to Calcutta and kept me in our Jorasanko lane, while the mustard fields are in bloom in Shilida [Shelidah] and wild ducks have set up their noisy households in the sandbanks of the Padma. I have already raised a howl of protests and vilifications in our papers by saying in plain words what was in my mind to a deputation who had come to Bolpur to offer me congratulations. This has been a relief to me – for honour is a heavy enough burden even when it is real but intolerable when meaningless and devoid of sincerity. However, I must not complain. Let me patiently wait for the time when all this tumult will be a thing of the past and truth will shine and peace will come even to a man whom the West has thought fit to honour.

Ever yours
Rabindranath Tagore

160 – RABINDRANATH TAGORE

# то Harriet Monroe

## (editor of *Poetry*)

........................................................................................................................................

Dear Miss Monroe

My destiny is furiously amusing herself [by] showering upon me dry leaves of correspondence thick and fast – and when, hidden among them, come down by chance a few stray flowers of friendship I have very little breath left to receive them with any show of welcome. Your last letter is of such a kind lying on my table in apparent neglect. I know you will pardon me and will have some sympathy for a poet whose latest acquisition in the shape of honour can, by no means, be described as a feather in his cap, judged by its weight. But still I must bear it proudly, rejoicing in the fact that the East and the West ever touch each other like twin gems in the circlet of humanity, that they had met long before Kipling was born and will meet long after his name is forgotten.

I have been polishing the English versions of some of my narrative poems since we last met. I find it difficult to impart to them the natural vigour of the original poems. Simplicity appears anaemic and spectre-like when she lacks her ruddy bloom of life, which is the case with these translations of mine. Some of these, with my latest revisions, have already appeared in the *Nation* in England, and as for the remaining ones are they worth the trouble of publishing?

I am, dear friend,

　Most sincerely yours

　　Rabindranath Tagore

........................................................................................................................................

# TO Thomas Sturge Moore

My dear Sturge Moore,

Our school is closed, and after a long interval of busy time a full day has been given to me to spend as I like. I took up your book, *The Sea is Kind*, finishing it at one sitting. It will be difficult for you to imagine this blazing summer sky of ours with hot blasts of air repeatedly troubling the fresh green leaves of a tree whose name will be of no use to you. This is as unlike the climate and the country where your poems were written as anything could be. I feel your environments in your poems. There is in them the reticence of your sky, the compactness of your indoor life and the general consciousness of strength ready to defy fate. Here in the East the transparent stillness of our dark nights, the glare of the noonday sun melting into a tender haze in the blue distance, the plaintive music of the life that feels itself afloat in the Endless, seem to whisper into our hearts some great secret of existence which is uncommunicable.

All the same, nay, all the more, your literature is precious to us. The untiring hold upon life which you never lose, the definiteness of your aims and the positive reliance you have upon things present before you, inspire us with a strong sense of reality which is so much needed both for the purposes of art and of life. Literature of a country is not chiefly for home consumption. Its value lies in the fact that it is imperatively necessary for the lands where it is foreign. I think it has been the good fortune of the West to have the opportunity of absorbing the spirit of the East through the medium of the Bible. It has added to the richness of your life because it is alien to your temperament. In course of time you may discard some of its doctrines and teachings but it has done its work — it has created a bifurcation in your mental system which is so needful for all life growth. The western literature is doing the same with us, bringing into our life elements some of which supplement and some contradict our tendencies. This is what we need.

It is not enough to charm or surprise us — we must receive shocks and be hurt. Therefore we seek in your writings not simply what is artistic but what is vivid and forceful. That is why Byron had such an immense influence over our youths of the last generation. Shelley, in spite of his vague idealism, roused our minds because of his fanatic impetuosity which is born of a faith in life. What I say here is from the point of view of a foreigner. We cannot but miss a great deal of the purely artistic element in your literature but whatever is broadly human and deeply true can be safely shipped for distant times and remote countries. We look for your literature to bring to us the thundering life flood of the West, even though it carries with it all the debris of the passing moments.

I am getting ready to go off to the hills to spend my vacation there.

  Ever yours,
  Rabindranath Tagore

# TO Lord Chelmsford

## (Viceroy of India)

Your Excellency,

The enormity of the measures taken by the Government in the Punjab[†] for quelling some local disturbances has, with a rude shock, revealed to our minds the helplessness of our position as British subjects in India. The disproportionate severity of the punishments inflicted upon the unfortunate people and the methods of carrying them out, we are convinced, are without parallel in the history of civilized governments, barring some conspicuous exceptions, recent and remote. Considering that such treatment has been meted out to a population, disarmed and resourceless, by a power which has the most terribly efficient organization for destruction of human lives, we must strongly assert that it can claim no political expediency, far less moral justification. The accounts of insults and sufferings undergone by our brothers in the Punjab have trickled through the gagged silence, reaching every corner of India, and the universal agony of indignation roused in the hearts of our people has been ignored by our rulers – possibly congratulating themselves for what they imagine as salutary lessons. This callousness has been praised by most of the Anglo-Indian papers, which have in some cases gone to the brutal length of making fun of our sufferings, without receiving the least check from the same authority –

† Beginning with the Amritsar massacre on 13 April.

relentlessly careful in smothering every cry of pain and expression of judgement from the organs representing the sufferers. Knowing that our appeals have been in vain and that the passion of vengeance is blinding the nobler vision of statesmanship in our Government, which could so easily afford to be magnanimous as befitting its physical strength and moral tradition, the very least I can do for my country is to take all consequences upon myself in giving voice to the protest of millions of my countrymen, surprised into a dumb anguish of terror. The time has come when badges of honour make our shame glaring in their incongruous context of humiliation, and I for my part wish to stand, shorn of all special distinctions, by the side of those of my countrymen, who, for their so-called insignificance, are liable to suffer a degradation not fit for human beings.

These are the reasons which have painfully compelled me to ask Your Excellency, with due deference and regret, to relieve me of my title of Knighthood, which I had the honour to accept from His Majesty the King at the hands of your predecessor, for whose nobleness of heart I still entertain great admiration.

Yours faithfully,
Rabindranath Tagore

# TO Romain Rolland

Dear Romain Rolland

Let me acknowledge with thanks your letter of 26 August. I had been hoping to come over to Europe and meet you, but the atmosphere there is troubled and in our country sufferings have accumulated in various forms making it hard for me to leave her just now.

It hurts me very deeply when I think that there is hardly a corner in the vast continent of Asia where men have come to feel any real love for Europe. The great event of the meeting of the East and the West has been desecrated by the spirit of contempt on the one side and a corresponding hatred on the other. The reason is, it was greed which brought Europe to Asia and threat of physical power which maintains her there. This prevents our mutual relationship from becoming truly human and this makes it degrading for both parties. Parasitism, whether based upon power or upon weakness, must breed degeneracy. We who in our blind pride of caste deprived man of his full dues of rights and respect, are paying the penalty now, and instead of the soul current running through our society we have left to us the dry sand-bed of dead customs. And the time seems fast approaching when the soul will be sucked dry from the civiliza-tion of Europe also by the growing lust [for] gain in her commerce and politics, unless she has the wisdom and power to change her mind and not merely her system.

Your idea of a Review of Asia and Europe, in which writers of the East and West may take part in dealing with the treasures of thought, of art, of science, of faith, is very attractive to me. I am sure it will rouse interest in cultured minds in our part of the world. At the same time, you must know that in the Asia of the present age, intellect and all means of expression remain unorganized. Our minds are disunited and our thoughts scattered. The vocal section of our countrymen is mainly occupied with mendicant politics and petty journalism. The cramping poverty of our life and its narrowness of prospect tend to make most of our efforts feeble and our aims immediate. We greatly need some outside call to make us conscious of our mission. So long proud Europe has only claimed our homage and gained but the least and the worst that man can give. But if your paper comes bearing to us Europe's claim to our best thoughts we may well hope that response will not be found wanting.

Yours

Rabindranath Tagore

# TO Charles Freer Andrews

........................................................................................................

*Andrews, an English missionary who became a close associate of both Tagore and Gandhi, was left in charge of Tagore's Shantiniketan school when Tagore visited the West in 1920–21. During this period, Gandhi launched his movement of non-cooperation with the Government.*

*2970 Ellis Avenue, Chicago*
*5 March 1921*

Dear friend, lately I have been receiving more and more news and newspaper cuttings from India giving rise in my mind to a painful struggle that presages a period of suffering which is waiting for me. I am striving with all my power to tune my mood of mind to be in accord with the great feeling of excitement sweeping across my country. But deep in my being why is there this spirit of resistance maintaining its place in spite of my strong desire to remove it? I fail to find a clear answer and through my gloom of dejection breaks out a smile and voice saying, 'Your place is on the seashore of worlds, with children; there is your truth, your peace, and I am with you there.' And this is why lately I have been playing with metres, with merest nothings. These are whims that are content to be borne away by the current of time, dancing in the sun and laughing as they disappear. But while I play, the whole creation is amused, for are not flowers and leaves never-ending experiments in metre, is not my God an eternal waster of time? He flings stars and planets in the whirlwind of changes, he floats paper boats of ages filled with his fancies on the rushing stream of appearance. When I tease

........................................................................................................

him and beg him to allow me to remain his little follower and accept a few trifles of mine as the cargo of his paper boat, he smiles and I trot behind him catching the hem of his robe. But where am I among the crowd, pushed from behind, pressed from all sides? And what is this noise about me? If it is a song then my own *sitar* can catch the tune and I can join in the chorus, for I am a singer. But if it is a shout then my voice is wrecked and I am lost in bewilderment. I have been trying all these days to find a melody, straining my ear, but the idea of non-cooperation, with its mighty volume of sound does not sing to me, its congregated menace of negation shouts. And I say to myself, 'If you cannot keep step with your countrymen at this great crisis of their history, never say that you are right and rest of them wrong; only give up your role as a soldier, go back to your corner as a poet, be ready to accept popular derision and disgrace.'

Rathi,[†] in support of the present movement, has often said to me that the passion for rejection is a stronger power in the beginning than the acceptance of an ideal. Though I know it to be a fact, I cannot accept it as a truth. We must choose our allies once for all, for they stick to us even when we might be glad to be rid of them. If we once claim strength from intoxication, then in the time of reaction our normal strength is bankrupt, and we go back again and again to the demon that lends us resources in a vessel whose bottom it takes away.

*Brahma-vidya*[‡] in India has for its object *mukti*, emancipation, while Buddhism has *nirvana*, extinction. It may be argued that both have the same idea [under] different names. But names represent attitudes of mind, emphasize particular aspects of truth. *Mukti* draws our attention to the positive, and *nirvana* to the negative side of truth. Buddha kept silence all through his teachings about the truth of the *Om*, the *everlasting yes*, his

† Son of Rabindranath Tagore.
‡ Branch of learning imparting knowledge of God.

implication being that by the negative path of destroying the self we naturally reach that truth. Therefore he emphasized the fact of *dukkha*, misery, which had to be avoided and the *Brahma-vidya* emphasized the fact of *anandam*† which had to be attained. The latter cult also needs for its fulfilment the discipline of self-abnegation, but it holds before its view the idea of Brahma, not only at the end but all through the process of realization. Therefore the idea of life's training was different in the Vedic period from that of the Buddhistic. In the former it was the purification of life's joy, in the latter it was the eradicating of it. The abnormal type of asceticism to which Buddhism gave rise in India revelled in celibacy and mutilation of life in all different forms. But the forest life of the *Brahmanas* was not antagonistic to the social life of man, but harmonious with it. It was like our musical instrument *tanpura* whose duty is to supply the fundamental notes to the music to save it from going astray into discordance. It believed in *anandam*, the music of the soul, and its own simplicity was not to kill it but to guide it.

The idea of non-cooperation is political asceticism. Our students are bringing their offering of sacrifices to what? Not to a fuller education but to non-education. It has at its back a fierce joy of annihilation which in its best form is asceticism and in its worst form is that orgy of frightfulness in which human nature, losing faith in the basic reality of normal life, finds a disinterested delight in unmeaning devastation, as has been shown in the late war and on other occasions which came nearer home to us. *No* in its passive moral form is asceticism and in its active moral form is violence. The desert is as much a form of *himsa* as is the raging sea in storm, they both are against life.

I remember the day, during the Swadeshi Movement‡ in

† Bliss.
‡ Nationalist movement in Bengal, started in 1905, akin to Ireland's Sinn Fein; Swadeshi means 'of our Country', i.e. indigenous.

Bengal, when a crowd of young students came to see me in the first floor of our Vichitra house. They said to me that if I ordered them to leave their schools and colleges they would instantly obey me. I was emphatic in my refusal to do so, and they went away angry, doubting the sincerity of my love for my motherland. Long before this ebullition of excitement, I myself had given a thousand rupees, when I had not five rupees to call my own, to open a *swadeshi* store and courted banter and bankruptcy. The reason for my refusing to advise those students to leave their schools was because the anarchy of a mere emptiness never tempts me, even when it is resorted to as a temporary shelter. I am frightened of an abstraction which is ready to ignore living reality. These students were no mere phantoms to me; their life was a great fact to them and to the All. I could not lightly take upon myself the tremendous responsibility of a mere negative programme for them which would uproot them from their soil, however thin and poor that soil might be. The great injury and injustice which had been done to those boys who were tempted away from their career before any *real* provision was made, could never be made good to them. Of course that is nothing from the point of view of an abstraction which can ignore the infinite value even of the smallest fraction of reality. But the throb of life in the heart of the most insignificant of men beats in the unison of love with the heart-throb of the infinite. I wish I were the little creature Jack whose one mission was to kill the giant abstraction which is claiming the sacrifice of individuals all over the world under highly painted masks of delusion.

I say again and again that I am a poet, that I am not a fighter by nature. I would give everything to be one with my surroundings. I love my fellow beings and I prize their love. Yet I have been chosen by destiny to ply my boat there where the current is against me. What irony of fate is this, that I should be preaching cooperation of cultures between East and West on this side of the sea just at the moment when the doctrine of non-cooperation is preached on the other side? You know that I do not believe in the material civilization of the West, just as I do not believe the physical body to be the highest truth in man. But I still less believe in the destruction of the physical body. What is needed is the establishment of harmony between the physical and the spiritual nature of man, maintaining of balance between the foundation and superstructure. I believe in the true meeting of the East and the West. Love is the ultimate truth of soul; we should do all we can not to outrage that truth, to carry its banner against all opposition. The idea of non-cooperation unnecessarily hurts that truth. It is not our hearth fire, but the fire that burns out our hearth.

While I have been considering the non-cooperation idea one thought has come to me over and over again which I must tell you. *Bara Dada*[†] and myself are zamindars, which means collectors of revenue under British Government. Until the time comes when we give up paying revenue and allow our lands to be sold we have not the right to ask students or anybody else to make any sacrifice which may be all they have. My father was about to give up all his property for the sake of truth and honesty. And likewise we may come to that point when we have to give up our means of livelihood. If we do not feel that that point has been reached by us then at least we should at once make ample provision out of our competency for others who are ready to risk their all. When I put to myself this problem the answer which I find is that by temperament and training all the good I am now capable of doing presupposes a certain amount of wealth. If I am to begin to earn my living, possibly I shall be able to support myself but nothing better than that. Which will mean not merely sacrificing my money but my mind. I know that my God may claim even that, and by the very reclaiming repay me. Utter privation and death may have to be my ultimate sacrifice for the

† Rabindranath's eldest brother, a keen supporter of Gandhi.

sake of some ideals which represent immortality. But so long as I do not feel the call or respond to it myself how can I urge others to follow the path which may prove to be the path of utter renunciation? Let the individuals choose their own responsibility of sacrifice, but are we ready to accept that responsibility for them? Do we fully realize what it may mean in suffering or in evil? or is it a mere abstraction for us which leaves us untouched [by] all the concrete possibilities of misery [for] individuals? Let us first of all try to think [of] them as the nearest and dearest to us and then ask them to choose danger and poverty for their share [in] life.

With love,

Ever yours

Rabindranath Tagore

# TO Edward John Thompson

## (biographer of Tagore)

........................................................................................................

*Santiniketan, West Bengal*
*20 September 1921*

Dear Thompson

I have just received your book dealing with myself. I believe it is my sensitiveness born of my egotism which makes me shrink from attending to any discussions concerning me. But I have read your book all through. I am sure you have tried to be fair in your estimate of my works. About the comparative merits of my individual productions I myself am undecided though I have my preferences with which I never expect my readers always to agree. In fact as a critic of my own writings my ideas do not often coincide with those of Ajit.[†]

All along my literary career I have run against the taste of my countrymen, at least those of them who represent the vocal portion of my province. It has hardly been pleasant to me, but it has had the effect of making me reconciled to my mental loneliness. In the West − for some little while in England and lately in the continental countries of Europe − the recognition which I met with came to me with a shock of surprise. When a poet's life's works are accepted by his fellow beings it gives him a sense of intellectual companionship with his readers which is precious. But it has a great danger of growing into a temptation − and I believe, consciously and unconsciously I have been

[†] Ajit Kumar Chakravarty, a friend of Tagore and literary critic, cited by Thompson.

........................................................................................................

succumbing to it with regard to my western readers. But I have this paradox in my nature that when I begin to enjoy my success I grow weary of it in the depth of my mind. It is not through any surfeit of it, but through something in it which hurts me. Reputation is the greatest bondage for an artist. I want to emancipate my mind from its grasp not only for the sake of my art, but for the higher purposes of life, for the dignity of soul. What an immense amount of unreality there is in literary reputation, and I am longing – even while appreciating it like a buffalo the luxury of its mud bath – to come out of it as a *sanyasi*, naked and aloof. A gift has been given to me – this great world – which I can truly enjoy when I am simple and natural. I am looking back to those days of my youth when I had easy access into the heart of this universe – and I believe I shall yet again recover my place there when I am able to sever my mind from the attraction of the literary world which with its offer of rewards tries to standardize creative visions according to criterions distractingly varied and variable.

You have spared yourself no trouble in your attempt to understand me, and I am sure your book is the best one that has yet appeared about myself. I must thank you for this – at the same time I wish I could altogether lose the memory of my fame as a poet.

Yours
    Rabindranath Tagore

[PS] In answer to your note just arrived: Surul is a village about two miles away from Shantiniketan where I have a garden containing a building.

The metrical forms in *Gitali* are the natural outcome of the structure of music which I follow in my songs. I shall explain it to you when we meet.

# TO Prashanta Chandra Mahalanobis

*Mahalanobis, a Bengali friend of Tagore, was a close adviser to Edward John Thompson in the writing of his studies of Tagore.*

Shantiniketan, West Bengal
September? 1921

*Kalyaniyeshu*†

I have read Thompson's book now. He has worked hard and read much in order to write it, and so it is better than any other book about me. However, that is not such a great thing. Other books should be entirely discarded.

But while reading it I found myself constantly thinking – the way the sahib describes the atmosphere of my life and works is a construct of his own preconceptions and lack of knowledge. And atmosphere is a vital element in a person's life. Unless one is an artist one cannot describe atmosphere properly, for it is something very delicate. The collecting and assembling of a few opinions and available materials produces a structure that hides the real person. And then, in matters of literary judgement Thompson relies heavily on Ajit. Ajit's drawback was that he could not function without a theory – whether an existing theory or one he had invented. He was not a leader in the area of literary perception; hence his inability to grasp [my] *Kshanika*.

All in all, Thompson's book will be a very convenient resort for those of my countrymen wishing to abuse me as a foreigner. And yet that idea is essentially not at all accurate. My own

† To him who deserves my good wishes.

conviction is that I was the first to introduce the land of Bengal to Bengalis as a subject fit for literature – neither Michael nor Nabin Sen nor Bankim did that. I could do it because the family I was born into did not detach my mind from my country. I never let myself become entangled in the usual conventions and rituals; and because I remained a loner by nature, I was able to associate freely with everyone. Thompson seems to me to exaggerate my isolation; he does not grasp my associations. This is why he makes too much of my 'unpopularity' and fails to understand that in spite of the opposition to me my country has accepted me almost unawares. He should have seen the crowd at my lectures. The general impression his book leaves on the reader's mind is a superficial one that is to a great extent incorrect. I feel very tired – but work must continue.

*Snehashakta*[†]

    Shri Rabindranath Thakur

    [signed in Bengali]

---

† Affectionately.

# TO Victoria Ocampo

*Ocampo was Tagore's hostess in Argentina from November 1924 to early January 1925, when he sailed for Europe.*

*S.S.* Giulio Cesare
*13 January 1925*

Dear Vijaya

I am drifting farther and farther away from your shore and now it has become possible for me to set the vision of my everyday surroundings at San Isidro against a background of separation. I am not a born traveller – I have not the energy and strength needed for knowing a strange country and helping the mind to gather materials from a wide area of new experience for building its foreign nest. And therefore when I am away from my own land I seek for some individuals who may represent to me the country to which they belong. For me the spirit of Latin America will ever dwell in my memory incarnated in your person. You rescued me from the organized hospitality of a reception committee and allowed me to receive through yourself the personal touch of your country. Unfortunately there was the barrier of language that prevented a free enough communication of minds between us, for you never felt fully at home in the only European language I happen to know. It was unfortunate because you have a richness of mind which naturally longs to offer its own tribute to those whom you accept as your friends, and I fully understand the pain which you must have suffered for not being able to reveal adequately to me your deeper thoughts and to dissolve the fog that screened off the world of your intellectual life from my vision. I am deeply sorry that it has not been possible for me to have an acquaintance of your complete personality – the difficulty having been enhanced owing to the literary character of your mind. For such a mind has its aristocratic code of honour about its manner of self-expression choosing to remain dumb [rather] than to send out its thoughts dressed in rags. But never for a moment imagine that I failed to recognize that you had a mind. To me it was like a star that was distant and not a planet that was dark. When we were together we mostly played with words and tried to laugh away our best opportunities to see each other clearly. Such laughter often disturbs the atmosphere of our mind, raising dust from its surface which only blurs our view. One thing most of my friends fail to know [is] that where I am real I am profoundly serious. Our reality is like treasure, it is not left exposed in the outer chamber of our personal self. It waits to be explored and only in our serious moments [can it] be approached. You have often found me homesick – it was not so much for India, it was for that abiding reality in me in which I can have my inner freedom. It becomes totally obscured when for some reason or other my attention is too much directed upon my own personal self. My true home is there where from my surroundings comes the call to me to bring out the best that I have, for that inevitably leads me to the touch with the universal. My mind must have a nest to which the voice of the sky can descend freely, the sky that has no other allurements but light and freedom. Whenever there is the least sign of the nest becoming a jealous rival of the sky, my mind, like a migrant bird, tries to take its flight to a distant shore. When my freedom of light is obstructed for some length of time I feel as if I am bearing the burden of a disguise, like the morning in its disguise of a mist. I do not see myself – and this obscurity, like a nightmare, seems to suffocate me with its heavy emptiness. I have often said to you that I am not free to give up my freedom – for this freedom is claimed by my Master for his own service. There have been times when I *did* forget this and allowed myself to drift into some easeful captivity – but every time it ended in catastrophe and I was driven by an angry power to the open, across broken walls.

I tell you all this because I know you love me. I trust my providence. I feel certain – and I say this in all humility – that he has chosen me for some special mission of his own and not merely for the purpose of linking the endless chain of generation. Therefore I believe that your love may, in some way, help me in my fulfilment. It will sound egoistic, only because the voice of our ego has in it the same masterful cry of insistence as the voice of that which infinitely surpasses it. I assure you, that through me a claim comes which is not mine. A child's claim upon its mother has a sublime origin – it is not a claim of an individual, it is that of humanity. Those who come on some special errand of God are like that child; if they ever attract love and service it should be for a higher end than merely their own enjoyment. Not only love, but hurts and insults, neglect and rejection come not to grind them into dust but to kindle their life into a brighter flame.

Your friendship has come to me unexpectedly. It will grow to its fulness of truth when you know and accept my real being and see clearly the deeper meaning of my life. I have lost most of my friends because they asked me for themselves, and when I said I was not free to offer away myself – they thought I was proud. I have deeply suffered from this over and over again – and therefore I always feel nervous whenever a new gift of friendship comes in my way. But I accept my destiny and if you also have the courage fully to accept it we shall ever remain friends.

Shri Rabindranath Thakur
[signed in Bengali]

Tomorrow we shall reach Barcelona and the day after Genoa. I am about to leave my easy chair in my cabin. That chair has been my real nest for these two weeks giving me rest and privacy and a feeling that my happiness is of value to somebody. I do not know when it will be possible for me to write to you again but I shall always remember you.

# TO Leonard Knight Elmhirst

## (co-founder of the Dartington Trust)

.................................................................................................

*Balatonfüred, [Hungary]*
*7 November 1926*

Dear Leonard

This is a delightful watering place. The bath here is charged with carbonic acid gas which I am told is good for distracted nerves. Doctors advise me to take the shorter eastern route to India through Yugoslavia, Serbia, Constantinople, Greece and Egypt. The prescription is very much like the French wine ordered for me in Milan; it is tempting. The people [in] this eastern corner of Europe are perfectly charming – their personality unshrouded by the grey monotony of a uniform civilization that has overspread the western world. It is mixed with something primitive and therefore is fresh and vital and warmly human. How naïvely simple and direct is the expression of their feeling for me. I am the guest of the people here, their one object being to nurse me into health taking real pride in rendering this service. Is there any other individual today in the whole world who is so fortunate as I am in gaining the adoration of such a multitude of peoples in spite of the insuperable obstacles against making himself fully known and dedicating to them what he has in store? They seem to offer me their love on trust without waiting to be sure that they do not deceive themselves. When I had my welcome in Germany and in Norway, the people very often shouting to me 'Come back to us', it made me wonder how I had deserved it. But in places like Budapest the attitude of the people towards me is so clingingly personal, so full of tender

.................................................................................................

solicitude that I forget to ask myself what price I had ever paid for it. It only reveals a spontaneous attraction of a mysterious feeling of kinship. I cannot help thinking that in spite of my numerous deficiencies my providence has found in me an instrument which he can use for his own great purpose, though it is a matter of perpetual puzzle to the instrument itself. I wish you were with me to realize how human these people are. I am sure they make terrible mistakes and can be frankly cruel to their neighbours – not because they are callous with the callousness of senility with its cold calculating and cautious unscrupulousness but because they have the passionate impetuosity of their youthfulness. They are too often chastised for their delinquencies by their big brothers [with] stronger muscles, but those old sinners themselves are waiting for their doom in God's own hands.

This time I have been able to see the state of things in Europe that has filled my mind with misgivings. There was a time when ideals of justice, love of freedom could find their voice from some corner or other of this continent. But today all the big nations seem to have gone half-seas-over in their reckless career of political ambition and adventures of greed. None of them has the natural privilege today to stand for right when any great wrong is done to humanity. The standard of life has become so complex and costly that these people cannot help thinking that righteousness is a luxury that can only be indulged in when all claims [by] their insatiable self [are] fairly satisfied. They are ashamed of the sentiments that help to keep life green and tender and in its place they cultivate the sneering spirit of cynicism brilliant and barren. Europe has got her science not as complementary to religion but as its substitute. Science is great, but it only affords us knowledge, power, efficiency, but no ideal of unity, no aspiration for the perfect – it is non-human, impersonal, and therefore is like things that are inorganic, useful in many ways but useless as our food of life. If it is allowed to go on extending its sole dominion in the human world then the living flesh of man will wither away and his skeleton will reign supreme in the midst of his dead wealth. I have very strongly felt this time that the European countries have found themselves [in] a vicious circle of mutual hatred and suspicion and they do not know how to stop, however much they may wish. Their passion of greed has been ignited to a terrible intensity and magnitude through the immense possibility of power that science has offered to them and they appear like a star suddenly flaring up into rapid and fatal brilliancy through some enormous accession of materials. The present European atmosphere has been very oppressive to me making me think over and over again what a terrible menace man has been for man.—But no more of this – and goodbye

Ever yours

Rabindranath Tagore

# TO Mahatma Gandhi

On 8 May 1933, Gandhi began a twenty-one-day fast, with a press statement that: 'Whether I survive the fast or not, is a matter of little moment. Without it I would, in all probability, have been useless for further service of Harijans [Untouchables], and for that matter, any other service.' Its intention, he concluded, was 'to remove bitterness, to purify hearts and to make it clear that the [non-cooperation] movement is wholly moral, to be prosecuted by wholly moral persons'.

Glen Eden, Darjeeling, West Bengal
11 May 1933

Dear Mahatmaji

I am trying clearly to find out the meaning of this last message of yours which is before the world today. In every important act of his life Buddha preached limitless love for all creatures. Christ said 'Love thine enemies' and that teaching of his found its final expression in the words of forgiveness he uttered for those who killed him. As far as I can understand, the fast that you have started carries in it the idea of expiation for the sins of your countrymen. But I ask to be excused when I say that the expiation can truly and heroically be done only by daily endeavours for the sake of those unfortunate beings who do not know what they do. The fasting which has no direct action upon the conduct of misdoers and which may abruptly terminate one's power further to serve those who need help, cannot be universally accepted and therefore it is all the more unacceptable for any individual who has the responsibility to represent humanity.

The logical consequence of your example, if followed, will be an elimination of all noble souls from the world leaving the morally feeble and downtrodden multitude to sink into the fathomless depth of ignorance and iniquity. You have no right to say that this process of penance can only be efficacious through your own individual endeavour and for others it has no meaning. If that were true you ought to have performed it in absolute secrecy as a special mystic rite which only claims its one sacrifice beginning and ending in yourself. You ask others actively to devote their energy to extirpate the evil which smothers our national life and enjoin only upon yourself an extreme form of sacrifice which is of a passive character. For lesser men than yourself it opens up an easy and futile path of duty by urging them to take a plunge into a dark abyss of self-mortification. You cannot blame them if they follow you in this special method of purification of their country, for all messages must be universal in their application and if not they should never be expressed at all.

The suffering that has been caused to me by the vow you have taken has compelled me to write to you thus – for I cannot bear the sight of a sublimely noble career journeying towards a finality which, to my mind, lacks a perfectly satisfying justification. And once again I appeal to you for the sake of the dignity of our nation which is truly impersonated in you, and for the sake of the millions of my countrymen who need your living touch and help to desist from any act that you think is good only for you and not for the rest of humanity.

With deepest pain and love
Rabindranath Tagore

# TO William Butler Yeats

*Santiniketan, West Bengal*
*16 July 1935*

Dear Yeats

Your letter seems to come to me from a remote age reminding me of those days of my acquaintance with you intense and intimate. Though I had already left behind one half of a century of my life when I visited your country I felt that I had come to the beginning of a fresh existence young with the surprise of an experience in an atmosphere of kindly personalities. I often remember a meeting with you in that chamber of yours, quaintly unique, that seemed to me, I do not know why, resonant of an old world silence, and though I find it difficult distinctly to recollect the subject of our talk the feeling of it lingers in my mind like the aroma of a rich and rare wine.

I know you have entered into an epoch of life which is vague to me and distant, but I shall always remember the generosity of your simple and sensitive poetic youth which exercised in my mind a profound attraction for your genius.

Ever yours
Rabindranath Tagore

# TO Jawaharlal Nehru

Santiniketan, West Bengal
9 October 1935

My dear Jawaharlal

We have been anxiously following in the daily papers the news of your wife's illness watching for some favourable signs of improvement. I earnestly hope that the amazing strength of mind which she has shown through all the vicissitudes of her life will help her. Please convey to her my kindest regards.

Every winter Visva-Bharati† rudely reminds me of the scantiness of her means, for that is the season when I have to stir myself to go out for gathering funds. It is a hateful trial for me – this begging business either in the guise of entertaining people or appealing to the generosity of those who are by no means generous. I try to exult in a sense of martyrdom accepting the thorny crown of humiliation and futility without complaining. Should I not keep in mind for consolation what you are going through yourself for the cause which is dearer to you than your life and your personal freedom? But the question which often troubles my mind is whether it is worth my while to exhaust my energy laboriously picking up minute crumbs of favour from the tables of parsimonious patrons or keep my mind fresh from the indignity of storing up disappointments. But possibly this is my excuse for shirking unpleasantness. I have asked Mahatmaji for lending me his voice which he has kindly consented to. Of course his influence is likely to meet with a greater success than I

† Tagore's university at Shantiniketan.

can ever hope to attain. I must not forget to tell you that Sir Tej Bahadur Sapru also has promised to support me.

Kindly remember me to dear Indira.‡ I hope some day or other she will find opportunity to revisit our ashram and revise her memory of those few months which she spent here making us happy.

With love,
    Yours
        Rabindranath Tagore

‡ Indira Nehru, later Indira Gandhi, was a student at Shantiniketan, 1934–5.

# TO Jawaharlal Nehru

......................................................................................................................

*Santiniketan, West Bengal*
*31 May 1936*

Dear Jawaharlal,

    I have just finished reading your great book[†] and I feel intensely impressed and proud of your achievement. Through all its details there runs a deep current of humanity which overpasses the tangles of facts and leads us to the person who is greater than his deeds and truer than his surroundings.

    Yours very sincerely

    Rabindranath Tagore

---

† *An Autobiography.*

......................................................................................................................

# TO Yone Noguchi

*Noguchi, a Japanese poet well known in the West in the early decades of this century, and a friend of Tagore, tried passionately to enlist his support for Japan's militarism in China.*

Santiniketan, West Bengal

*1 September 1938*

Dear Noguchi,

I am profoundly surprised by the letter that you have written to me: neither its temper nor its contents harmonize with the spirit of Japan which I learnt to admire in your writings and came to love through my personal contacts with you. It is sad to think that the passion of collective militarism may on occasion helplessly overwhelm even the creative artist, that genuine intellectual power should be led to offer its dignity and truth to be sacrificed at the shrine of the dark gods of war.

You seem to agree with me in your condemnation of the massacre of Ethiopia by Fascist Italy but you would reserve the murderous attack on Chinese millions for judgement under a different category. But surely judgements are based on principle, and no amount of special pleading can change the fact that in launching a ravening war on Chinese humanity, with all the deadly methods learnt from the West, Japan is infringing every moral principle on which civilization is based. You claim that Japan's situation is unique, forgetting that military situations are always unique, and that pious warlords, convinced of peculiarly individual justification for their atrocities have never failed to arrange for special alliances with divinity for annihilation and torture on a large scale.

Humanity, in spite of its many failures, has believed in a fundamental moral structure of society. When you speak, therefore, of 'the inevitable means, terrible it is though, for establishing a new great world in the Asiatic continent' – signifying, I suppose, the bombing of Chinese women and children and the desecration of ancient temples and universities as a means of saving China for Asia – you are ascribing to humanity a way of life which is not even inevitable among the animals and would certainly not apply to the East, in spite of her occasional aberrations. You are building your conception of an Asia which would be raised on a tower of skulls. I have, as you rightly point out, believed in the message of Asia, but I never dreamt that this message could be identified with deeds which brought exaltation to the heart of Tamerlane at his terrible efficiency in manslaughter. When I protested against 'westernization' in my lectures in Japan, I contrasted the rapacious imperialism which some of the *nations* of Europe were cultivating with the ideal of perfection preached by Buddha and Christ, with the great heritages of culture and good neighbourliness that went [in]to the making of Asiatic and other civilizations. I felt it to be my duty to warn the land of *bushido*, of great art and traditions of noble heroism, that this phase of scientific savagery which victimized western humanity and led their helpless masses to a moral cannibalism was never to be imitated by a virile people who had entered upon a glorious renascence and had every promise of a creative future before them. The doctrine of 'Asia for Asia' which you enunciate in your letter, as an instrument of political blackmail, has all the virtues of the lesser Europe which I repudiate and nothing of the larger humanity that makes us one across the barriers of political labels and divisions. I was amused to read the recent statement of a Tokyo politician that the military alliance of Japan with Italy and Germany was made for 'highly spiritual and moral reasons' and 'had no materialistic considerations behind it'. Quite so. What is not amusing is that artists and thinkers should echo such remarkable sentiments that translate military swagger into spiritual bravado. In the West, even in the critical days of war madness, there is never any dearth of great spirits who can raise their voice above the din of battle, and defy their own warmongers in the name of humanity. Such men have suffered, but never betrayed the conscience of their peoples which they represented. Asia will not be westernized if she can learn from such men: I still believe that there are such souls in Japan though we do not hear of them in those newspapers that are compelled at the cost of their extinction to reproduce their military master's voice.

'The betrayal of intellectuals' of which the great French writer spoke after the European war, is a dangerous symptom of our age. You speak of the savings of the poor people of Japan, their silent sacrifice and suffering and take pride in betraying that this pathetic sacrifice is being exploited for gun-running and invasion of a neighbour's hearth and home, that human wealth of greatness is pillaged for inhuman purposes. Propaganda, I know, has been reduced to a fine art, and it is almost impossible for peoples in non-democratic countries to resist hourly doses of poison, but one had imagined that at least the men of intellect and imagination would themselves retain their gift of independent judgement. Evidently such is not always the case: behind sophisticated arguments seems to lie a mentality of perverted nationalism which makes the 'intellectuals' of today go blustering about their 'ideologies' dragooning their own 'masses' into paths of dissolution. I have known your people and I hate to believe that they could deliberately participate in the organized drugging of Chinese men and women by opium and heroin, but they do not know; in the meanwhile, representatives of Japanese culture in China are busy practising their craft on the multitudes caught in the grip of an organization of wholesale human pollution. Proofs of such forcible drugging in Manchukuo and China have been adduced by unimpeachable authorities. But from Japan there has come no protest, not even from her poets.

Holding such opinions as many of your intellectuals do, I am not surprised that they are left 'free' by your Government to express themselves. I hope they enjoy their freedom. Retiring from such freedom into 'a snail's shell' in order to savour the bliss of meditation 'on life's hopeful future', appears to me to be an unnecessary act, even though you advise Japanese artists to do so by way of change. I cannot accept such separation between an artist's function and his moral conscience. The luxury of enjoying special favouritism by virtue of identity with a Government which is engaged in demolition, in its neighbourhood, of all salient bases of life, and of escaping, at the same time, from any direct responsibility by a philosophy of escapism, seems to me to be another authentic symptom of the modern intellectual's betrayal of humanity. Unfortunately the rest of the world is almost cowardly in any adequate expression of its judgement owing to ugly possibilities that it may be hatching for its own future, and those who are bent upon doing mischief are left alone to defile their history and blacken their reputation for all time to come. But such impunity in the long run bodes disaster, like unconsciousness of disease in its painless progress of ravage.

I speak with utter sorrow for your people; your letter has hurt me to the depths of my being. I know that one day the disillusionment of your people will be complete, and through laborious centuries they will have to clear the debris of their civilization wrought to ruin by their own warlords run amok. They will realize that the aggressive war on China is insignificant as compared to the destruction of their inner spirit of chivalry of Japan which is proceeding with a ferocious severity. China is unconquerable, her civilization, under the dauntless leadership of Chiang Kai-shek, is displaying marvellous resources; the desperate loyalty of her peoples, united as never before, is creating a new age for that land. Caught unprepared by a gigantic machinery of war, hurled upon her peoples, China is holding her own; no temporary defeats can ever crush her fully aroused spirit. Faced by the borrowed science of Japanese militarism which is crudely western in character, China's stand reveals an inherently superior moral stature. And today I understand more than ever before the meaning of the enthusiasm with which the big-hearted Japanese thinker Okakura assured me that 'China is great'.

You do not realize that you are glorifying your neighbour at your own cost. But these are considerations on another plane: the sorrow remains that Japan, in the words of Madame Chiang Kai-shek which you must have read in the *Spectator*, is creating so many ghosts. Ghosts of immemorial works of Chinese art, of irreplaceable Chinese institutions, of great peace-loving communities drugged, tortured, and destroyed. 'Who will lay the ghosts?' she asks. Japanese and Chinese people, let us hope, will join hands together, in no distant future, in wiping off memories of a bitter past. True Asian humanity will be reborn. Poets will raise their song and be unashamed, one believes, to declare their faith again in a human destiny which cannot admit of a scientific mass production of fratricide.

Yours sincerely,
Rabindranath Tagore

PS I find that you have already released your letter to the press; I take it that you want me to publish my answer in the same manner.

# TO FOSS WESTCOTT

*In June 1941, Eleanor Rathbone, a British MP, publicly appealed to Indians to support the Allied war effort. A dying Tagore made a vitriolic public response, which attracted a letter from Foss Westcott, the head of the Anglican Church in India.*

Santiniketan, West Bengal
*16 June 1941*

My dear Lord Bishop

I thank you for the trouble you have taken to acquaint me with your reaction to my recent reply to Miss Rathbone's open letter. I respect your sentiments and share your conviction that never was mutual understanding more necessary between your people and ours than today. I have, as you are no doubt aware, worked all my life for the promotion of racial, communal and religious harmony among the different peoples of the world. I have also, at considerable personal cost and often at the risk of being misunderstood by my own people, set my face against all claims of narrow and aggressive nationalism, believing in the common destiny and oneness of all mankind. I hold many of your people in the highest regard and count among them some of my best friends. Both my faith and my practice during the last so many decades should be ample guarantee that I was not carried away by any racial, religious or merely national prejudice in my recent statement. I have neither the right nor the desire to judge the British people as such; but I cannot help being concerned at the conduct of the British Government in India, since it directly involves the life and well-being of millions of my countrymen. I am too painfully conscious of the extreme poverty, helplessness and misery of our people not to deplore the supineness of the Government that has tolerated this condition for so long. I have nothing against Miss Rathbone personally, and I am glad to be assured by you of her estimable qualities and of her love for our people. But I had hoped that the leaders of the British nation, who had grown apathetic to our suffering and forgetful of their own sacred trust in India during their days of prosperity and success, would at last, in the time of their own great trial, awake to the justice and humanity of our cause. It has been a most grievous disappointment to me to find that fondly cherished hope receding farther and farther from realization each day. Believe me, nothing would give me greater happiness than to see the people of the West and the East march in a common crusade against all that robs the human spirit of its significance.

With kind regards,
    Yours sincerely
    Rabindranath Tagore

# ESSAYS,
# STATEMENTS
# AND
# CONVERSATIONS

In Calcutta, in 1917, when Tagore gave one of his most powerful lectures in Bengali, repeated by public demand in a large theatre hall, mounted police had to be called to clear the crowd. In New York, in 1930, when he spoke at Carnegie Hall, which held 4,000 people, thousands had to be turned away, according to the *New York Times*. Over the years, countless observers, Bengalis and non-Bengalis, testified to Tagore's power to hold an audience with his speech.

In a long lifetime, he gave an enormous number of lectures and talks which were later published, and wrote copious essays, besides issuing press statements, giving interviews and holding recorded conversations with distinguished figures such as Albert Einstein. His subjects were extraordinarily varied, but with the emphasis on literature, philosophy, religion, social reform, education and the history of India. Inevitably there was much repetition and some woolliness: many of these published pieces remain decently buried in the pages of Tagore's collected Bengali works or in western and Indian journals (if they were originally in English). Nevertheless, a great body of fine prose remains, and to choose ten of the best pieces is difficult.

This selection covers all the above categories and one or two others, such as music (a conversation with Einstein in Germany in 1930) and art (a talk about his own paintings at an exhibition in London in 1930). With the exception of 'Poet Yeats', which was an appreciation of W. B. Yeats written for a Bengali audience, all the pieces were originally spoken or written in English.

The first five are oriented to the West, either by design or by virtue of their subject matter, while the last four more directly concern India. The remaining piece, Tagore's reply to Gandhi's controversial statement on the great Bihar earthquake of 1934 – that it was 'a divine chastisement sent by God for our sins', i.e. Untouchability – acts as a kind of link between Tagore's western and Indian concerns. For in arguing with Einstein on the nature of reality (another conversation printed here), Tagore had said, 'This world is a human world – the scientific view of it is also that of the scientific man. Therefore, the world apart from us does not exist; it is a relative world, depending for its reality upon our consciousness.' Whereas in 1934, by contrast, he told Gandhi, 'We feel perfectly secure in the faith that our own sins and errors, however enormous, have not enough force to drag down the structure of creation to ruins. We can depend upon it, sinners and saints, bigots and breakers of convention.' Gandhi profoundly disagreed, saying, 'I have the faith that our own sins have more force to ruin that structure than any mere physical phenomenon.' Paradoxically, Einstein agreed with Tagore's 1934 position, contra Gandhi, and not with his 1930 position – and yet Einstein admired Gandhi much more than he admired Tagore.

# East and West

*1*

It is not always a profound interest in man that carries travellers nowadays to distant lands. More often it is the facility for rapid movement. For lack of time and for the sake of convenience we generalize and crush our human facts into the packages within the steel trunks that hold our travellers' reports.

Our knowledge of our own countrymen and our feelings about them have slowly and unconsciously grown out of innumerable facts which are full of contradictions and subject to incessant change. They have the elusive mystery and fluidity of life. We cannot define to ourselves what we are as a whole, because we know too much; because our knowledge is more than knowledge. It is an immediate consciousness of personality, any evaluation of which carries some emotion, joy or sorrow, shame or exaltation. But in a foreign land we try to find our compensation for the meagreness of our data by the compactness of the generalization which our imperfect sympathy helps us to form. When a stranger from the West travels in the eastern world he takes the facts that displease him and readily makes use of them for his rigid conclusions, fixed upon the unchallengeable authority of his personal experience. It is like a man who has his own boat for crossing his village stream, but, on being compelled to wade across some strange watercourse, draws angry comparisons as he goes from every patch of mud and every pebble which his feet encounter.

Our mind has faculties which are universal, but its habits are insular. There are men who become impatient and angry at the least discomfort when their habits are incommoded. In their idea of the next world they probably conjure up the ghosts of their slippers and dressing-gowns, and expect the latchkey that opens their lodging-house door on earth to fit their front door in the other world. As travellers they are a failure; for they have grown too accustomed to their mental easy chairs, and in their intellectual nature love home comforts, which are of local make, more than the realities of life, which, like earth itself, are full of ups and downs, yet are one in their rounded completeness.

The modern age has brought the geography of the earth near to us, but made it difficult for us to come into touch with man. We go to strange lands and observe; we do not live there. We hardly meet men: but only specimens of knowledge. We are in haste to seek for general types and overlook individuals.

When we fall into the habit of neglecting to use the understanding that comes of sympathy in our travels, our knowledge of foreign people grows insensitive, and therefore easily becomes both unjust and cruel in its character, and also selfish and contemptuous in its application. Such has, too often, been the case with regard to the meeting of western people in our days with others for whom they do not recognize any obligation of kinship.

It has been admitted that the dealings between races of men are not merely between individuals; that our mutual understanding is either aided, or else obstructed, by the general emanations forming the social atmosphere. These emanations are our collective ideas and collective feelings, generated according to special historical circumstances.

For instance, the caste idea is a collective idea in India. When we approach an Indian who is under the influence of this collective idea, he is no longer a pure individual with his conscience fully awake to the judging of the value of a human being. He is more or less a passive medium for giving expression to the sentiment of a whole community.

It is evident that the caste idea is not creative; it is merely institutional. It adjusts human beings according to some mechanical arrangement. It emphasizes the negative side of the individual – his separateness. It hurts the complete truth in man.

In the West, also, the people have a certain collective idea that obscures their humanity. Let me try to explain what I feel about it.

## 2

Lately I went to visit some battlefields of France which had been devastated by war. The awful calm of desolation, which still bore wrinkles of pain – death struggles stiffened into ugly ridges – brought before my mind the vision of a huge demon, which had no shape, no meaning, yet had two arms that could strike and break and tear, a gaping mouth that could devour, and bulging brains that could conspire and plan. It was a purpose, which had a living body, but no complete humanity to temper it. Because it was passion – belonging to life, and yet not having the wholeness of life – it was the most terrible of life's enemies.

Something of the same sense of oppression in a different degree, the same desolation in a different aspect, is produced in my mind when I realize the effect of the West upon eastern life – the West which, in its relation to us, is all plan and purpose incarnate, without any superfluous humanity.

I feel the contrast very strongly in Japan. In that country the old world presents itself with some ideal of perfection, in which man has his varied opportunities of self-revelation in art, in ceremonial, in religious faith, and in customs expressing the poetry of social relationship. There one feels that deep delight of hospitality which life offers to life. And side by side, in the same soil, stands the modern world, which is stupendously big and powerful, but inhospitable. It has no simple-hearted welcome for man. It is living; yet the incompleteness of life's idea within it cannot but hurt humanity.

The wriggling tentacles of a cold-blooded utilitarianism, with which the West has grasped all the easily yielding succulent portions of the East, are causing pain and indignation throughout the eastern countries. The West comes to us, not with the imagination and sympathy that create and unite, but with a shock of passion – passion for power and wealth. This passion is a mere force, which has in it the principle of separation, of conflict.

I have been fortunate in coming into close touch with individual men and women of the western countries, and have felt with them their sorrows and shared their aspirations. I have known that they seek the same God, who is my God – even those who deny Him. I feel certain that, if the great light of culture be extinct in Europe, our horizon in the East will mourn in darkness. It does not hurt my pride to acknowledge that, in the present age, western humanity has received its mission to be the teacher of the world; that her science, through the mastery of laws of nature, is to liberate human souls from the dark dungeon of matter. For this very reason I have realized all the more strongly, on the other hand, that the dominant collective idea in the western countries is not creative. It is ready to enslave or kill individuals, to drug a great people with soul-killing poison, darkening their whole future with the black mist of stupefaction, and emasculating entire races of men to the utmost degree of helplessness. It is wholly wanting in spiritual power to blend and harmonize; it lacks the sense of the great personality of man.

The most significant fact of modern days is this, that the West has met the East. Such a momentous meeting of humanity, in order to be fruitful, must have in its heart some great emotional idea, generous and creative. There can be no doubt that God's choice has fallen upon the knights-errant of the West for the service of the present age; arms and armour have been given to them; but have they yet realized in their hearts the single-minded loyalty to their cause which can resist all temptations of bribery from the devil? The world today is offered to the West. She will destroy it, if she does not use it for a great creation of man. The materials for such a creation are in the hands of science; but the creative genius is in man's spiritual ideal.

## 3

When I was young a stranger from Europe came to Bengal. He chose his lodging among the people of the country, shared with them his service. He found employment in the houses of the rich, teaching them French and German, and the money thus earned he spent to help poor students in buying books. This meant for him hours of walking in the midday heat of a tropical summer; for, intent upon exercising the utmost economy, he refused to hire conveyances. He was pitiless in his exaction from himself of his resources, in money, time and strength, to the point of privation; and all this for the sake of a people who were obscure, to whom he was not born, yet whom he dearly loved. He did not come to us with a professional mission of teaching sectarian creeds; he had not in his nature the least trace of that self-sufficiency of goodness, which humiliates by gifts the victims of its insolent benevolence. Though he did not know our language, he took every occasion to frequent our meetings and ceremonies; yet he was always afraid of intrusion, and tenderly anxious lest he might offend us by his ignorance of our customs. At last, under the continual strain of work in an alien climate and surroundings, his health broke down. He died, and was cremated at our burning ground, according to his express desire.

The attitude of his mind, the manner of his living, the object of his life, his modesty, his unstinted self-sacrifice for a people to any benefaction bestowed upon them, were so utterly unlike anything we were accustomed to associate with the Europeans in

India, that it gave rise in our mind to a feeling of love bordering upon awe.

We all have a realm, a private paradise, in our mind, where dwell deathless memories of persons who brought some divine light to our life's experience, who may not be known to others, and whose names have no place in the pages of history. Let me confess to you that this man lives as one of those immortals in the paradise of my individual life.

He came from Sweden, his name was Hammargren. What was most remarkable in the event of his coming to us in Bengal was the fact that in his own country he had chanced to read some works of my great countryman, Ram Mohan Roy,[†] and felt an immense veneration for his genius and his character. Ram Mohan Roy lived in the beginning of the last century, and it is no exaggeration when I describe him as one of the immortal personalities of modern time. This young Swede had the unusual gift of a far-sighted intellect and sympathy, which enabled him even from his distance of space and time, and in spite of racial differences, to realize the greatness of Ram Mohan Roy. It moved him so deeply that he resolved to go to the country which produced this great man, and offer her his service. He was poor, and he had to wait some time in England before he could earn his passage money to India. There he came at last, and in reckless generosity of love utterly spent himself to the last breath of his life, away from home and kindred and all the inheritances of his motherland. His stay among us was too short to produce any outward result. He failed even to achieve during his life what he had in his mind, which was to found by the help of his scanty earnings a library as a memorial to Ram Mohan Roy, and thus to leave behind him a visible symbol of his devotion. But what I prize most in this European youth, who left no record of his life behind him, is not the memory of any service of goodwill, but

† See 'Ram Mohan Roy', p. 243.

the precious gift of respect which he offered to a people who are fallen upon evil times, and whom it is so easy to ignore or to humiliate. For the first time in the modern days this obscure individual from Sweden brought to our country the chivalrous courtesy of the West, a greeting of human fellowship.

The coincidence came to me with a great and delightful surprise when the Nobel prize was offered to me from Sweden. As a recognition of individual merit it was of great value to me, no doubt; but it was the acknowledgement of the East as a collaborator with the western continents, in contributing its riches to the common stock of civilization, which had the chief significance for the present age. It meant joining hands in comradeship by the two great hemispheres of the human world across the sea.

## 4

Today the real East remains unexplored. The blindness of contempt is more hopeless than the blindness of ignorance; for contempt kills the light which ignorance merely leaves unignited. The East is waiting to be understood by the western races, in order not only to be able to give what is true in her, but also to be confident of her own mission.

In Indian history, the meeting of the Mussulman and the Hindu produced Akbar, the object of whose dream was the unification of hearts and ideals. It had all the glowing enthusiasm of a religion, and it produced an immediate and a vast result even in his own lifetime.

But the fact still remains that the western mind, after centuries of contact with the East, has not evolved the enthusiasm of a chivalrous mind which can bring this age to its fulfilment. It is everywhere raising thorny hedges of exclusion and offering human sacrifices to national self-seeking. It has intensified the mutual feelings of envy among western races themselves, as they fight over their spoils and display a carnivorous pride in their snarling rows of teeth.

We must again guard our minds from any encroaching distrust of the individuals of a nation. The active love of humanity and the spirit of martyrdom for the cause of justice and truth which I have met with in the western countries have been a great lesson and inspiration to me. I have no doubt in my mind that the West owes its true greatness, not so much to its marvellous training of intellect, as to its spirit of service devoted to the welfare of man. Therefore I speak with a personal feeling of pain and sadness about the collective power which is guiding the helm of western civilization. It is a passion, not an ideal. The more success it has brought to Europe, the more costly it will prove to her at last, when the accounts have to be rendered. And the signs are unmistakable, that the accounts have been called for. The time has come when Europe must know that the forcible parasitism which she has been practising upon the two large continents of the world – the two most unwieldy whales of humanity – must be causing to her moral nature a gradual atrophy and degeneration.

As an example, let me quote the following extract from the concluding chapter of *From the Cape to Cairo*, by Messrs Grogan and Sharp, two writers who have the power to inculcate their doctrines by precept and example. In their reference to the African they are candid, as when they say, 'We have stolen his land. Now we must steal his limbs.' These two sentences, carefully articulated, with a smack of enjoyment, have been more clearly explained in the following statement, where some sense of that decency which is the attenuated ghost of a buried conscience, prompts the writers to use the phrase 'compulsory labour' in place of the honest word 'slavery'; just as the modern politician adroitly avoids the word 'injunction' and uses the word 'mandate'. 'Compulsory labour in some form', they say, 'is the corollary of our occupation of the country.' And they add: 'It is

Tagore, aged twenty-one, in Calcutta, 1882

At the wedding of his son, in Calcutta, 1910: daughter Mira, son Rathindranath, daughter-in-law Pratima, daughter Bela

Acting as Fakir in his play *The Post Office*, in Calcutta, 1917

As zamindar on his family estates, East Bengal

With Mahatma Gandhi, in Shantiniketan, 1940

At the exhibition opening of his paintings, in Paris, 1930: Countess Anna de Noailles, the French minister of fine arts, Victoria Ocampo

With Albert Einstein, in New York, 1930

Self-portrait, dated 1935

Untitled painting by Tagore, dated 1932

Untitled painting by Tagore, n.d. (exhibited in 1930)

Mrinmayi and Apurba in *The Conclusion* (*Shamapti*) by Satyajit Ray, 1961, adapted from a Tagore short story

Mani Malika in *The Lost Jewels* (*Manihara*) by Satyajit Ray, 1961, adapted from a Tagore short story

pathetic, but it is history,' implying thereby that moral sentiments have no serious effect in the history of human beings.

Elsewhere they write: 'Either we must give up the country commercially, or we must make the African work. And mere abuse of those who point out the impasse cannot change the facts. We must decide, and soon. Or rather the white man of South Africa will decide.' The authors also confess that they have seen too much of the world 'to have any lingering belief that western civilization benefits native races'.

The logic is simple – the logic of egoism. But the argument is simplified by lopping off the greater part of the premise. For these writers seem to hold that the only important question for the white men of South Africa is, how indefinitely to grow fat on ostrich feathers and diamond mines, and dance jazz dances over the misery and degradation of a whole race of fellow beings of a different colour from their own. Possibly they believe that moral laws have a special domesticated breed of comfortable concessions for the service of the people in power. Possibly they ignore the fact that commercial and political cannibalism, profitably practised upon foreign races, creeps back nearer home; that the cultivation of unwholesome appetites has its final reckoning with the stomach which has been made to serve it. For, after all, man is a spiritual being, and not a mere living money bag jumping from profit to profit, and breaking the backbone of human races in its financial leapfrog.

Such, however, has been the condition of things for more than a century; and today, trying to read the future by the light of the European conflagration, we are asking ourselves everywhere in the East: 'Is this frightfully overgrown power really great? It can bruise us from without, but can it add to our wealth of spirit? It can sign peace treaties, but can it give peace?'

It was about two thousand years ago that all-powerful Rome in one of its eastern provinces executed on a cross a simple teacher of an obscure tribe of fishermen. On that day the Roman governor felt no falling off of his appetite or sleep. On that day there was, on the one hand, the agony, the humiliation, the death; on the other, the pomp of pride and festivity in the governor's palace.

And today? To whom, then, shall we bow the head?

> Kasmai devaya havisha vidhema?
> 'To which God shall we offer oblation?'

We know of an instance in our own history of India, when a great personality, both in his life and voice, struck the keynote of the solemn music of the soul – love for all creatures. And that music crossed seas, mountains and deserts. Races belonging to different climates, habits and languages were drawn together, not in the clash of arms, not in the conflict of exploitation, but in harmony of life, in amity and peace. That was creation.

When we think of it, we see at once what the confusion of thought was to which the western poet, dwelling upon the difference between East and West, referred when he said, 'Never the twain shall meet.' It is true that they are not yet showing any real sign of meeting. But the reason is because the West has not sent out its humanity to meet the man in the East, but only its machine. Therefore the poet's line has to be changed into something like this:

> Man is man, machine is machine,
> And never the twain shall wed.

You must know that red tape can never be a common human bond; that official sealing-wax can never provide means of mutual attachment; that it is a painful ordeal for human beings to have to receive favours from animated pigeon-holes, and condescensions from printed circulars that give notice but never speak. The presence of the western people in the East is a human fact. If we are to gain anything from them, it must not be a mere sum-total of legal codes and systems of civil and military services. Man is a great deal more to man than that. We have our human birthright to claim direct help from the man of the West, if he has anything great to give us. It must come to us, not through mere facts in a juxtaposition, but through the spontaneous sacrifice made by those who have the gift, and therefore the responsibility.

Earnestly I ask the poet of the western world to realize and sing to you with all the great power of music which he has, that the East and the West are ever in search of each other, and that they must meet not merely in the fulness of physical strength, but in fulness of truth; that the right hand, which wields the sword, has need of the left, which holds the shield of safety.

The East has its seat in the vast plains watched over by the snow-peaked mountains and fertilized by rivers carrying mighty volumes of water to the sea. There, under the blaze of a tropical sun, the physical life has bedimmed the light of its vigour and lessened its claims. There man has had the repose of mind which has ever tried to set itself in harmony with the inner notes of existence. In the silence of sunrise and sunset, and on star-crowded nights, he has sat face to face with the Infinite, waiting for the revelation that opens up the heart of all that there is. He has said, in a rapture of realization: 'Hearken to me, ye children of the Immortal, who dwell in the Kingdom of Heaven. I have known, from beyond darkness, the Supreme Person, shining with the radiance of the sun.'

The man from the East, with his faith in the eternal, who in his soul had met the touch of the Supreme Person – did he never come to you in the West and speak to you of the Kingdom of Heaven? Did he not unite the East and the West in truth, in the unity of one spiritual bond between all children of the Immortal, in the realization of one great Personality in all human persons?

Yes, the East did once meet the West profoundly in the growth of her life. Such union became possible, because the East came to the West with the ideal that is creative, and not with the passion that destroys moral bonds. The mystic consciousness of the Infinite, which she brought with her, was greatly needed by the man of the West to give him his balance.

On the other hand, the East must find her own balance in science – the magnificent gift that the West can bring to her. Truth has its nest as well as its sky. That nest is definite in structure, accurate in law of construction; and though it has to be changed and rebuilt over and over again, the need of it is never-ending and its laws are eternal. For some centuries the East has neglected the nest-building of truth. She has not been attentive to learn its secret. Trying to cross the trackless infinite, the East has relied solely upon her wings. She has spurned the earth, till, buffeted by storms, her wings are hurt and she is tired, sorely needing help. But has she then to be told that the messenger of the sky and the builder of the nest shall never meet?

# Poet Yeats

Yeats can never be one of the crowd, his uniqueness is obvious to all. Just as his height sets him physically above almost everyone, so one notices in his personality a certain affluence which, like a fountain, wells up from the ordinary rut surrounding him, as if propelled by the power of divine creativity. One feels that his esse is inexhaustible.

When I read today's English poets I am often struck by the thought that they are not poets of the world as a whole, but rather poets of the world of letters. Here in England poets have a long literary tradition, with a plentiful supply of similes, metaphors and other stylistic devices. The result is that they do not have to go to the springs of poetic inspiration to make poetry. Instead they emulate those *ustads* in music who no longer feel the call to sing from the heart and thereby reduce music to a series of phrases and tunes, however complex and adroit their technique may be. When passion does not come from deep sensitivity, it becomes just a series of well-crafted words. Then it has to make up for its lack of candour and inner assurance with exaggeration; since it cannot be natural, it resorts to artifice in order to prove its originality.

My meaning will become clearer if we compare Wordsworth with Swinburne. Swinburne is the principal poet of poetry as opposed to life. He is so extraordinarily adroit at verbal music that he is besotted by his skill. Out of suggestive sounds he fashions a gorgeously variegated tapestry of images. His is a striking achievement, no doubt; but it has not established him as a world poet.

The poetry of Wordsworth arose from the direct touch of the

world upon his heart. Hence its simplicity – which is not the same thing as being easy of understanding by the reader. Whenever a poet writes out of a direct response to life, his poetry blooms like the flowers and fruits on a tree. It is not conscious of itself, nor does it feel obliged to present itself as being beautiful or deeply felt. Whatever it appears to be, it is: to appreciate and enjoy it is the onus upon the reader.

Certain individuals are born with a need for direct experience, and they do not permit any barrier to come between that experience and its inner realization. With absolute self-confidence and sincerity, they express the essence of the natural and human worlds in their own idiom. They have the courage to break all the conventions of contemporary poetry.

Burns was born in an age of literary artifice. His feelings sprang straight from the heart and he could express them in words. And so he was able to pierce through the bonds of literary usage and give unrestrained expression to the soul of Scotland.

In our own time, the poetry of Yeats has been received very warmly for the same basic reason. His poetry does not echo contemporary poetry, it is an expression of his own soul. When I say 'his own soul', I ought to make the idea a bit clearer. Like a cut diamond that needs the light of the sky to show itself, the human soul on its own cannot express its essence, and remains dark. Only when it reflects the light from something greater than itself, does it come into its own. In Yeats's poetry, the soul of Ireland is manifest.

Again this statement requires some clarification. Consider how, when the sun shines upon clouds, different portions reflect back different colours, depending on their condition and position. But this variety of colours does not create a clash; there is harmony in it, which would be inconceivable with clouds made of painted cotton wool.

Thus, whether the country is Ireland, Scotland or anywhere else, the genius of its people gives its own hue to the light of universal humanity. Universal man is something many-splendoured.

But a universal poet, while reflecting universal ideas, also belongs to his country, and his ideas are coloured by the special passions of his native land. The one who can express these well is considered blessed. In our country Vaishnava poetry, by virtue of its being genuinely Bengali, must be considered world poetry. It gives the world its due, but in doing so, it adds a particular flavour, it renders the universal in a particular form.

Those who dedicate themselves to fighting life's battles must put on armour; they require protection against the world and the blows that fall upon them from all sides. But those whose only goal is self-expression, find lack of protection to be their proper garb. On meeting Yeats, I felt that here was such a man. Here was someone capable of comprehending the world through the un trammelled power of his soul. His gaze was different from that of other men: he saw not by learning, nor by habit, nor by imitation.

When a man has this kind of unmediated perception of the world and can convey it, we observe a similarity between his vision and the vision of previous men; and this is not accidental. For all those who look candidly, see similarly. The Vedic poets too saw the life spirit in nature. The rivers and clouds, dawn, fire and storm were not scientific facts to them but manifestations of the working of the divine law. Their own experiences of joy and sorrow seemed to be re-enacted in the earth and heavens in wonderful disguise. As it is in our minds, so it is throughout nature. The whole drama of the human heart, with its laughter and tears, its desires, fulfilments and failures, is played out on the grandest scale in the light and shade and colour of the firmament. So vast is it, we cannot grasp its totality, we see just its parts, the waters, the land: we miss the overall picture, the underlying structure of the play. Only when man casts off his blinkers of habit and learning, when he looks with his whole heart, does he perceive the great drama in all its epic yearning – and this he cannot express except through myths and metaphors. His mind is now awakened and he experiences a realization – that there is nothing in the world that is not within him also, and that whatever is within him is immanent in the world in a deeper form. He thus attains the vision of the poet, which is to say that he sees with his heart, not with his eyeball, nerves or brain. This is a truth not of objective fact, but of the inner eye. And the language of his expression is consonant; it is the language of melody and beauty, the most ancient of human languages. Even today, when a poet shares such a universal perception, he speaks in the same language used by the old poets – which is why, although such language is outdated in a scientific age, poets still use it. Every new human experience revivifies the old stories and leaves its mark upon them. It stimulates the poet's mind and naturally induces him to return to the ancient modes.

Yeats has made his poetry confluent with the ancient poetic tradition of Ireland. Because he has achieved this naturally, he has won extraordinary recognition. With all his vitality he has been in contact with this traditional world; his knowledge of it is not second-hand. And so he sees beyond the physical world: its mountains and open spaces are a mysterious field for him, traversable only by meditation. Had he tried to express this feeling through the channels of modern literature, his sentiment and vigour would have been spoilt; for such modernity is not really fresh, but rather something worn out, rendered stiff and unresponsive by constant use. It is like the ashes that hide the fire: the fire predates the ash and yet is always new; the ash is 'modern' but decrepit. And so every time one finds that the real poetry cuts through the contemporary diction.

Everyone knows that for some time past Ireland has been undergoing a national awakening. As a result of the suppression of the Irish spirit by British rule, this movement has grown in strength. For a long time its chief expression was political, in the shape of a rebellion. But in due course it acquired a new form. Ireland now understood that she need depend on no one and stood ready to give of herself.

Her situation is reminiscent of our own country. Our educated community made a determined attempt to secure political rights. But in the course of this it became obvious that the leaders of the movement had no concern for the language, literature and traditions of the country. Their efforts were almost unrelated to the life of the vast majority of the people. Whatever they did in the way of national uplift was done in the English language and directed at the British Government. The idea that national work might involve the people as a whole, did not occur to them.

Fortunately, however, at least in Bengal, through our literature we started to find ourselves. The chief glory of Bankim Chandra [Chatterji] is that he ushered in an age in which Bengalis felt pleased and proud to speak and write in their own tongue. Before that we were just schoolboys, doing our English exercises using our dictionary and grammar book; and we treated our own language and literature with contempt. Suddenly, *Bangadarshan*† appeared, and showed us our own power. We discovered that we too could create literature and that it could satisfy our mental hunger. Once begun, we could not stop. Before, we had shut our eyes and told ourselves that we had nothing; now, we went looking for our own wealth. Where previously in the pages of *Bangadarshan* Comte and Mill had reigned, our writers now assiduously enthroned indigenous gods.

This enterprise in due time spread itself through various fields of endeavour. Whether or not we would manage to increase the number of native seats in the legislative council had been

† *The Mirror of Bengal*: celebrated journal of Bankim Chandra Chatterji, started in 1873.

something in the gift of the Government; but whether or not we would advance in the direction of national liberation, was dependant on our own will-power. We saw that any one of us willing to apply his powers in any sphere would help fit us to realize our national potential. The satisfaction inherent in this realization is the only true path of progress for us.

Arrogance accompanies the awakening of a sense of power and is an obstacle to the realization of truth. It inclines us to self-delusion rather than self-appraisal. It equates the bogus and the genuine, thus downgrading the genuine. It causes us to forget that only by clearly defining what we lack, may we truly understand what we have. Such clarity of self-knowledge is our sole means of access of strength. Arrogance obscures our grasp of the limits of our strength and leads us into weakness and futility. The foundation of our new pride must be truth: arrogance will get us nowhere. It is when arrogance repeatedly dashes itself against the fort of truth, to no avail, that we start to find our true selves.

In Ireland, as in our country, there has been an earnest effort to achieve self-expression. The first products of any such mental churning are bound to be frothy, and for a fair while it is not worth attaching much importance to what is often ludicrous – as witness, in Ireland, the work of the well-known writer George Moore, *Hail and Farewell*. But notwithstanding, a few Irish writers of real genius did find their voices and by drawing upon the ancient stories and legends, gave new voice to the soul of Ireland. Yeats was one of them. He has won Ireland a place in world literature.

When he raised Ireland's standard in the field of literature, it was even then showing signs of weakening. She had already wandered from the path of political rebellion and entered a period of political chicanery; the patriotic spirit had become dominated by diplomacy.

A critic has written of Yeats: [Here Tagore gives his rendition in Bengali of some writing in English, describing Yeats's emergence from within the Celtic tradition.]

The critic continues: 'It was with the publication of the *Wanderings of Oisin* in 1889, if I remember aright — that Yeats sprang to the front rank of contemporary poets, and threatened to add to the august company of the immortals. In the qualities by which he succeeded — an exquisitely delicate music, intensity of imaginative conviction, intimacy with natural and (dare I say?) supernatural manifestations — he was typically Celtic.'[†]

This notion of 'imaginative conviction' is profoundly true of Yeats. Imagination to him is not just the faculty of invention, it is the light whereby that which he sees is truly seized and becomes part of his life. In other words, imagination is not a mere device in his hands for making poetry, it is the stuff of life, which enables Yeats to extract sustenance from the world. Whenever I have chanced to meet him in private, I have sensed this. Though I have not yet had the opportunity to know him fully as a poet, by knowing him as a man I have come to feel that his is a soul in contact with life in all essentials.

[†] Tagore translated the first passage from this critic into Bengali, but left the second passage as a direct quotation from the original English. The first passage is not important to the argument, and since the English original is not available, we have omitted it. *Eds*

# On His Drawings

I have been asked to say something about these pictures, but I really do not know what to say about them. It is not for me to explain what they are, because I have not yet discovered them. The desire to draw came suddenly, and until I arrived in Europe I had a very great diffidence about the merit of these pictures, but I was encouraged by some artists whom I chanced to meet when I was in the south of France. They showed very great enthusiasm for the drawings, and insisted upon my exhibiting some of them in Paris. I was reluctant to do so, for I felt Paris to be a rather dangerous place for the purpose. The French are a very critical people, not only in respect to pictures, but also in respect of everything else, and so I felt rather nervous and undecided about the proposal. While I was staying in Paris a writer of great eminence, well known in literary circles, visited me, and when I showed him some of the drawings his remarks were very flattering to my vanity. This lightened somewhat the burden of diffidence from which I had been suffering, and then some friends of mine brought some of the famous art critics of Paris to see me and to pronounce judgement on these works, and they were also extremely favourable. It was then arranged that there should be an exhibition of these pictures, and a selection from the drawings was made. I tried to know what was in these pictures which would explain the enthusiasm of the reception given to them. One authority told me that I had achieved something in these pictures which their own artists had been trying to achieve without success. I could not believe it myself, but there it is; the observations were made by experts belonging to a people who are very critical, and who can indulge in what may be termed the cruelty of laughter. Bearing these things in mind, I came to the conclusion that I might have some little faith in my own powers as an artist.

Some people have asked me, 'What was your preliminary training?' I can only say that my training was in words, not in lines. From my childhood I think I had an inborn sense of rhythm. Even when I did not fully understand poetry, verse, especially Sanskrit verse, had an intense satisfaction for me, and since then, as you know, I have been doing nothing better than to turn out verse. I do not know what is in this task which gives one such a deep sense of ecstasy, but I believe the explanation is in the words themselves. Words are barren, dismal and uninspiring by themselves, but when they are bound together by some bond of rhythm they attain their significance as a reality which can be described as creative. We need not ask the question what they mean. They have something which appeals to our recognition. They have a reality; they have a value – a reality which is ultimate, and they have the quality of permanence. In their rhythmic interrelation the words come to a completeness and wholeness so that we cannot help recognizing them and acknowledging them as part of our own selves.

This correlation of words has been my study from boyhood, but I had been working with verse as my medium, and you all know that verse inevitably is designed to deal with thoughts and sentiments. Verse becomes immortal when we have the form of something which is a perfect harmonious unity as in a great poem. The felicitous expression of an idea has in it something beautiful and profound. If the same sentiment were expressed in bald prose, it would not have that intense value. The reality of the sentiment is found in its poetic perfection. It is some quality of ultimate reality, some value which is beyond the mere intellectual meaning – a primary quality, which may have significance as well as a secondary quality residing in itself or in the sentiments expressed. Music has the same quality. The notes when they are dissociated have no meaning. They are only of value when they are made into a perfect unity. This means an eternal unity, a quality that can never become stale. I had thoughts of this sort from my very young days. It came to my mind that the whole world can be viewed as a unity of life and creation. Only those creations of the poet or the artist have a right to survive which have their proper balance, for interrelation is a principle of creation. I often think what significance there may be in the long neck of the giraffe. When it suddenly developed the extra demand for its neck, the whole body was troubled, and until the process was completed it was a misfit, and so the whole body did its best in order to prepare for and give appropriate welcome to the newcomer. Such things are going on all over the world. There are innumerable animals which have pursued and, I believe, have achieved the balance of their life by something developing to bring them to their ultimate goal. Not until it was reached was the whole scheme of things completed.

If I had known you would be asking me about the genesis of these pictures, I should have thought out some ideas regarding them. It may be said that some of the drawings are weird; but then there are weird pictures in the history of creation. Camels are very weird; but in its own surroundings in the desert the camel is complete. The prudent people, the utilitarian people, say: 'What are these, and what use are these? What does the picture stand for?' I say do not bother about what they are. You do not ask the jasmine what is the philosophy of jasminehood, but when you see the jasmine you rejoice in its beauty, and the wonder and satisfaction is that it should be there at all. Creation is art in its most literal meaning, for it is the meaning of reality. In the last year or two I have found in drawing a means for the expression of reality. The discovery has given me intense satisfaction and pride – a pride such as the artist should have in achievement. I shall not be turned aside from my satisfaction if it is remarked by some people that a poet should keep to his verse and not bother about the making of pictures, for I am proud to have been told by some of the great critics of Europe that my pictures are better than the work of some of the well-known artists of the day. You will think that I am growing more and more vain as I grow older. Well, I can plead the excuse that painting is new to me, and that I have not yet grown used to and hardened in this form of expression.

# On Music

TAGORE  There is in human affairs an element of elasticity –
some freedom within a small range, which is for the
expression of our personality. It is like the musical system in
India, which is not so rigidly fixed as it is in western music.
Our composers give a certain definite outline, a system of
melody and rhythmic arrangement, and within a certain limit
the player can improvise upon it. He must be one with the
law of that particular melody, and then he can give
spontaneous expression to his musical feeling within the
prescribed regulation. We praise the composer for his genius
in creating a foundation along with a superstructure of
melodies, but we expect from the player his own skill in the
creation of variations of melodic flourish and ornamentation.

EINSTEIN  That is only possible where there is a strong artistic
tradition in music to guide the people's mind. In Europe,
music has come too far away from popular art and popular
feeling and has become something like a secret art with
conventions and traditions of its own.

TAGORE  So you have to be absolutely obedient to this too
complicated music. In India the measure of a singer's freedom
is in his own creative personality. He can sing the composer's
song as his own, if he has the power creatively to assert
himself in his interpretation of the general law of the melody
which he is given to interpret.

EINSTEIN  It requires a very high standard of art fully to realize
the great idea in the original music, so that one can make
variations upon it. In our country the variations are often
prescribed.

TAGORE If in our conduct we can follow the law of goodness, we can have real liberty of self-expression. The principle of conduct is there, but the character which makes it true and individual is our own creation. In our music there is a duality of freedom and prescribed order.

EINSTEIN Are the words of a song also free? I mean to say, is the singer at liberty to add his own words to the song which he is singing?

TAGORE Yes. In Bengal we have a kind of song – *kirtan* we call it – which gives freedom to the singer to introduce parenthetical comments, phrases not in the original song. This occasions great enthusiasm, since the audience is constantly thrilled by some beautiful, spontaneous sentiment added by the singer.

EINSTEIN Is the metrical form quite severe?

TAGORE Yes, quite. You cannot exceed the limits of versification; the singer in all his variations must keep the rhythm and the time, which is fixed. In European music you have comparative liberty about time, but not about melody. But in India we have freedom of melody with no freedom of time.

EINSTEIN Can Indian music be sung without words? Can one understand a song without words?

TAGORE Yes, we have songs with unmeaning words, sounds which just help to act as carriers of the notes. In north India music is an independent art, not the interpretation of words and thoughts, as in Bengal. The music is very intricate and subtle and is a complete world of melody by itself.

EINSTEIN It is not polyphonic?

TAGORE Instruments are used, not for harmony, but for keeping time and for adding to the volume and depth. Has melody suffered in your music by the imposition of harmony?

EINSTEIN Sometimes it does suffer very much. Sometimes the harmony swallows up the melody altogether.

TAGORE Melody and harmony are like lines and colours in

pictures. A simple linear picture may be completely beautiful; the introduction of colour may make it vague and insignificant. Yet colour may, by combination with lines, create great pictures, so long as it does not smother and destroy their value.

EINSTEIN  It is a beautiful comparison; line is also much older than colour. It seems that your melody is much richer in structure than ours. Japanese music seems to be so.

TAGORE  It is difficult to analyse the effect of eastern and western music on our minds. I am deeply moved by western music — I feel that it is great, that it is vast in its structure and grand in its composition. Our own music touches me more deeply by its fundamental lyrical appeal. European music is epic in character; it has a broad background and is Gothic in its structure.

EINSTEIN  Yes, yes, that is very true. When did you first hear European music?

TAGORE  At seventeen, when I first came to Europe, I came to know it intimately, but even before that time I had heard European music in our own household. I had heard the music of Chopin and others at an early age.

EINSTEIN  There is a question we Europeans cannot properly answer, we are so used to our own music. We want to know whether our own music is a conventional or a fundamental human feeling; whether to feel consonance and dissonance is natural or a convention which we accept.

TAGORE  Somehow the piano confounds me. The violin pleases me much more.

EINSTEIN  It would be interesting to study the effects of European music on an Indian who had never heard it when he was young.

TAGORE  Once I asked an English musician to analyse for me some classical music and explain to me what elements make for the beauty of a piece.

EINSTEIN  The difficulty is that the really good music, whether of the East or of the West, cannot be analysed.

TAGORE  Yes, and what deeply affects the hearer is beyond himself.

EINSTEIN  The same uncertainty will always be there about everything fundamental in our experience, in our reaction to art, whether in Europe or in Asia. Even the red flower I see before me on your table may not be the same to you and me.

TAGORE  And yet there is always going on the process of reconciliation between the two reactions, the individual taste conforming to the universal standard.

# On the Nature of Reality

TAGORE You have been busy, hunting down with
mathematics, the two ancient entities, time and space, while I
have been lecturing in this country on the eternal world of
man, the universe of reality.

EINSTEIN Do you believe in the divine isolated from the
world?

TAGORE Not isolated. The infinite personality of man
comprehends the universe. There cannot be anything that
cannot be subsumed by the human personality, and this
proves that the truth of the universe is human truth.

EINSTEIN There are two different conceptions about the
nature of the universe – the world as a unity dependent on
humanity, and the world as reality independent of the human
factor.

TAGORE When our universe is in harmony with man, the
eternal, we know it as truth, we feel it as beauty.

EINSTEIN This is a purely human conception of the universe.

TAGORE This world is a human world – the scientific view of
it is also that of the scientific man. Therefore, the world apart
from us does not exist; it is a relative world, depending for its
reality upon our consciousness. There is some standard of
reason and enjoyment which gives it truth, the standard of the
eternal man whose experiences are made possible through our
experiences.

EINSTEIN This is a realization of the human entity.

TAGORE Yes, one eternal entity. We have to realize it through
our emotions and activities. We realize the supreme man,
who has no individual limitations, through our limitations.

Science is concerned with that which is not confined to individuals; it is the impersonal human world of truths. Religion realizes these truths and links them up with our deeper needs. Our individual consciousness of truth gains universal significance. Religion applies values to truth, and we know truth as good through own harmony with it.

EINSTEIN Truth, then, or beauty, is not independent of man?

TAGORE No, I do not say so.

EINSTEIN If there were no human beings any more, the Apollo Belvedere no longer would be beautiful?

TAGORE No!

EINSTEIN I agree with this conception of beauty, but not with regard to truth.

TAGORE Why not? Truth is realized through men.

EINSTEIN I cannot prove my conception is right, but that is my religion.

TAGORE Beauty is in the ideal of perfect harmony, which is in the universal being; truth is the perfect comprehension of the universal mind. We individuals approach it through our own mistakes and blunders, through our accumulated experience, through our illumined consciousness. How otherwise can we know truth?

EINSTEIN I cannot prove, but I believe in the Pythagorean argument, that the truth is independent of human beings. It is the problem of the logic of continuity.

TAGORE Truth, which is one with the universal being, must be essentially human; otherwise, whatever we individuals realize as true, never can be called truth. At least, the truth which is described as scientific and which only can be reached through the process of logic – in other words, by an organ of thought which is human. According to the Indian philosophy there is Brahman, the absolute truth, which cannot be conceived by the isolation of the individual mind or described by words, but can be realized only by merging the individual in its infinity. But such a truth cannot belong to science. The nature of truth which we are discussing is an appearance; that is to say, what appears to be true to the human mind, and therefore is human, and may be called maya, or illusion.

EINSTEIN It is no illusion of the individual, but of the species.

TAGORE The species also belongs to a unity, to humanity. Therefore the entire human mind realizes truth; the Indian and the European mind meet in a common realization.

EINSTEIN The word species is used in German for all human beings; as a matter of fact, even the apes and the frogs would belong to it. The problem is whether truth is independent of our consciousness.

TAGORE What we call truth lies in the rational harmony between the subjective and objective aspects of reality, both of which belong to the superpersonal man.

EINSTEIN We do things with our mind, even in our everyday life, for which we are not responsible. The mind acknowledges realities outside of it, independent of it. For instance, nobody may be in this house, yet that table remains where it is.

TAGORE Yes, it remains outside the individual mind, but not the universal mind. The table is that which is perceptible by some kind of consciousness we possess.

EINSTEIN If nobody were in the house the table would exist all the same, but this is already illegitimate from your point of view, because we cannot explain what it means, that the table is there, independently of us. Our natural point of view in regard to the existence of truth apart from humanity cannot be explained or proved, but it is a belief which nobody can lack — not even primitive beings. We attribute to truth a superhuman objectivity. It is indispensable for us — this reality which is independent of our existence and our experience and our mind — though we cannot say what it means.

TAGORE  In any case, if there be any truth absolutely unrelated to humanity, then for us it is absolutely non-existing.

EINSTEIN  Then I am more religious than you are!

TAGORE  My religion is in the reconciliation of the superpersonal man, the universal human spirit, in my own individual being.

# The Bihar Earthquake

It has caused me painful surprise to find Mahatma Gandhi accusing those who blindly follow their own social custom of Untouchability of having brought down God's vengeance upon certain parts of Bihar, evidently specially selected for his desolating displeasure. It is all the more unfortunate, because this kind of unscientific view of things is too readily accepted by a large section of our countrymen. I keenly feel the iniquity of it when I am compelled to utter a truism in asserting that physical catastrophes have their inevitable and exclusive origin in certain combinations of physical facts. Unless we believe in the exorability of the universal law in the working of which God himself never interferes, we find it impossible to justify his ways on occasions like the one which has sorely stricken us in an overwhelming manner and scale.

If we associate ethical principles with cosmic phenomena, we shall have to admit that human nature preaches its lessons in good behaviour in orgies of the worst behaviour possible. For, we can never imagine any civilized ruler of men making indiscriminate examples of casual victims, including children and members of the Untouchable community, in order to impress others dwelling at a safe distance who possibly deserve severer condemnation. Though we cannot point out any period of human history that is free from iniquities of the darkest kind, we still find citadels of malevolence yet remain unshaken, that the factories that cruelly thrive upon abject poverty and the ignorance of the famished cultivators, or prison-houses in all parts of the world where a penal system is pursued, which most often is a special form of licensed criminality, still stand firm. It only shows that the law of gravitation does not in the least respond to the stupendous load of callousness that accumulates till the moral foundation of our society begins to show dangerous cracks and civilizations are undermined. What is truly tragic about it is the fact that the kind of argument that Mahatmaji uses by exploiting an event of cosmic disturbance far better suits the psychology of his opponents than his own, and it would not have surprised me at all if they had taken this opportunity of holding him and his followers responsible for the visitation of Divine anger. As for us, we feel perfectly secure in the faith that our own sins and errors, however enormous, have not enough force to drag down the structure of creation to ruins. We can depend upon it, sinners and saints, bigots and breakers of convention. We, who are immensely grateful to Mahatmaji for inducing, by his wonder-working inspiration, freedom from fear and feebleness in the minds of his countrymen, feel profoundly hurt when any words from his mouth may emphasize the elements of unreason in those very minds – unreason, which is a fundamental source of all the blind powers that drive us against freedom and self-respect.

# The Problem of India

*This statement, in the form of a letter, was addressed to an American lawyer, Myron H. Phelps, sympathetic to India.*

Shantiniketan, West Bengal
*4 January 1909*

My dear Sir,

I am exceedingly gratified to receive your very kind letter and to know of your desire for our welfare.

In regard to the assistance you expect from me, I am afraid that as I have never been used to express myself in the English language I shall not be able to give an adequate or effective idea of what I feel to be the truth about our country. However, I shall attempt as best I may to give you an outline of my views, more as a response to your message of goodwill than with the hope of rendering any help in your friendly endeavours.

One need not dive deep, it seems to me, to discover the problem of India; it is so plainly evident on the surface. Our country is divided by numberless differences – physical, social, linguistic, religious; and this obvious fact must be taken into account in any course which is destined to lead us into our own place among the nations who are building up the history of man. The trite maxim 'History repeats itself' is like most other sayings but half the truth. The conditions which have prevailed in India from a remote antiquity have guided its history along a particular channel, which does not and cannot coincide with the lines of evolution taken by other countries under different sets of influences. It would be a sad misreading of the lessons of the past to apply our energies to tread too closely in the footsteps of any other nation, however successful in its own career. I feel strongly that our country has been entrusted with a message which is not a mere echo of the living voices that resound from western shores, and to be true to her trust she must realize the divine purpose that has been manifest throughout her history; she must become conscious of the situation she has been instrumental in creating – of its meaning and possibilities.

It has ever been India's lot to accept alien races as factors in her civilization. You know very well how the caste that proceeds from colour takes elsewhere a most virulent form. I need not cite modern instances of the animosity which divides white men from negroes in your own country, and excludes Asiatics from European colonies. When, however, the white-skinned Aryans on encountering the dark aboriginal races of India found themselves face to face with the same problem, the solution of which was either extermination, as has happened in America and Australia, or a modification in the social system of the superior race calculated to accommodate the inferior without the possibility of either friction or fusion, they chose the latter. Now the principle underlying this choice obviously involves mechanical arrangement and juxtaposition, not cohesion and amalgamation. By making very careful provision for the differences, it keeps them ever alive. Unfortunately, the principle once accepted inevitably grows deeper and deeper into the constitution of the race even after the stress of the original necessity ceases to exist.

Thus secure in her rigid system of seclusion, in the very process of inclusion, India in different periods of her history received with open arms the medley of races that poured in on her without any attempt at shutting out indesirable elements. I need not dwell at length on the evils of the resulting caste system. It cannot be denied, and this is a fact which foreign onlookers too often overlook, that it served a very useful purpose in its day and has been even up to a late age of immense protective benefit to

India. It has largely contributed to the freedom from narrowness and intolerance which distinguishes the Hindu religion and has enabled races with widely different culture and even antagonistic social and religious usages and ideals to settle down peaceably side by side – a phenomenon which cannot fail to astonish Europeans, who, with comparatively less jarring elements, have struggled for ages to establish peace and harmony among themselves. But this very absence of struggle, developing into a ready acquiescence in any position assigned by the social system, has crushed individual manhood and has accustomed us for centuries not only to submit to every form of domination, but sometimes actually to venerate the power that holds us down. The assignment of the business of government almost entirely to the military class reacted upon the whole social organism by permanently excluding the rest of the people from all political cooperation, so that now it is hardly surprising to find the almost entire absence of any feeling of common interest, any sense of national responsibility, in the general consciousness of a people of whom as a whole it has seldom been any part of their pride, their honour, their dharma, to take thought or stand up for their country. This completeness of stratification, this utter submergence of the lower by the higher, this immutable and all-pervading system, has no doubt imposed a mechanical uniformity upon the people but has at the same time kept their different sections inflexibly and unalterably separate, with the consequent loss of all power of adaptation and readjustment to new conditions and forces. The regeneration of the Indian people, to my mind, directly and perhaps solely depends upon the removal of this condition. Whenever I realize the hypnotic hold which this gigantic system of cold-blooded repression has taken on the minds of our people whose social body it has so completely entwined in its endless coils that the free expression of manhood even under the direst necessity has become almost an impossibility, the only remedy that suggests itself to me and which even at the risk of uttering a truism I cannot but repeat, is – to educate them out of their trance.

I know I shall be told that foreign dominion is also one of the things not conducive to the free growth of manhood. But it must be remembered that with us foreign dominion is not an excrescence the forcible extirpation of which will restore a condition of normal health and vigour. It has manifested itself as a political symptom of our social disease, and at present it has become necessary to us for effecting the dispersal of all internal obstructive agencies. For we have now come under the domination not of a dead system, but of a living power, which, while holding us under subjection, cannot fail to impart to us some of its own life. This vivifying warmth from outside is gradually making us conscious of our own vitality and the newly awakened life is making its way slowly, but surely, even through the barriers of caste.

The mechanical incompatibility and consequent friction between the American colonies and the parent country was completely done away with by means of a forcible severance. The external force which in eighteenth-century France stood to divide class from class [could] only be overcome by *vis major* to bring emancipation to a homogeneous people. But here in India are working deep-seated social forces, complex internal reactions, for in no other country under the sun has such a juxtaposition of races, ideas and religions occurred; and the great problem which from time immemorial India has undertaken to solve is what in the absence of a better name may be called the race problem. At the sacrifice of her own political welfare she has through long ages borne this great burden of heterogeneity, patiently working all the time to evolve out of these warring contradictions a great synthesis. Her first effort was spent in the arrangement of vast materials, and in this she had attained a perhaps somewhat dearly bought success. Now has come the time when she must begin to build, and dead arrangement must gradually give way to living construction, organic growth. If at this stage vital help has come from the West even in the guise of an alien rule, India must submit – nay welcome it, for above all she must achieve her life's work.

She must take it as a significant fact in her history that when on the point of being overcome with a torpor that well nigh caused her to forget the purpose of what she had accomplished, a rude shock of life should have thus burst in upon her reminding her of her mission and giving her strength to carry it on. It is now manifestly her destiny that East and West should find their meeting place in her ever-hospitable bosom. The unification of the East which has been her splendid if unconscious achievement must now be consciously realized in order that the process may be continued with equal success and England's contribution thereto utilized to full advantage.

For us, there can be no question of blind revolution, but of steady and purposeful education. If to break up the feudal system and the tyrannical conventionalism of the Latin Church which had outraged the healthier instincts of humanity, Europe needed the thought impetus of the Renaissance and the fierce struggle of the Reformation, do we not in a greater degree need an overwhelming influx of higher social ideals before a place can be found for true political thinking? Must we not have that greater vision of humanity which will impel us to shake off the fetters that shackle our individual life before we begin to dream of national freedom?

It must be kept in mind, however, that there never has been a time when India completely lost sight of the need of such reformation. In fact she had no other history but the history of this social education. In the earliest dawn of her civilization there appeared amidst the fiercest conflict of races, factions and creeds, the genius of Ramachandra and Krishna introducing a new epoch of unification and tolerance and allaying the endless struggle of antagonism. India has ever since accepted them as the divine will incarnate, because in their life and teachings her innermost truth has taken an immortal shape. Since then all the illustrious names of our country have been of those who came to bridge over the differences of colours and scriptures and to recognize all that is highest and best as the common heritage of humanity. Such have been our emperors Asoka and Akbar, our philosophers Shankara and Ramanuja, our spiritual masters Kabir, Nanak, Chaitanya and others not less glorious because knit closer to us in time and perspective. They belong to various sects and castes, some of them of the very 'lowest', but still they occupy the ever-sacred seat of the guru, which is the greatest honour that India confers on her children. This shows that even in the darkest of her days the consciousness of her true power and purpose has never forsaken her.

The present unrest in India of which various accounts must have reached you is to me one of the most hopeful signs of the times. Different causes are assigned and remedies proposed by those whose spheres of activity necessarily lead them to a narrow and one-sided view of the situation. From my seclusion it seems to me clear, that it is not this or that measure, this or that instance of injustice or oppression, which is at the bottom. We have been on the whole comfortable with a comfort unknown for a long time, we have peace and protection and many of the opportunities for prosperity which these imply. Why then this anguish at heart? Because the contact of East and West has done its work and quickened the dormant life of our soul. We have begun to be dimly conscious of the value of the time we have allowed to slip by, of the weight of the clogging effete matter which we have allowed to accumulate, and are angry with ourselves. We have also begun vaguely to realize the failure of England to rise to the great occasion, and to miss more and more the invaluable cooperation which it was so clearly England's mission to offer. And so we are troubled with a trouble which we know not yet how to name. How England can best be made to perceive that the mere establishment of the *Pax Britannica* cannot either justify or make possible her continued dominion, I have no idea; but of this I am sure that the sooner we come to our senses, and take up the broken thread of our appointed task, the earlier will come the final consummation.

With kindest regards,

Yours sincerely,

Rabindranath Tagore

# Ram Mohan Roy

It takes time to understand and appreciate any rare personality who comes at an age when his country has lost itself and contradicts its own majesty. His voice sounds painfully discordant only because the people have allowed the strings of their own instrument to slacken and fail to make them harmonize with the music of truth which once originated in the sublime height of their nature.

Ram Mohan Roy was one such man who had been rudely rejected by his country which refused to be reminded of the responsibility of its great inheritance while clinging with desperate infatuation to its degeneracy. But the occasion was urgent and therefore his appearance in the midst of an angry annoyance was inevitable. He came to represent the change of season which must follow the long indigence of drought and bring the wealth of shower which inspires in the heart of a parched-up bareness a magnificence of life. It seems like a bewildering surprise, such a shifting of scene, and its fulness of meaning must wait to be unfolded till the harvest ripens and the reapers no longer hesitate to acknowledge it. Ram Mohan came to his countrymen as an unwelcome accident stupendously out of proportion to his surroundings, and yet he was the man for whom our history has been watching through the night, the man who was to represent in his life the complete significance of the spirit and mission of the land to which he belonged. It was a lonely life, but it had for its comrades the noble path-seekers who preceded him in India, whose courage was supreme in their adventure of truth.

It is a matter of infinite wonder that at an obscure age of narrow provincialism Ram Mohan should be able to bring, as a gift to his people who did not understand him, the mind that in its generous sympathy and understanding comprehended the best aspirations of the East and West, the mind that opened to itself the confluence of cultures on which have ever come sailing great epochs of civilization. The vision of the modern age with its multitude of claims and activities shone clear before his mind's eye and it was he who truly introduced it to his country before that age itself completely found its own mind.

We in India have occasions to blame our destiny, we have reasons to deplore our past and despair of our future but at the same time we have the right to hope for the best when we know that Ram Mohan has been born to us. Such a marvellous fact has to be fully realized by us through series of years, and great as is the glory that it carries in itself, great will be our shame in proportion if we fail in the least to offer him our best recognition even after a century of his death. Let us be worthy to own him by our capacity to understand him and willingness to dedicate to him our proud homage of gratitude. For a long time we have kept him aloof from us as an alien and thus proved ourselves small, but the opportunity has come today when we can show that the country that produces great messengers of truth knows how greatly to receive them.

# Hindu Scriptures

That religion, though not infrequently administered as opiate of the people, did not always originate as such, is often ignored by thinkers whose intellectual bias inclines them to purely economic interpretations of social phenomena. . . .

Perhaps the most significant thing that strikes the intelligent and impartial reader of the Vedic hymns is that they read, not like so many commandments, enjoined by priests or prophets, which in the European mind are identified with Oriental religions, including Christianity, but as a poetic testament of a people's collective reaction to the wonder and awe of existence. A people of vigorous and unsophisticated imagination awakened at the very dawn of civilization to a sense of the inexhaustible mystery that is implicit in life. It was a simple faith of theirs that attributed divinity to every element and force of nature, but was a brave and joyous one, in which fear of the gods was balanced by trust in them, in which the sense of mystery only gave enchantment to life, without weighing it down with bafflement – the faith of a race unburdened with intellectual brooding on the conflicting diversity of the objective universe, though now and then illumined by such flashes of intuitive experience as 'Truth is one: (though) the wise call it by various names.' (*Rig Veda*)

It is this brooding on the meaning of existence that chiefly distinguishes the spirit of the hymns from that of the *Upanishads*. The same wonder and poetry are there, but deepened and widened by the calm of meditation. Keener spiritual longing shifts the emphasis from the wonder of the outside universe to the significance of the self within. The quest for Reality rebukes the emotional exuberance of the early poet, and compels him inwards to explore the infinite depths of the soul in which the central principle of creation is reflected.

The early authors were childlike in their reaction, fascinated by what they beheld and naïvely seeking to adjust to it their hopes and fears; but as when children grow they gather an increasing awareness of their selves, the later authors sought more and more a centre of reference in their own consciousness, a subjective counterpart to the objective majesty that had so long held them enthralled in awe, an answer in their own being to the cosmic challenge of the visible universe.

A transcendental spirit of enquiry challenges the old gods, and their mechanical propitiation prescribed by the sacred texts. Says Narada: 'I know the *Rig Veda*, the *Yajur*, the *Sama Veda*, with all these I know only the mantras and the sacred books, I do not know the Self.' (*Chandogya Upanishad*) The eternal, the unchanging, the one without a second, is proclaimed, for fear of whom fire burns, for fear of whom the sun shines, and for fear of whom the winds, the clouds and death perform their offices. And if this Supreme Self is unknowable and incomprehensible, it is yet realizable through self-discipline and knowledge by the Self in man, for the two are ultimately one. Thus man is delivered from the fear of cosmic forces and is made part of the Divine Will.

But the *Upanishads*, though they measured the highest reaches of the philosophic imagination of our people, were yet incomplete in their answer to the complex longing of the human soul. Their emphasis was too intellectual, and did not sufficiently explore the approach to Reality through love and devotion. Man can never be fully and wholly fulfilled through self-discipline and knowledge, though that self-discipline be superhuman and knowledge transcendental. A more human approach lies through love, which easily withdraws most of the obstacles that the Self interposes between the contemplator and the contemplated, though love too needs self-discipline for its disinterested expression.

This lesson was duly emphasized by the *Bhagavad Gita*, which finally expounded the harmony between diverse approaches to the Reality that is one, through knowledge, through love, through righteous and detached living, and developed the thesis, that any means that helped the individual to rise above the demands of the ego to his identity with the Supreme Self that is in all being, were the truly legitimate means of that individual's spiritual fulfilment. Thus was rounded up the entire range of Indian spiritual and philosophic speculation and practice, and were reconciled the paths of dispassionate contemplation of the impersonal, of ecstatic devotion to the personal, of disinterested living in the world of the actual. Sacrifice of desire and not of the object, renunciation of the Self, not of the world, were made the keynote of this harmony of spiritual endeavours.

Such, in brief, is the impression left on the mind of an Indian as he surveys the many many centuries that stretch between the hymns of the *Vedas* and the arguments of the *Bhagavad Gita*.

# A Poet's School

From questions that have often been put to me, I have come to feel that the public claims an apology from the poet for having founded a school, as I in my rashness have done. One must admit that the silkworm which spins and the butterfly that floats on the air represent two different stages of existence, contrary to each other. The silkworm seems to have a cash value credited in its favour somewhere in nature's accounting department, according to the amount of work it performs. But the butterfly is irresponsible. The significance which it may possess has neither weight nor use and is lightly carried on its pair of dancing wings. Perhaps it pleases someone in the heart of the sunlight, the lord of colours, who has nothing to do with account books and has a perfect mastery in the great art of wastefulness.

The poet may be compared to that foolish butterfly. He also tries to translate in verse the festive colours of creation. Then why should he imprison himself in duty? Why should he make himself accountable to those who would assess his produce by the amount of profit it would earn?

I suppose this poet's answer would be that, when he brought together a few boys, one sunny day in winter, among the warm shadows of the tall straight *shal* trees with their branches of quiet dignity, he started to write a poem in a medium not of words.

In these self-conscious days of psychoanalysis clever minds have discovered the secret spring of poetry in some obscure stratum of repressed freedom, in some constant fretfulness of thwarted self-realization. Evidently in this instance they are right. The phantom of my long-ago boyhood did come to haunt its early beginning; it sought to live in the lives of other boys, and to build its missing paradise with ingredients which may not have any orthodox material, prescribed measure, or standard value.

This brings to my mind Kalidasa, a poet of ancient India. Happily for the scholars, Kalidasa has left behind him no clear indication of his birth-place, and there is ample scope for endless disagreement. My scholarship does not pretend to go deep, but I remember having read somewhere that he was born in beautiful Kashmir. Since then I have given up reading discussions about his birth-place lest I find some learned contradiction equally convincing. Anyhow, it is in the fitness of things that Kalidasa should have been born in Kashmir – and I envy him, for I was born in Calcutta.

But psychoanalysis need not be disappointed, for he was banished to a city in the plains and his *Meghaduta*† vibrates with the music of sorrow that has its keynote 'in the remembrance of happier things'. It is significant that in this poem the lover's errant fancy, in quest of the beloved who dwelt in the paradise of eternal beauty, lingered with enjoyment about every hill, stream, or forest over which it passed; watched the grateful dark eyes of the peasant girls welcoming the rain-laden clouds of June; listened to some village elder reciting under the banyan tree a familiar love legend fresh with the tears and smiles of simple-souled generations. We feel in all this the prisoner of the stony-hearted city revelling in a vision of joy that, in his imaginary journey, followed him from hill to hill, waited at every turn of the path which bore the finger-posts of heaven for separated loves banished on the earth.

It was not a physical homesickness from which the poet suffered, it was something far more fundamental – the nostalgia of the soul. We feel in almost all his works the oppressive atmosphere of the king's palaces of those days, thick with luxury

† *The Cloud Messenger.*

and the callousness of self-indulgence, and yet an atmosphere of refined culture, of an extravagant civilization.

The poet in the royal court lived in exile, as it were. It was, he knew, not merely his own exile but that of the whole age to which he was born, the age that had amassed wealth and well-being, and lost its background of the great universe. What was the image in which his desire of perfection persistently appeared in his poems and dramas? It was the *tapovana*, the forest resort of the patriarchal community of ancient India. Those who are familiar with Sanskrit literature know that this was not a colony of people with a primitive culture. They were seekers of truth, for the sake of which they lived in purity but not puritanism; they led a simple life, but not one of self-mortification. They did not advocate celibacy and were in close touch with people who pursued worldly interests. Their aim was briefly suggested in the *Upanishad* in these lines:

> Te sarvagam sarvatah prapya dhira
> Yuktatmanah sarvamevavisanti.

'Those men of serene mind enter into the All, having realized and being everywhere in union with the omnipresent Spirit.'

It was no negative philosophy of renunciation. Kalidasa, living in the prosperous city of Ujjain in the glorious days of Vikram-aditya, his mind oppressed by material objects and by its own demands, let his thoughts escape to the vision of *tapovana*, and into life, light and freedom.

It was no deliberate copying but natural coincidence, that a poet of modern India should have a like vision when he felt within him the misery of a spiritual exile. In Kalidasa's time the people strongly believed in the ideal of *tapovana*, the forest colony, and there can be no doubt that even in that late age there were communities of men living in the heart of nature – not ascetics intent on a slow suicide but men of serene intellect who sought to realize the inward meaning of their life. When Kalidasa sang of the *tapovana*, his verses instantly touched the living faith of his listeners. But today the idea of the *tapovana* has lost all semblance with reality and has slipped into legend; therefore, in a modern poem, it would merely be 'literary'. Then again, the *tapovana* concept would be a fantastic anachronism in the present age, unless recast under the current conditions of life. That, indeed, was the reason why the poet of today had to compose his verse in a plausible language.

But I must give that history in some detail.

Civilized man has come far away from the orbit of his normal life. He has gradually formed and intensified some habits, like those of the bees, for adapting himself to his hive world. We so often see modern men suffering from world-weariness, from a sense of revolt against their environment. Social revolutions are ushered in with a suicidal violence that is rooted in our dissatisfaction with our hive-wall arrangements – the too-exclusive enclosure that deprives us of the perspective needed in our art of living. All this is an indication that man has not really been moulded in the model of the bee, and therefore he becomes recklessly antisocial when his freedom to be more than social is ignored.

In our highly complex modern conditions, mechanical forces are organized with such efficiency that the materials produced grow far in advance of man's capacity to select and assimilate them to suit his nature and needs. Such an overgrowth, like the rank vegetation of the tropics, creates confinement for man. The nest is simple. It has an easy relationship with the sky; the cage is complex and costly, it is too much itself, excommunicating whatever lies outside. And modern man is busy building his cage. He is always occupied in adapting himself to its dead angularities, limiting himself to its limitations, and so he becomes a part of it.

This talk may seem too oriental to some of my listeners. I am told that they believe in a constant high pressure of living produced by an artificially cultivated hunger for material objects.

This according to them generates and feeds the energy driving civilization upon its endless journey. Personally, I do not believe that this has ever been the main driving force behind any great civilization. But I have touched on this theme in order to explain the conduct of a poet trespassing into a region reserved for experts and for those who have academic distinction.

I was born in what was then the metropolis of British India. Our ancestors came floating to Calcutta upon the earliest tide of the fluctuating fortune of the East India Company. The code of life for our family became composed of three cultures, Hindu, Muslim and British. My grandfather belonged to that period when an extravagance in dress and courtesy and a generous leisure were gradually being clipped and curtailed into Victorian manners. I came to a world in which the modern city-bred spirit of progress had just triumphed over the lush green life of our ancient village community.

Though the trampling process was almost complete around me, something of the past lingered over the wreckage. In my boyhood days I often listened to my eldest brother dwelling regretfully on a society that had been hospitable, kindly, and filled with a simple faith and the ceremonial poetry of life. All that was a vanishing shadow in the twilight haze of the horizon; the all-pervading fact was the modern city, newly built by a Company of western traders, and the spirit of the new times striking upon our life, even if it had to face countless anomalies. But it has always been a surprise to me that while this hard crust of a city was my only experience of the world, I was constantly haunted by the nostalgic fancies of an exile.

It seems that the subconscious remembrance of some primeval dwelling-place, where in our ancestors' minds were figured and voiced the mysteries of the inarticulate rocks, the rushing water and the dark whispers of the forest, was constantly stirring my blood with its call. (Some living memory in me seemed to ache for the playground it had once shared with the primal life in the illimitable magic of land, water and air.) The thin, shrill cry of the high-flying kite in the blazing sun of a dazed Indian midday sent a solitary boy the signal of a dumb distant kinship. The few coconut palms growing by the boundary wall of our house, like some war captives from an older army of invaders of this earth, spoke to me of the eternal companionship which the great brotherhood of trees have ever offered to man. They made my heart thrill to the invitation of the forest. I had the good fortune of answering this invitation when as a boy of ten I stood alone on the Himalayas under the shade of great deodars, awed by the dark dignity of life's first-born aristocracy, by its sturdy fortitude that was terrible as well as courteous.

Looking back upon those moments of my boyhood when all my mind seemed to float poised upon a large feeling of the sky, of the light, I cannot help believing that my Indian ancestry has left deep in my being the legacy of its philosophy, the philosophy which speaks of fulfilment through harmony with nature. It arouses in us a great desire to seek our freedom, not in the manmade world but in the depth of the universe; and it makes us offer our reverence to the divinity inherent in fire, water and trees, in everything moving and growing. The founding of my school had its origin in the memory of that longing for freedom, the memory which seems to go back beyond the skyline of my birth.

Freedom in the mere sense of independence is meaningless. Perfect freedom lies in the harmony of relationship which we realize not through *knowing*, but in *being*. Objects of knowledge maintain an infinite distance from us who are the knowers. For knowledge is not union. We attain the world of freedom only through perfect sympathy.

Children with the freshness of their senses come directly to the intimacy of this world. This is the first great gift they have. They must accept it naked and simple and never lose their power of quick communication. For our perfection we have to be at once savage and civilized; we must be natural with nature and human with human society. The misery which I felt was due to the crowded solitude in which I dwelt in a city where man was everywhere, with no gap for the immense non-human. My banished soul, in the isolation of town life, cried within me for new horizons. I was like the torn-away line of a verse, always in a state of suspense, the other line with which it rhymed and which could give it fullness having been smudged. The easy power to be happy which, along with other children, I brought with me to this world, was being constantly worn away by friction with the brick-and-mortar arrangement of life, the mechanical habits and the customary code of respectability.

In the usual course I was sent to school, but possibly my suffering was unusual, greater than that of most other children. The non-civilized in me was sensitive; it had a great thirst for colour, for music, for the movements of life. Our city-built education took no heed of that living fact. It had its luggage van waiting for branded bales of marketable result. The non-civilized and the civilized in man should be in the same proportion as water and land on our globe, the former predominating. But the school had for its object a continual reclamation of the non-civilized. Such a drain of the living water causes an aridity which may not be considered deplorable in a city, but my nature never became accustomed in those conditions. The non-civilized triumphed in me too soon and drove me away from school when I had just entered my teens. I found myself stranded on a solitary island of ignorance and had to reply solely on my own instincts to build up my education from the very beginning.

This reminds me that when I was young I had the great good fortune of coming upon a Bengali translation of *Robinson Crusoe*. I still believe that it is one of the best books for boys ever written. I have already spoken in this paper about my longing when young to run away from my own self and be one with everything in nature. I have described this mood as particularly Indian, the outcome of traditional desire for the expansion of consciousness. One has to admit that such a desire is too subjective, but this is inevitable in our geographical circumstances. We live under the tyranny of the tropics, paying heavy toll every moment for the barest right of existence. The heat, the damp, the unspeakable fecundity of minute life feeding upon big life, the perpetual sources of irritation, visible and invisible, leave little margin of capital for extravagant experiments.

Excess of energy seeks obstacles to fight with and overcome. That is why we find so often in western literature a constant emphasis on the malignant aspect of nature; in her the people of the West discover an enemy, for the sheer pleasure of challenging her to fight. The same reason which made Alexander wish for other worlds to conquer when his conquest of this world was complete made these enormously vital people go out of their way and spread their coat-tails in other peoples' thoroughfares, claiming indemnity when these are trodden upon. To enjoy the risk of hurting themselves they are ready to hurt others who are inoffensive; the birds which know how to fly away, the timid beasts which inhabit inaccessible regions, and . . . I shall avoid the discourtesy of mentioning higher races.

Life needs hurdles on its path for its advance. The stream would lose the speed of its flow without the resistance of the soil through which it must cut its way. The spirit of combat is part of the genius of life. The tuning of an instrument helps music to be perfectly realized. Let us rejoice that, in the West, life's instrument is being tuned in all its chords through the contest with obstacles. The creativeness in the heart of the universe will never let obstacles be completely removed. It is only because there is an ideal of perfection to attain that the spirit of combat is great.

In *Robinson Crusoe*, the delight in union with nature finds its expression in a story of adventure where the solitary man is face to face with solitary nature, coaxing her, cooperating with her, exploring her secrets, using all his faculties to win her help. The pleasure I felt in reading this book was not in sharing the pride of human success against the closed fist of a parsimonious nature, but in the harmony with nature attained through intelligent dealings. And this is the heroic love-adventure of the West, the active wooing of the earth.

I remember how in my youth, in the course of a railway journey across Europe from Brindisi to Calais, I watched with keen delight and wonder that continent glowing with richness under the age-long attention of her chivalrous lover, western humanity. He had gained her, made her his own, unlocked the inexhaustible generosity of her heart. And I had intently wished that the introspective vision of the universal soul which an eastern devotee experiences in the solitude of his mind could be united with this spirit of service.

I remember a morning when a beggar woman in a Bengal village gathered in the loose end of her sari the stale flowers that were about to be thrown away from the vase on my table; and with a look of ecstatic tenderness she buried her face in them, exclaiming, 'Beloved of my heart!' Her eyes could easily pierce the veil of the outward form and reach the realm of the infinite in these flowers where she found the intimate touch of her beloved. But in spite of it all she lacked that energy of worship, the western form of direct divine service, which helps the earth to bring out her flowers and spread the reign of beauty on the desolate dust. I refuse to think that the twin spirits of East and West, the Mary and the Martha, can never meet to make perfect the realization of truth. And in spite of our material poverty and the antagonism of time I wait patiently for this meeting.

Robinson Crusoe's island comes to my mind when I think of an institution where the first great lesson in the perfect union of man and nature, not only through love and through active communication, may be learnt unobstructed. We have to keep in mind the fact that love and action are the only media through which perfect knowledge can be obtained, for the object of knowledge is not pedantry but wisdom. An institution of this kind should not only train up one's limbs and mind to be ready for all emergencies, but be attuned to the response between life and the world, to find the balance of their harmony which is wisdom. The first important lesson for children in such a place would be that of improvisation, the ready-made having been banished in order to give constant occasion to explore one's capacity through surprise achievements. I must make it plain that this implies a lesson not in simple life, but in creative life. For life may grow complex, and yet, if there is a living personality at its centre, it will have the unity of creation, it will carry its own weight in perfect grace, and will not be a mere addition to the number of facts that only go to swell a crowd.

I wish I could say that we have fulfilled this dream in our school. We have only made a beginning. We have given the children an opportunity to find their freedom in nature by being able to love it. For love is freedom; it saves us from paying with our soul for objects that are all too cheap. I know men who preach the cult of the simple life by glorifying the spiritual merit of poverty. I refuse to imagine any special value in poverty when it is a mere negation. Only when the mind is sensitive to the deeper call of reality is it weaned away from the lure of the fictitious. It is callousness which robs us of our simple power to enjoy and dooms us to the indignity of snobbish pride in furniture and the foolish burden of expensive things. But to pit the callousness of asceticism against the callousness of luxury is to fight one evil with another, inviting the pitiless demon of the desert in place of the indiscriminate demon of the jungle.

With the help of literature, festive ceremonials and religious teachings I tried to develop in the children of my school their feelings for nature as also a sensitiveness to their human surroundings. I prepared for them a real homecoming into this world. Among the subjects they learnt in the open air, in the shade of trees, were music and painting, and they had their dramatic performances.

But this was not sufficient, and I waited for men and the means to be able to introduce into our school activities that would build up character. I felt the need of the western genius for imparting to my educational ideal the strength of reality which knew how to achieve a definite end of practical good.

The obstacles were numerous. The tradition of the community which calls itself educated, the parents' expectations, the upbringing of the teachers themselves, the claim and the constitution of the official University, were all overwhelmingly arrayed against the idea I cherished. In addition, we attracted hardly any contributions from my countrymen as our funds were inadequate to support an institution in which the number of boys had necessarily to be small.

Fortunately, help came to us from an English friend who took the leading part in creating and guiding the rural organization connected with Visva-Bharati. He believes, as I do, in an education which takes account of the organic wholeness of human individuality, needing a general stimulation of all faculties, bodily and mental. In order to have the freedom to give effect to this idea, we started our work with a few boys who were orphans or whose parents were too poor to be able to send them to any kind of school.

Before long we discovered that minds actively engaged in constructive work fast developed energies which sought eager outlet in the pursuit of knowledge, even to the extent of undertaking extra tasks. The minds of these boys became so alert that a very simple fact made them at once see the advantage of learning English, which was not in their course of studies. The idea came to them one day when they were posting some letters: on the envelopes the postmaster wrote in English the addresses that had already been written in Bengali. Immediately they went to their teacher asking that they be taught English in an additional hour. These boys never regretted their rash request. Yet I remember to this day what criminal thoughts used to fill my young mind when my own teacher of English showed himself at the bend of the lane leading to our house!

For these boys vacation has no meaning. Their studies, though strenuous, are not a task, being permeated by a holiday spirit which takes shape in activities in their kitchen, their vegetable garden, their weaving, their work, of small repairs. It is because their classwork has not been separated from their normal activities, but forms a part of their daily current of life, that it really carries itself by its own onward flow.

Most of our boys when they first came were weak in body and mind; the ravages of malaria and other tropical diseases had been their fatal inheritance. They brought with them an intolerable mental perversity; the Brahmin was supercilious, the non-Brahmin pitiable in his shrinking self-abasement. They hated to do any work of common good lest others beside themselves should get the least advantage. They sulked when they were asked to do for their own benefit the kind of work that, they thought, should be done by a paid servant. They were not averse to living on charity but ashamed of self-help.

It might have been thought that this meanness and moral lethargy were inherent in their nature. But within a very short time all that changed. The spirit of sacrifice and comradeship which these boys have developed is rare even in children who have had better opportunities. It was the active, healthy life which brought out all that was good in them and the accumulated rubbish of impurities was swept off. The daily work which they were doing gave rise to problems which demanded a solution. The logic of facts showed to them the reality of moral principles in life, and now they feel astonished when other boys do not understand such principles. They take great pleasure in cooking, weaving, gardening, improving their surroundings, and in rendering services to other boys, very often secretly, lest they should feel embarrassed. The members of a mess usually clamour for more than is provided for them, but these boys willingly simplify their needs. They have developed a sense of responsibility. Instead of grumbling at deficiencies, they think and manage for themselves. To improve their dietary they must apply extra zest on their vegetable patches. Even if they get poor results, these have a value not to be assessed in terms of market price.

To give an artistic touch to my description, I wish I could speak of some breakdown in our plan, of some unexpected element of misfit trying to wreck the symmetry of our arrangements. I have to confess, however, that it has not yet happened. Perhaps our tropical climate is accountable for this dull calm in our atmosphere, for the lack of that excess energy which often loves to upset things. Maybe it is not too late to hope that this experiment of ours is not going to be a model paradise for harmless boys. Some incalculable problems, I am sure, will presently arise, challenging our theories and our faith in our ideal.

Meanwhile, having realized that this daily practice in the adaptation of mind and body to life's necessities has made these boys intellectually alert, we have mustered courage to extend the system to the primary section of our school. The children of that section, under an ideal teacher who believes that to teach is to learn, have just finished constructing their first hut of which they are absurdly proud. They have apparently begun to think that education is a permanent part of the adventure of life; it is not like a painful hospital treatment for curing them of the congenital malady of their ignorance, but is a function of health, the natural expression of their mind's vitality. Thus, I have just had the good fortune to watch the first shoot of life peeping out in a humble corner of our organization. My idea is to allow this creeper to grow, with no special label of learned nomenclature attached to it; grow till it completely hides the dead pole that bears no natural flower or fruit, but flourishes the parchment flag of examination success.

Before I stop I must say a few more words about a most important item on our educational programme.

Children have their active subconscious mind which, like the tree, has the power to draw food from the surrounding atmosphere. For them the atmosphere is a great deal more important than rules and methods, equipment, textbooks and lessons. The earth has her mass of substance in her land and water; but, if I may use figurative language, she finds her stimulus in her atmosphere. It evokes from her responses in colour and perfume, music and movement. In his society man has about himself a diffuse atmosphere of culture. It keeps his mind sensitive to his racial inheritance, to the current of influences that come from tradition; it enables him to imbibe unconsciously the concentrated wisdom of ages. But in our educational organizations we behave like miners, digging only for things and not like the tillers of the earth whose work is a perfect collaboration with nature.

I tried to create an atmosphere in my school – this was the main task. In educational institutions our faculties have to be nourished in order to give our mind its freedom, to make our imagination fit for the world which belongs to art, and to stir our sympathy for human relationships. This last is even more important than learning the geography of foreign lands.

The minds of the children of today are almost deliberately made incapable of understanding other people with different languages and customs. The result is that, later, they hurt one another out of ignorance and suffer from the worst form of the blindness of the age. The Christian missionaries themselves help in this cultivation of contempt for alien races and civilizations. Led by sectarian pride while they profess brotherhood for all, they use school textbooks to corrupt young susceptible minds. I have tried to save our children from such aberrations, and here the help of friends from the West, with their sympathetic hearts, has been of the greatest service.

# SHORT
# STORIES

The short story in Bengali was invented by Tagore. Beginning in 1891 and continuing almost to his death, he wrote nearly a hundred stories. Some of them are generally agreed to have universal appeal. Anita Desai wrote of them: 'Almost every story contains enough observation to fill a novel.' Satyajit Ray judged them to be 'among the best short stories ever written', and in 1961, for Tagore's birth centenary, he made three short films out of three Tagore stories under the title *Three Daughters* (*Tin Kanya*); two of these stories, 'The Conclusion' and 'The Lost Jewels', are included here.

'The Conclusion' is one of Tagore's most lyrical stories and among the very few to have a happy ending, being a romance between a Calcutta-returned village graduate, a budding *babu*, and a way-ward, illiterate village girl. It requires little introduction, except perhaps to remind the reader that in 1890s Bengal, in the villages, child brides were the norm, even among the college educated.

'The Raj Seal', by contrast, deals with a fully fledged Calcutta *babu*, and is packed with irony, exploiting to the hilt the *babu*'s twin incompatible urges to be both British title-holder and patriotic hero. Tagore wrote the story in 1898, a year in which he began by delivering a paper at the Calcutta Town Hall entitled 'Kantharodh' (The Throttled) in protest against the Govern-ment's Sedition Bill; then attacked the Government for arresting a leading Indian nationalist on a charge of sedition; and finally had a go at Bengalis too, insisting that the presidential address of the Bengal Provincial Conference should be read in Bengali as well as in English (the usual language of Bengali politicians in that period) and at the same time severely criticizing the servile mentality and orthodox mores of some leading Bengali land-owners. Although the world of Raj politicking that Tagore depicts in this story has long since passed into history, 'The Raj Seal' shows that Tagore was acutely alive to the risible and corrupt character of the politics that might easily replace the Raj, once his countrymen had a free hand in government.

In 'The Lost Jewels', a story of the same period, a different kind of *babu* has centre stage: though he dresses like the British, he is not obsequious to them. Modern education on British lines in Calcutta has given him an independent and rational outlook. And as a result, there is a psychological gap between him and his traditional wife, of a kind very common in Bengal at this time, when well-educated men married largely illiterate wives (as Tagore himself had). With the passing of time, the gap widens into a gulf; there are no children to fill it; and the wife becomes increasingly obsessed instead with the gold and jewellery poured on her by her uncomprehending husband (again, a state of mind that was quite common among Bengali wives at this time). The final outcome is bound to be disaster.

The story is a horror story. Its tone is not dissimilar to that of a well-known horror story by Satyajit Ray, 'Khagam', in which a sceptical character remarks, 'This is the land of tall stories. You'll hear of strange happenings all the time, but never see one yourself. Look at our *Ramayana* and *Mahabharata*. It is said they're history, but actually they're no more than a bundle of non-sense. . . . Yet everyone – even the educated – swallows them whole.' Eventually, of course, it is Ray's sceptic who gets swallowed by the supernatural forces he has deliberately provoked. While 'The Lost Jewels' is intended to have an air of menace too, both Tagore (and Ray in his film) aim to make the spine tingle rather than to give the reader goose-flesh. The ending is by way of a sophisticated joke which unfortunately does not translate; we have therefore provided a brief footnote which we trust will be adequate, if not fully equivalent.

The final two stories are more straightforward. 'Purification' was written in 1928, more than a generation after the earlier stories, and deals with a recognizably contemporary western urban dilemma – how to treat beggars and outcasts in society – though the details are of course specific to the India of the time. Besides demonstrating Tagore's ability to treat a clearly political theme without being remotely propagandistic, the story shows how fierce his irony could be when turned upon the non-cooperation movement. 'The Parrot's Training' is ironic too but in a much gentler vein. It is really a fable about the failings of orthodox education, and was written in 1918 at the time of the Calcutta University Commission; indeed, when it was published in English with some amusing illustrations, Tagore sent copies to some of the members of the commission, presumably hoping that a tall story might have more impact on the educated mind than factual history.

# The Conclusion

Apurba Krishna had just passed his BA examination in Calcutta and was returning to his village. On the way his boat had to cross a small river. Later in the year, after the close of the rainy season, it would have been almost dry. Now at the end of Shraban, the monsoon month, it had reached the edge of the village and was lapping at the ruins of the bamboo grove. But after days and days of heavy rain, the sun shone in a cloudless sky.

Apurba's thoughts as he sat in the boat were brimming too. Had we access to the pictures in his young mind we would have seen them dancing like the sun's rays on the wind-ruffled water.

The boat drew up at the usual ghat. From the riverbank Apurba could see the tiled roof of his house through a gap in the trees. No one there knew of his arrival, and so no one had come to meet him. The boatman offered a hand with the luggage, but Apurba refused it and stepped gaily ashore. His feet touched the mud of the ghat, and he fell over, luggage and all. At that instant a melodious peal of high-pitched laughter came from somewhere and startled the birds in a nearby peepul tree.

Extremely embarrassed, Apurba quickly recovered his balance and looked about him. On top of a pile of bricks in course of being unloaded for the local money-lender, a girl sat doubled up with giggles. Apurba recognized her as Mrinmayi, daughter of their recently arrived neighbours. He knew they had previously lived by a big river some distance away, but when the river had swallowed their land they had settled in the village two or three years ago.

Apurba knew much about this girl's reputation. The men of the village referred to her affectionately as Pagli – 'Madcap' – but their wives were in a constant state of alarm at her wayward behaviour. All her playmates were boys, and she had vast scorn for girls her own age. In the ranks of biddable children she was regarded as a scourge.

Being her father's favourite made her all the more unruly. Her mother never stopped grumbling about it to her friends. Yet because the father loved Mrinmayi, her tears would have hurt him deeply if he had been at home. That fact, and natural deference to her absent husband, kept the mother from imposing too strict a discipline.

Mrinmayi was dark complexioned with wavy hair that straggled over her shoulders. Her expression was boyish. Her enormous black eyes held no shame or fear, and not the slightest coyness. She was tall, well built, healthy, strong – but of an age people found hard to estimate; otherwise they would have criticized her parents because she was still unmarried. If the boat of some distant zamindar arrived at the ghat, the villagers became impressively alert. As if at a signal, the women pulled their veils down to the tips of their noses, thus concealing their faces like curtains on a stage. But Mrinmayi would arrive holding a naked child to her chest, her unbound hair hanging free. She would stand like a young doe gazing inquisitively in a land where there was neither hunter nor danger. Eventually she would return to her boy playmates and give them elaborate descriptions of the new arrival's manners and mores.

Our Apurba had set eyes on this untamed creature several times during holidays at home, and had occasionally thought of her in a casual way, and sometimes in a not-so-casual way. In the course of life one sees a great many faces, but only a few become fixed in the mind, not for their external appeal but for some other quality – a transparency perhaps. Most faces do not give away much of the personality; but the transparent face – the face in a thousand – clearly reveals the mystery behind it and immediately impresses itself on the mind. Mrinmayi's face was one of these. Her eyes held all the wilful femininity of a nimble, unfettered fawn. It was a face that, once seen, was not easy to forget.

Of course its melodious laughter, however charming it might have been to others, sounded rather painful to the unlucky Apurba. Hastily handing the suitcase to the boatman, he set off red-faced towards home.

And so the scene was beautifully set, with the riverbank, the shady trees, the birdsong, the morning sun, the joy of being twenty – no need to mention a pile of bricks: but as for the person sitting on top of them, she bestowed grace even on that dull and solid heap. How cruel of fate to have turned poetry into farce at the first entrance of the first act.

## 2

The peal of laughter from that pile was still echoing in Apurba's ears when he picked up his mud-smeared case and chadar, took the path beneath the trees, and arrived at his house. His widowed mother was ecstatic at his unexpected arrival. She sent out at once for rice pudding, curds and *rui* fish and caused a bit of a flurry in the neighbourhood. Once the meal was over she introduced the subject of marriage. Apurba had expected it. He had already received many proposals, and in keeping with the slogan of the day had obstinately insisted 'BA pass before bride'. But now he was a BA, and his mother had been expectant for so long that he knew further excuses would be useless. He said, 'Very well, first let me see the girl. Then I'll decide.'

His mother said, 'I've seen her. You needn't give it a thought.'

Apurba was quite prepared to give it a thought himself and

said, 'Bride must be seen before marriage.' His mother thought she had never heard anything so outrageous, but she consented.

That night, after Apurba had put out the lamp and lain down to sleep in his solitary bed, he caught a sound from beyond the patter of midnight rain and the stillness of the village, the sound of sweet high-pitched laughter. His morning downfall bothered him very much, and he pondered how to rectify the impression he had created. The girl doesn't know that I, Apurba Krishna, am an erudite fellow, he thought, who has spent long periods in Calcutta – not a village bumpkin to be dismissed with a laugh because of a trifling slip in some mud.

The next day Apurba had to inspect the potential bride. She was not far away; the family lived in a neighbouring village. He dressed with some care. Discarding his usual dhoti and chadar, he wore a long silk *chapkan*, a puggree on his head, and his best varnished shoes, and set out at dawn with a silk umbrella in his hand.

The instant he entered the prospective father-in-law's house, he was received with pomp and circumstance. In due time a trembling creature, painted and polished, tinsel round the bun in her hair, and wrapped in a fine colourful sari, was produced before him. She was led silently to a corner, where she remained with her head bent almost to her knees and an elderly maidservant at her back to give her courage. Her small brother Rakhal now concentrated his total attention upon this latest intruder into the family and scrutinized its puggree, gold watch-chain and newly sprouted beard. After stroking this last a few times, Apurba finally asked with a solemn air, 'What have you read?' The dumb-founded ornamented bundle made no response. After a few more questions and some encouraging prods in the ribs from the maid, the girl blurted out in a faint voice, '*Charupath*-Volume-Two-Grammar - Volume - One - Descriptive - Geography - Arithmetic - History-of-India.' Simultaneously there came a sudden series of repeated thuds outside the room, and a moment later Mrinmayi raced breathlessly into the room with her hair flying. Without so much as a glance at Apurba Krishna, she grabbed the brother of the bride-to-be by the hand and began to pull him out of the room. But Rakhal refused to cooperate, so absorbing was the situation indoors. The maid did her best to retrieve this by berating Mrinmayi as sharply as propriety permitted. Apurba Krishna meanwhile preserved his own dignity as best he could by sitting bolt upright in his lofty turban and fiddling with the watch-chain across his stomach. When Mrinmayi finally grasped that she could not distract Rakhal, she slapped him loudly on the back, whipped the veil off the girl's head, and dashed out like a whirlwind. The maid growled in fury, and Rakhal tittered at the sudden sight of his sister minus her precious veil. The slap on the back he did not object to at all, for such exchanges often took place between them. Mrinmayi's hair, for instance, once hung halfway down her back, rather than to her shoulders. One day Rakhal had sneaked up behind her and snipped off a handful with a pair of scissors. She had grabbed the scissors from him in anger and finished the job with a few slashes. Waves of hair had fallen to the ground and lain there like clusters of black grapes. This was the system of discipline between them.

The inspection session fell silent and did not endure much longer. Somehow the girl uncurled herself, regained a perpendicular position and returned to the inner rooms escorted by the old maid. Apurba, still stroking his sparse moustache, rose as solemnly as possible and prepared to depart. But when he reached the door he saw that his new pair of varnished shoes had vanished, and no one could find them. Everyone in the house was frightfully put out and hurled endless reproaches in the direction of the culprit. Eventually a desperate Apurba borrowed an old, torn and flapping pair of slippers belonging to the master of the house. With this additional touch to his fancy *chapkan* and puggree, he very gingerly set out along the village path.

By the edge of a pond, at a deserted point on the path, the high-pitched laughter caught him again. It was as if some fun-loving nymph in the forest had seen the slippers and could not suppress her giggles. While Apurba stood hesitating, she emerged brazenly, placed his new pair of shoes on the path, and was about to take to her heels when Apurba managed to grab both her hands and capture her.

Twisting and turning, Mrinmayi tried to free herself but could not. A stray sunbeam slanted through the trees on to her full, mischievous face. Like a curious traveller stooping to see the sunlit bed of a moving stream through clear water, Apurba gravely gazed on Mrinmayi's upturned face with its sparkling eyes, very gradually loosened his grip on his prisoner, and released her. If he had struck her in anger Mrinmayi would not have been at all surprised, but this gentle sentence of punishment in this empty glade quite baffled her.

The whole sky seemed to ring with laughter like the sound of celestial ankle bells. Lost in thought Apurba Krishna plodded home.

## 3

All day Apurba made up excuses for not joining his mother in the inner rooms. He had an invitation elsewhere; he ate there. The fact is – though it may be hard to swallow – that even someone as erudite, serious minded and original as Apurba was remarkably eager to regain his lost dignity in the eyes of this simple village girl. What did it matter if she had momentarily reduced him to a laughing-stock, then ignored him in favour of some ignoramus named Rakhal? Must he prove to her that he reviewed books for a magazine called *Visvadip* and carried in his suitcase cologne, shoes, Rubini's camphor, coloured letter paper, and a book on how to play the harmonium, not to mention a notebook awaiting future publication like the dawn in the womb of night? Nevertheless, whatever common sense might say, Mr Apurba Krishna Ray was definitely unprepared to admit defeat at the hands of this flighty rustic girl.

When he appeared in the inner rooms that evening, his mother asked, 'Well Apu, you saw the girl. Do you approve?'

Somewhat awkwardly Apurba replied, 'I saw the girl, Mother, and there was one I liked.'

Astounded, his mother said, 'You saw *girls*?'

Then, after much shilly-shallying, he revealed that he had selected Mrinmayi, daughter of their neighbour. What a choice after so much education and study!

At first Apurba was considerably abashed, but he was no longer so when his mother began to object vehemently. He sat there insisting doggedly that he would marry no one but Mrinmayi. The more he thought of the dolled-up kind of girl, the more repulsive became the idea of marrying one.

Battle was joined between them, in the form of tiffs, sulks, fasts and sleepless nights, and after two or three days Apurba was victorious. His mother managed to convince herself that Mrinmayi was still immature, that her own mother had been unable to bring her up properly, but that if taken in hand after marriage Mrinmayi's nature would change. Gradually, she came to believe that the girl had a pretty face. It was when she thought of the girl's cropped hair that her heart filled with despair. Yet even that, she hoped, if tied up firmly and thoroughly soaked in oil, might in time respond to treatment.

To the village people Apurba's choice of bride quickly became labelled *apurba* – original. Many of them rather liked 'Pagli Mrinmayi', but not, it had to be said, as a possible daughter-in-law.

Her father, Ishan Majumdar, was informed. He was a clerk in a steamship company, responsible for the correct loading and unloading of goods and the sale of tickets from a decrepit tin-roofed hut at a distant riverside station. When he heard the news, he shed tears of sorrow and joy, mingled in proportions unknown. He petitioned his boss, a head-office sahib, for leave of absence to attend his daughter's wedding. The sahib considered this insufficient grounds and turned down the request. Then, expecting a week's holiday at Puja time, Ishan wrote home to postpone the wedding. But Apurba's mother said, 'The auspicious days fall in the present month, the wedding cannot be put off.' Twice rejected, the distressed father protested no more and went back to weighing goods and selling tickets.

Whereupon Mrinmayi's mother and all the older women of the village assembled and began to instruct Mrinmayi day and night in her future duties. Their stern prohibitions against playfulness and frolicking around, loud laughter, gossip with boys, and eating when hungry succeeded in making marriage sound like a nightmare. An alarmed Mrinmayi thought she had been sentenced to life imprisonment with hanging at the end of it. Like an unbroken pony she stiffened her neck, reared back, and said, 'I'm not going to get married.'

4

Nevertheless, she did.

Then her lessons began. Overnight, Mrinmayi's world contracted to the confines of her mother-in-law's inner rooms. Her mother-in-law began the task of correcting her. Assuming a minatory expression, she said, 'Look, dear, you are not a little girl any longer. We don't tolerate disgraceful manners in our house.' Mrinmayi did not grasp what she meant. If my manners are not tolerated here, I'd better go elsewhere, she thought. That afternoon she went missing. A thorough search was launched. Finally the traitor Rakhal led them to her secret hideout, the abandoned old chariot of the village deity Radha Kanta under a banyan tree. It is easy to imagine how the mother-in-law and willing well-wishers set upon the girl.

That night the clouds gathered and rain began with a pattering sound. Apurba Krishna edged a little closer to Mrinmayi as she lay in bed and whispered in her ear, 'Mrinmayi, don't you love me?'

'No!' she said violently, 'I will never ever love you!' And then she unleashed all her rage and humiliation on Apurba's head like a thunderbolt.

In a wounded voice he said, 'Why, what have I done?'

'Why did you marry me?'

A satisfactory counter to this accusation was tricky. But then and there Apurba decided he must win her over.

The next day the mother-in-law saw all the signs of rebellion and locked Mrinmayi in. At first and for some time she fluttered about the room like a newly captured bird. When she could not escape she shredded the bedsheets with her teeth in futile anger and then, lying prone on the floor, pined for her father and wept.

In time someone slowly came and sat beside her. Affectionately he tried to lift her hair off the floor and away from her face. Mrinmayi shook her head vigorously and threw off the hand. Then Apurba bent down to her and said softly, 'I've opened the door. Come, let's get away to the back garden.' But Mrinmayi's head shook vehemently and said, 'No.' Apurba tried to lift her chin and said, 'Just look who's here.' Rakhal, bewildered at seeing Mrinmayi prostrate on the floor, stood at the door. Without looking up she pushed away Apurba's hand. 'Rakhal's come to play with you. Won't you go with him?' In a voice loud with irritation she repeated 'No!' Rakhal realized he had chosen the wrong moment and fled with a sigh of relief. Apurba sat on in silence. Mrinmayi wept and wept, until she exhausted herself and fell asleep. Apurba tiptoed out and fastened the door behind him.

The next day she received a letter from her father. He grieved over his inability to attend his darling's marriage, and he sent the newly-weds his heartfelt blessings. Mrinmayi went to her mother-in-law and said, 'I want to go to my father.' The astonished woman exploded at this outlandish request. 'Who knows where her father lives, and she wants to go to him! A fantastic notion!' Mrinmayi went away without replying. She went to her room, bolted the door, and in utter hopelessness began to pray to her father as if to God: 'Father, come and take me away. I have no one here. I'll die if I stay here.'

In the dead of night, while her husband slept, Mrinmayi very carefully opened the door and left the house. Clouds passed over now and then, but the paths were plain in the moonlight. How to choose one leading to her father was beyond her. She assumed that if she followed the route of the mail runner it would take her to any address in the world. She set off on this familiar path. After walking quite a way she grew weary, and night was nearly over. As a few birds uncertain of the time began to give tentative chirps, she found herself on a riverbank in a place like a large market. She paused to think, and then recognized the 'jham jham' sound of the mail runner's ankle bells. Then he himself appeared, out of breath, with the mail bag on his shoulder. Mrinmayi rushed up to him and begged, 'I want to go to my father at Kushiganj. Will you take me?'

'I don't know where Kushiganj is.' With barely a pause for breath he roused the boatman on the mail boat tied up at the ghat, and the boat cast off. He was not allowed to take time to answer questions.

By and by the market awoke. Mrinmayi went down to the ghat and called to another boatman, 'Will you take me to Kushiganj?' Before he could reply, someone in the next boat called out, 'So it's you, Minu Ma? What are you doing here?' Bursting with impatience she called back, 'Banamali, I'm going to my father at Kushiganj. Can you take me in your boat?'

Banamali was a boatman from their village and knew this wilful girl very well. 'You're going to your father? That's good. Come on, I'll take you.' Mrinmayi jumped in.

The boatman cast off. The clouds descended and a torrential downpour began. The boat tossed in a current swollen with the rains of the month of Bhadra. Mrinmayi was overwhelmed with fatigue. She spread the loose end of her sari, lay down, and went tamely to sleep, rocked by the river like a baby in mother nature's arms.

She awoke in her bed in her married home. Seeing her eyes open the maid began to scold. This brought the mother-in-law and a stream of harsh words. Mrinmayi, wide-eyed, stared at her. But when she made a dig at Mrinmayi's father's bad training, Mrinmayi got up, went to the next room, and bolted the door.

Apurba forsook his usual timidity, went to his mother and said, 'What harm is there in sending her to her father for a few days?'

His mother turned on him: 'She's bewitched!' and then she took up an old theme: with so many girls to choose from, why had he brought home this bone-burning good-for-nothing?

5

All day the downpour continued, and the atmosphere indoors was equally foul. That night, in the early hours, Apurba woke Mrinmayi and said, 'Do you want to go to your father?' Suddenly alert, she clutched his hand and said simply, 'Yes!' Apurba whispered, 'Come then. We'll escape very quietly. I've arranged a boat.'

Mrinmayi looked at her husband with profound gratitude. She got up quickly, dressed, and prepared to leave. Apurba left a note to allay his mother's anxiety, and the two of them stepped out. In the dark, without a soul or a sound nearby, she first put her hand in her husband's of her own free will; the tingle of her excitement thrilled his every nerve.

The boat moved out into the night. In spite of her ecstasy Mrinmayi fell asleep almost at once. The next day, what freedom! what delight! On both banks were so many villages, markets, fields of grain, forests, other boats passing back and forth. Soon she was plying her husband with a thousand questions about the tiniest and most trivial of sights. What is in that boat? Where have those people come from? What is the name of this place? Questions whose answers could not be found in any of Apurba's college books or extracted from his Calcutta experience. His friends there would have been embarrassed to know that he answered every one of them and that most of his replies did not tally with the truth. He asserted, for instance, that a boat carrying sesame carried linseed, and he called a magistrate's court a zamindar's warehouse and confused the town of Panchberia with that of Rainagar. His wrong replies did not impede in the slightest the satisfaction in the heart of his trustful questioner.

The following evening they reached Kushiganj. In a tin-roofed hut half lit by an oily old lantern Ishan Chandra sat bare-chested on a stool, bent over a huge leather-bound account book resting on a small desk. The newly-weds entered and Mrinmayi said, 'Father!' in a tone of voice quite alien to that room. Ishan wept. He could not think what to say or what to do. His daughter and son-in-law were standing in his hut like the princess and prince of an empire, and all he could offer them for thrones were some bales of jute. He was absolutely disoriented. And what about food? As a poor clerk he cooked his own dal and rice – but this was a joyous occasion. Mrinmayi said, 'Father, today we'll all cook.' Apurba agreed with alacrity.

The room was without space, servants and food, but joy sprang in abundance from the constricted circumstances of poverty, as a fountain gushes with increased force from a tiny aperture.

Three days went by. Twice the river steamer appeared on

schedule with many passengers and much hubbub; but by evening the riverbank had emptied, and then the three of them were at liberty once more. They cooked together, making mistakes, and ended up with meals not quite what they had intended, which Mrinmayi, now the devoted wife, served to son-in-law and father-in-law, while they teased her about a thousand shortcomings in her household arrangements and she jingled her bangles in pretended pique. At last Apurba said they really had to leave. Though Mrinmayi pleaded with him for a few more days, her father said, 'Better not.'

On the last day he hugged his daughter, stroked her head, and said in a choked voice, 'Darling, you must be a Lakshmi to brighten your husband's home. Let no one find fault with my Minu.' A sobbing Mrinmayi bade farewell and departed with her husband. Ishan turned and went back to his hut, now twice as cramped and cheerless, and resumed weighing goods, day after day, month after month.

## 6

When this guilty couple returned home, Apurba's mother wore a long face and said nothing. She blamed no one, and they did not try to exonerate themselves. Unspoken reproof and reproach sat sternly upon the house like a stone. At last the atmosphere became unbearable, and Apurba said, 'Mother, college has opened, and I had better return to start my law degree.'

His mother said indifferently, 'What will you do with your wife?'

'She'll stay here.'

'No son, it won't work. You must take her with you.' She did not employ the usual affectionate form of address.

Apurba in a mortified tone said, 'All right.' He began to prepare. On the night before his departure he came to bed and found Mrinmayi in tears. Sorrowfully he asked, 'I suppose you don't want to go with me to Calcutta?'

'No.'

'Don't you love me?' There was no answer. Sometimes an answer comes easily, but other times the psychology of it is so complex that a shy girl can only keep silent. Apurba asked, 'Will you mind leaving Rakhal?'

'Yes,' said Mrinmayi without hesitation.

A pang of jealousy as piercing as the point of a needle passed through this Bachelor of Arts at the thought of the boy Rakhal. He said, 'I won't be able to return for a long time.'

No reply.

'I think it could even be two years or more.'

'When you return, bring a Rogers three-bladed knife for Rakhal,' Mrinmayi ordered.

Apurba, who had been reclining against a bolster, rose a little at this and said, 'So you really do want to stay here.'

'Yes, I'll go and stay with my mother.'

Apurba sighed and said, 'All right, that's that. I won't come back until you write me a letter. Does that make you very happy?'

Mrinmayi felt that this question did not require a reply and dropped off to sleep. But Apurba did not sleep. He propped himself up with a pillow and remained alert.

Late at night the moon rose, and moonlight fell across the bed. Apurba looked at Mrinmayi and thought he saw a fairy princess put to sleep by the touch of a silver wand. If he could only find a wand of gold he could awaken her and exchange a garland of love. But he knew that such a wand would only bring him heartache instead of happiness, while the silver wand had turned her into a blissfully sleeping beauty.

At dawn he woke her and said, 'Mrinmayi, it's time for me to go. Let me take you to your mother's house.' She got out of bed and stood there, and Apurba took her hands. 'I want you to grant me a wish. I have helped you many times. Now that I am going will you give me a reward?'

Mrinmayi was puzzled. 'What?'

'Give me one loving kiss.'

Apurba's ridiculous request and earnest voice made Mrinmayi burst into laughter. Then she pulled a long face and prepared to kiss him. She came close and could not, giggled and began to laugh again. Twice she tried, and at last gave up, muffling her hilarity with her sari. Apurba pulled her ears as a punishment but made a stern vow: he must not lower his dignity by snatching his reward by force. It must come spontaneously, as a sacred offering – or not at all.

Mrinmayi laughed no more. They set out together for her mother's house in the hush of early morning. When he returned he said to his own mother, 'I thought it over and decided to take her to her mother. Having a wife with me in Calcutta would restrict my studies. She'd have no company there. You don't seem to want her here, so I left her with her own mother.' In deep resentment, mother and son parted.


7


In her mother's house Mrinmayi found that she could not settle to anything. The entire house seemed to have altered. Time dragged. What to do, where to go, whom to see, she could not decide. It was as if the house and the village had been obliterated by a total eclipse of the sun at midday. And another thing: the desire to go to Calcutta that overwhelmed her now – where had that been last night? Only a day ago, she had had no conception that the life she loved could completely lose its savour. Today, like a mature leaf ready to detach itself from a tree, she effortlessly rejected her former existence.

There is a tale told of a swordsmith so skilled he could make a weapon keen enough to slice a man in two without his feeling a thing; only when he moved would the two parts divide. Mrinmayi was unaware when the Creator's sword severed her childhood from her youth. She looked around her, astonished and bruised, and saw herself anew. Her bedroom in her old home was no longer familiar. The girl who had lived there had disappeared. Now all her memorable moments gathered around another house, another room, another bed.

No one saw Mrinmayi out of doors any more. No one heard her peals of laughter. Rakhal was afraid even to look at her. Games together were out of the question. She said to her mother, 'Take me back to my mother-in-law's house.'

There Apurba's mother had been grieving, remembering her son's face at farewell. She agonized over his going away angry and leaving his wife with her own mother. Then the mournful Mrinmayi, veiled with due respect, came to touch her mother-in-law's feet. No wonder the old woman wept, embraced the younger, and in a moment was reconciled. Then the mother-in-law looked into the newly married girl's face and was amazed. The Mrinmayi she had known was no more. Could ordinary beings be so transformed? Such an enormous change would require enormous strength. The mother-in-law had intended to correct Mrinmayi's faults one by one, but an invisible Rectifier had taken charge of her and in one fell swoop had moulded her anew. Now Mrinmayi could understand her mother-in-law, and her mother-in-law Mrinmayi. They intertwined as one household like the branches and twigs of a tree.

A profound sense of womanhood filled every fibre of Mrinmayi and made her feel as tender as heartache. Tears of contrition welled up in her like the inky-black rain-clouds that herald the monsoon. They cast deep shadows beneath her eye-lashes. She kept thinking to herself: I didn't know my own mind. You could see that. So why didn't you make it up for me? Why didn't you punish me? I didn't want to go to Calcutta with you and behaved like a witch. Why didn't you make me go? You shouldn't have taken any notice of me and my obstinacy.

She thought of that morning when Apurba had captured her on the lonely road by the pond, had said nothing, only looked at her. She saw the path, the spot beneath the trees, the morning sunbeams, the expression in his eyes and all of a sudden she sensed their full meaning. The half-kiss she had given him before he went away now tormented her like a thirsty bird in the desert darting forward and hesitating before a mirage. Over and over again she thought: I wish I'd done that then, I wish I'd said that, if only it had been like that!

Apurba was similarly despairing. He was telling himself: Mrinmayi has never seen my best self. While Mrinmayi was asking herself: what must he think of me? What must he take me for? A difficult, thoughtless, silly girl, not a mature woman capable of returning his love from an unquenchable heart. She felt sick with shame and remorse and began to repay all her debts to Apurba with kisses and caresses on his pillow.

When he had gone away he had said, 'If you don't write, I won't come home.' When she remembered that, she shut the door and began a letter on the gold-bordered coloured paper that he had given her. Very carefully she drew some lines and then, after smudging her fingers, without bothering to address her husband with a formal salutation she wrote: 'Why don't you write to me? How are you?' and 'You come home.' What more could she say? Everything worth saying had surely been said, but not perhaps with quite the flair for expression to which humans are accustomed. Mrinmayi understood that and racked her brain for ways to put some new words together. 'Now write me a letter, and write how you are and come home, mother is well, Bishu and Puti are well, yesterday our black cow had a calf.' With this she ended the letter. She put it in an envelope and in drops of love inscribed each letter: Shrijukta Babu Apurba Krishna Ray. But even so much love could not make the lines straight, the letters neatly formed, the spelling faultless. And on an envelope, besides the name, something else is required. This Mrinmayi did not know. To keep the letter private she gave it to a trusted maid for posting. Needless to say, nothing came of it. Apurba did not come home.

8

His mother knew he had a holiday, yet Apurba had not returned. She and Mrinmayi assumed that he was still angry, and when Mrinmayi thought of her letter she was overcome with shame. It had conveyed nothing she really wanted to say, and Apurba would think her even more immature and even less worthy of his efforts. She was transfixed with anxiety. Again and again she asked the maid, 'That letter, did you post it?' A thousand times the maid reassured her, 'Yes, I dropped it into the box myself. The master should have got it days ago.'

A day eventually came when Apurba's mother called Mrinmayi and told her, 'Daughter, Apu has been gone a long time, so I am thinking of going to Calcutta to see him. Will you come?' Mrinmayi nodded in agreement, went to her room, shut the door, fell on the bed, embraced the pillow and shook with silent laughter. Then all her pent-up emotion spilled out and she became serious, gloomy and apprehensive. Finally she started to cry.

With no prior warning these two repentant women set out for Calcutta to plead with Apurba for absolution. There they stayed at the home of his married sister.

That evening Apurba, who had given up hope of a letter from Mrinmayi, broke his vow and sat down to write to her. No words came. He groped for one to convey mingled love and hurt. Not finding it, he became contemptuous of his mother tongue. Just then a note arrived from his brother-in-law: 'Mother

is here. Come at once and have your meal with us. All is well.'
In spite of this assurance, Apurba went along in a mood of
gloomy apprehension. As he entered his sister's house he
promptly asked, 'Mother, is everything all right?'

'Everything is perfectly all right. You didn't come home for
the holiday, so I have come to fetch you.'

'You needn't have troubled,' Apurba said. 'You know I have
to prepare for the law exams . . .' And so on.

When it was time to eat his sister asked, '*Dada*, why isn't your
wife with you?'

'My studies, you know . . .' her brother said solemnly.

His brother-in-law laughed. 'All these feeble excuses! You
were afraid of us.'

The sister said, 'You look ferocious enough to frighten any
young person.'

The banter continued, but Apurba remained downcast.
Nothing made him feel happier. All he could think was that since
his mother had come, Mrinmayi could easily have come too if
she had wished. Perhaps his mother had tried but been turned
down. It was hardly something he felt he could question her
about: one must simply accept that all human intercourse, in fact
all creation, was a maze of deception and error.

After the meal a blustery wind arose and heavy rain came
down. Apurba's sister proposed, '*Dada*, do stay with us tonight.'

'No, I must get back. I have to work.'

'What can you achieve at this hour?' asked his brother-in-law.
'Stay. You're not obliged to anyone. Why worry?'

After more urging Apurba acquiesced. His sister said, '*Dada*,
you look tired. Don't stay up. Go to bed.' That was Apurba's
wish as well. He wanted to be alone in bed in the dark and away
from all this chatter. At the bedroom door he saw that the room
was dark. His sister said, 'That wind has blown out your lamp.
Shall I bring another?'

'No need. I sleep without a lamp.' His sister left.

Apurba began to feel his way towards the bed. He was about to climb into it when with a sudden sound of bangles, a soft arm took him in its embrace, and a pair of lips like a flowering bud smothered him with a flood of passionate kisses that left no space to express surprise. He was startled only for a moment. Then he knew that the half-kiss interrupted by fits of laughter was at long last being concluded among uninhibited tears.

# The Raj Seal

When Nabendu Shekhar tied the knot with Aruna Lekha, behind the haze of holy incense the marriage god Prajapati had a good laugh. Alas, the things that amuse Prajapati are not always funny for us human beings.

Nabendu Shekhar's father was someone with quite a reputation among the British. He, Purnendu Shekhar, had skilfully navigated his path in the world and successfully salaamed his way to that summit of social prestige, a Rai Bahadurship; even greater heights, more difficult of access and more laden with honours, had been within his grasp when, at the age of fifty-five, his gaze still avidly and dolefully fixed upon the misty peaks of a Raja-hood, he unexpectedly departed the world unfavoured, and the joints in his neck, fatigued by salaaming, finally found rest as his body was laid out at the cremation ground.

But energy, so scientists tell us, is conserved, it shifts only in form and location and is never destroyed: and so like the fidgety goddess Lakshmi and her motionless consort, the father's salaam-ing power transferred itself to the son. Soon young Nabendu Shekhar's head was bobbing up and down tirelessly at the doorsteps of the British, like a pumpkin carried by a swiftly flowing river.

In his childless state, following the death of his first wife, Nabendu took a second wife. But the traditions of Aruna Lekha's family differed greatly from those of the first wife.

The elder brother of the new family was its guiding light. Everyone at home and in the neighbourhood revered his opin-ions on all matters. He was a BA and had a capable mind, but a fat salary and a position of authority did not appeal to him, neither did the whole business of contacts and patronage; the British kept their distance from him, and he, likewise, preferred to keep them at arm's length. Thus, though his presence dazzled his domestic circle, he exerted little influence further afield.

Earlier, he had spent three years away in England. The courtesy of English people there had so captivated him that he had forgotten the humiliating condition of his country and had returned home suited and booted in the English style.

His family had been a bit embarrassed at first, but soon they began to say that no one wore sahib's clothes as well as their elder brother. In due course, the glory of English dress penetrated to their very hearts.

The brother's own idea when he came back was: 'I shall set the first example of how to be on equal terms with the British.' By always bowing and scraping when we meet them, he maintained, we simply make ourselves inferior and at the same time do the sahibs an injustice.

He had brought back many cordial testimonials from important figures in England, and so in Bengal he managed to attain some slight position in the councils of the British. Accompanied by his wife, he partook of English tea, dinner, sports and humour. His success made his blood tingle and go to his head.

It was around this time, on the occasion of the opening of a new railway line, that some respectable native gentlemen, a favoured few, were invited by the company to travel along the new track with the lieutenant-governor. The elder brother of the family was among them.

On the way back a railway sergeant insulted the party by compelling them to leave their special carriage. The brother, dressed in his usual English attire, was about to get out when the official politely said, 'Why are you getting up? You may stay.'

The privilege puffed him up a little, to begin with. But as the carriage rolled on and the arid ashen-coloured fields of Bengal rolled by, the dying glow of the sun setting on the western horizon seemed like a shameful stain across the whole country; the mind of the lonely passenger, observing it unwinkingly, felt abashed. The thought of his Motherland cleft his whole heart and made his eyes sting with tears.

An old story came to his mind. An ass was pulling a temple car along the sacred way, and the passers-by, prostrating themselves in the dust before it were offering their *pranams*. 'They are all worshipping me,' the foolish ass thought.

'There's only one small difference between that ass and me,' the elder brother told himself. 'I have at last realized that it is not my person the British sahibs respect, but the jacket weighing on my shoulders.'

As soon as he reached home, he called everyone together, lit a fire and cast into it all his English clothes, one by one, as sacrificial offerings.

The higher the flames leapt, the more excitedly the children danced for joy. From now on their respected elder renounced his sipping of tea and munching of crumbs with the British, and made himself once more inaccessible inside his domestic fortress; while the rest of the aforementioned degree-and-title holders donned their puggrees once more and went off to buzz around British doors.

This, then, was the family whose second daughter, by divine conspiracy, Nabendu Shekhar married. All the girls in it were as well educated as they were attractive. Nabendu thought, 'I've struck lucky.'

The reverse notion, that they were in luck to have acquired him, he lost no time in substantiating. Various letters which various sahibs had at various times written to his father kept somehow popping out of his pockets quite by chance, upon which he would casually hand them to his sisters-in-law. But when he noticed the cutting little smiles that appeared on their cherry-shaped lips like daggers glinting in some gorgeous velvet scabbard, the unfortunate fellow became aware that he had misjudged his audience. 'I've made a blunder,' he told himself.

The eldest of the sisters-in-law, who was also the most appealing and accomplished of them, was Labanya Lekha. One day, an auspicious day, she arranged a small shrine in an alcove of Nabendu Shekhar's bedroom, consisting of a pair of English shoes anointed with vermilion, and then proceeded to place in front of it flowers and sandalwood paste and to burn two candles and incense. The minute Nabendu entered the room two of the sisters-in-law commanded him, 'Prostrate yourself before your beloved god, whose blessings will promotion bring.'

The third sister-in-law laboured long and hard to embroider a sacred scarf, a *namabali* – but instead of the usual names of the gods it bore well-known English names like Jones, Smith, Brown and Thomas. This she presented to Nabendu with due ceremony.

The fourth sister-in-law, not yet of an age for such things, nevertheless said to her brother-in-law, '*Bhai*, I promise you a rosary, so that you will be able to count the names of your sahib friends.'

Her eldest sister ticked her off: 'Look here, don't be so cheeky.'

Nabendu was inwardly annoyed, but he found it impossible to break away from his sisters-in-law, especially from the pretty eldest one. They were like nectar as well as thorns; they drew him to them and scratched him at one and the same time. He was like a maddened insect circling around them, wounding his wings but continuing to hover in blind intoxication.

Destiny, however, had willed that the lure of intimacy with sisters-in-law would eventually overcome lust for the company of sahibs.

The latter had reached such a pitch that when Nabendu wanted to pay humble court to the most senior sahib – the Burra Sahib – he would tell his sisters-in-law, 'I'm off to hear Suren Banerji's latest speech against the Government.' Or if he planned

to pay his respects to the sahib next in rank – the Chota Sahib –
on his arrival at the station from Darjeeling, he would announce,
'I'm going out to visit Uncle.'

The wretched fellow had landed himself in a real fix, with a
foot in both boats. His sisters-in-law vowed to themselves, 'We
shan't let you go until we hole the enemy vessel.'

A rumour now reached Nabendu's ears that in the next
Queen's birthday honours he would at last step into a Rai
Bahadurship, would ascend the first rung on the ladder to heaven.
Alas, he did not have the courage to break the joyful news of the
likely preferment to his sisters-in-law. That is, not until one
autumn evening when the bright moonlight struck him and he
suddenly revealed his passionate excitement to his wife. The very
next day she climbed into her palanquin, went straight to her
elder sister, and in a voice choked with tears poured out her
troubles.

Labanya listened and said, 'Calm down a bit, it's not as if Rai
Bahadurs have tails – why be so ashamed?'

Aruna Lekha could only repeat, 'No *Didi*, I don't mind what
else I become, but not a Rai Bahadur*ni*.'

The fact was, Aruna was already acquainted with a Rai Bahadur
and had well-founded reasons for her objection.

Labanya firmly assured her, 'All right, stop worrying. Leave
this to me.'

The husband of Labanya, Nil Ratan, was then working at
Buxar, many hundreds of miles west of Calcutta, near Varanasi.
Towards the close of autumn Nabendu received an invitation
from Labanya to join her. Delighted, without hesitation he set
out. As he boarded the train the left side of his body did not
twitch – which only goes to prove that the superstition about a
twitch in one's left side being a bad omen is just that, a
superstition.

The climate of early winter in western India had made Labanya
Lekha glow with health and charm like the radiant streaks of

dawn. She sparkled and rippled with laughter like the billowing fronds of a bunch of *kash* grass beside some lonely riverbank. To the enchanted eyes of Nabendu a blossoming jasmine creeper seemed to be scattering dewdrops that flashed in the sunbeams of early morning.

The pleasure in his mind and the air in the west cured his usual indigestion. What with the delights of good health and natural beauty and the thrill of his sister-in-law's ministrations he felt as if he had soared away from the ground. The river Ganges flowing past the foot of the garden, flushed with water, seemed to embody his own wild emotions as it swept swiftly on towards its unknown destination.

When, bathed in the rays of the dawn sun, he ambled back along the bank from his morning walk, his entire body felt gratified, as if embraced by a lover. And after that, when he attempted to help his sister-in-law to cook, he allowed his ignorance and incompetence to stand exposed at every step. He showed not the slightest desire to attend to his faults; in fact each day he repeated them. Measuring out ingredients, lifting pots on and off the stove, preventing vegetables from burning – in whatever domestic activity was required of him, Nabendu proved helpless, as feeble as a new-born child. The laughter that greeted him, sometimes affectionate, sometimes contemptuous, he revelled in.

At the midday meal, prompted by hunger on the one hand and his sister-in-law's insistence on the other, not to speak of his own greediness, the deliciousness of the food and the delectability of the cook, Nabendu found it hard to restrain himself.

Even at cards, after eating, he demonstrated no sign of genius. He fiddled the pack, he looked at others' hands, he snatched and bickered – but he did not win. The fact that he could not accept his defeats brought him endless ridicule; but in spite of that, the reprobate was completely insensitive to reform.

Only in one respect did he totally change. He abandoned the

belief that to be in favour with the sahibs was the ultimate goal in life, at least he did for the time being. Instead, he basked in the glory of the attention and affection of his family and friends.

The atmosphere he was now moving in was of course new to him. Although Labanya's husband Nil Ratan was a senior advocate at the courts he did not keep up contacts with the local sahibs, a fact that had provoked comment. He said: 'What's the point? When courtesies are not returned, whatever I give will not be repaid. What joy is to be had in sowing seed in the desert, however fair it may look? If you want a harvest, better sow in black soil.'

Nabendu too came to accept this attitude. He ceased to worry about a return on his former investments. Once, both he and his father before him had ploughed furrows in the hope of reaping Rai Bahadurships. Now he no longer felt the need to sprinkle water on this particular ground. After all, hadn't he already at great cost had a racecourse built in a favourite resort of the British?

The time of the annual Indian National Congress session approached. Nil Ratan Babu received a letter requesting him to collect contributions. Nabendu was contentedly playing cards with Labanya when Nil Ratan appeared one day, subscription book in hand, and said, 'We'd like your signature here.'

Recalling his allegiances, Nabendu could not prevent his face from falling. Labanya remarked, as if in desperation, 'Careful! Don't do it, your racecourse will be ruined.'

This made Nabendu brag, 'Why should I lose sleep over a thing like that!'

Nil Ratan reassured him, 'We won't print your name in the papers, don't worry.'

Labanya replied with an air of great deliberation, 'But think of the consequences. What if someone happened to—'

Nabendu interrupted impatiently, 'If my name gets printed will that diminish it?'

So saying, he took the subscription book from Nil Ratan's hands, abruptly inscribed a figure of a thousand rupees and signed. But all the while his mind was hoping: let my name not appear in print.

Labanya struck her forehead in a gesture of great concern: 'What have you done!'

The proud Nabendu said, 'Why, what's wrong with it?'

'But what about the guard at Sealdah Station, the sales assistant at Whiteaway's, and the sahib who grooms the horses at Hart Brothers – won't they take offence and be angry with you? Will they still come to your Puja celebrations and drink your champagne, pat you on the back when they see you?'

'So what to all that,' said Nabendu haughtily. 'You want me to stick to "at homes" and die of shame?'

Some days later he was sitting sipping tea at breakfast, reading the newspaper when his eye alighted on an anonymously published letter. It expressed fulsome thanks for his contribution to the Congress and added that the support of such a figure as Nabendu Shekhar was of incalculable benefit in building up the Congress.

Building up the Congress! Oh late lamented Father Purnendu Shekhar! Was it for this that you procreated your miserable son on the soil of India!

Still, hand in hand with sorrow goes joy. Plainly, this fellow Nabendu, for whose influence both the British and the Congress were covetously and singlemindedly angling, could hardly be regarded as a nobody: the fact was now public knowledge. Nabendu therefore presented the item to Labanya with a broad smile. She read it with a bemused expression, as if she had no idea of who had written it: 'O my! Now the cat's really out of the bag! Too bad! It's really too bad! Who could be your enemy? Let his pen wither, let his ink become full of sand, let white ants eat his paper—'

Nabendu was benign: 'Don't curse him too much. I've already

pardoned him and given him my blessing. Let his pen and ink turn to gold!'

Within two days the post brought Nabendu a reply to the letter in the form of a second letter printed in another newspaper, this one opposed to the Congress, edited by an Englishman. The letter was signed, 'One who knows'. According to its writer, those who were familiar with Nabendu Shekhar could never give credence to the scandalous report that had recently been linked with his name: for it was impossible that he should wish to turn Congresswallah; that would be as if a leopard were trying to expunge the black spots on its skin. Babu Nabendu Shekhar was a man of substance, the writer continued, not a job-seeker or a briefless pleader. He was not one of those who had gone abroad to England for a short stay to ape English manners and dress and try to bluff his way into English society before returning home a frustrated failure. Why therefore would he do such a — etc., etc.

Woe to the late Father Purnendu Shekhar in his abode of the dead! To think how assiduously you once cultivated your good name in the eyes of the British!

This was a letter fit to be displayed before a sister-in-law like a peacock's tail. Before anything else, it showed Nabendu to be by no means a worthless nonentity, but actually a substantial and significant figure.

Once again Labanya looked bemused: 'Who is this bosom friend of yours who writes like this? Must be some ticket collector, leather dealer or bandsman at Fort William?'

Her husband Nil Ratan said, 'You ought to write a reply, don't you think?'

Nabendu was lofty: 'There's no need, surely. One cannot respond to everything people say.'

Labanya burst into such peals of laughter they seemed to spill over the entire room like a fountain.

Nabendu was put out: 'Why are you laughing so much?'

This made her giggle so unstoppably that her blooming young body seemed about to disintegrate.

Nabendu felt completely drenched by this spray of mirth. In a rather injured voice he said, 'I suppose you think I'm afraid to write?'

'Not at all,' said Labanya. 'I was only thinking of that racecourse. You haven't quite given up hope yet, have you? – where there's life, there's hope.'

'You think that's why I don't want to write?' Nabendu cried angrily, and at once he took up pen and ink. But while writing, the warmth of his feelings did not find full expression, and so Labanya and Nil Ratan took it upon themselves to redress the balance. The process was akin to the frying of a *luchi*: Nabendu would dip his pen in water to cool it and in ghee to soften it and then roll his words as flat as possible; while his two assistants would promptly take these words and puff them up crisp and hot. Ultimately, Nabendu's letter asserted that an enemy within was far worse than an enemy without. Pathans and Russians were less of a threat to the good government of India than the arrogance of the Anglo-Indian governing class. It was this group that constituted an impenetrable barrier to the permanence of the bond between the Government and its subjects. Congress was anxious to open a broad avenue of lasting friendship between rulers and ruled, but the Anglo-Indian press had covered the path with thorns. And so on.

Nabendu was quite alarmed – and yet the quality of the writing pleased him.

For some time after the appearance of this fine piece, controversy raged back and forth in various papers concerning Nabendu's donation and support for Congress. He became a fearless patriot, so keen was he to impress his sisters-in-law. Labanya laughed to herself and thought, 'All right, but you have yet to pass through fire.'

Prior to taking his bath one morning, Nabendu was in the

midst of trying to oil the inaccessible regions of his back, having already oiled his chest, when a bearer entered holding a visiting card printed with the name of the District Magistrate himself.

To encounter the magistrate with a body covered in oil – it was unthinkable! Like a well-marinated *koi*-fish about to be tossed into the frying-pan, Nabendu thrashed in an agony of futile indecision. Then somehow, in a trice, he bathed, dressed and breathlessly emerged into the drawing-room. The bearer said, 'The sahib waited a long time and then left.' Exactly how much blame for this total lie should be attributed to the bearer and how much to the nearby Labanya would make a pointed exercise in ethics.

At any rate, Nabendu's heart sank and began palpitating distractedly like a fragment of tail chopped off a house lizard. The whole day, whatever he did, he felt bothered.

Labanya, with a great effort, suppressed her laughter some-where in her innermost recesses and persistently questioned her brother-in-law, 'What's the matter with you today? You're not ill, are you?'

Nabendu managed to crank his features into a smile and produce a fitting response: 'How can I be ill here in your domain? Aren't you my very own heavenly physician, my Dhanantari sent by the gods?'

But a moment later his good humour evaporated and he began to ponder, 'First I made a donation to the Congress, then I wrote that letter to the papers, and then to cap it all, when the District Magistrate himself came calling, I kept him waiting – what must he be thinking of me?'

'Woe betide me!' thought the son of Father Purnendu Shek-har. 'Through the slings and arrows of fate I have been made out to be someone I am not.'

The very next morning, sporting a watch-chain and an enormous puggree on his head Nabendu stepped out. 'Where are you off to?' asked Labanya.

'An urgent engagement,' Nabendu replied.

Labanya said nothing.

When Nabendu presented his card to the orderly at the sahib's house the latter said, 'You cannot see him now.'

Nabendu reached into his pocket and produced two rupees. There was a quick salaam and then – 'There are five of us here.' Promptly Nabendu offered a ten-rupee note.

The summons came from the sahib. He was sitting at his desk working in his dressing-gown and slippers. Nabendu salaamed, the District Magistrate jabbed his finger in the direction of a seat and without looking up said, 'What's your business, Babu.'

Nabendu fiddled with his watch-chain and said in a slightly trembling voice, 'Yesterday you did me the honour of paying me a visit, but—'

The brows of the sahib knitted, then he raised his eyes from his papers and said, 'I paid you a visit? Babu, what nonsense are you talking!'

Nabendu sweated. 'Beg your pardon! It's a mistake, I must be confused,' he mumbled, and somehow made his escape. Much later, lying in bed, a sentence would keep running in his head like a chant in a nightmare: 'Babu, you are a howling idiot!'

On the way back in his carriage a thought struck him: 'The Magistrate did really call, but out of annoyance he didn't want to admit it.' Then he thought, 'I wish the ground would crack open!' But the earth refused to oblige him and he arrived home safe and sound.

He told Labanya, 'I went to buy some of the local rose-water to send back to Calcutta.'

Before he could say more, half a dozen peons in the uniform of the Collector's office presented themselves before him. After salaaming him they stood silently smiling.

Labanya too smiled: 'That donation to Congress you made – do you think they've come to arrest you?'

The peons now grinned in unison, revealing six sets of pointed teeth: 'Bakshish, Babu Sahib!'

Labanya's husband Nil Ratan appeared from a nearby room and said in an irritated tone, 'Why bakshish?'

The teeth gnashed gloriously: 'Bakshish for seeing the Magistrate Sahib.'

Still smiling, Labanya remarked, 'So the Magistrate Sahib sells rose-water now, does he? So much more soothing than his previous trade.'

The wretched Nabendu, desperate to reconcile rose-water and magistrate, uttered some words that no one could follow.

Nil Ratan spoke sharply to the peons: 'No bakshish for you here. You haven't done anything.'

Nabendu diffidently pulled a note from his pocket, saying, 'They are poor people, what's the harm . . .'

'There are much poorer people than they in the world,' said Nil Ratan, snatching the note from Nabendu's hand. 'I'll give this to them.'

Deprived of his chance to placate these demon followers of Lord Shiva – well, in this case, the Great Red-Face Shiva Sahib – Nabendu could only gaze piteously at the peons as if wordlessly pleading, 'Don't blame me, my friends, it's not my fault you know.'

The week of the Congress session arrived. To attend it Nil Ratan and his wife journeyed to the capital. Nabendu accompanied them.

The moment he set foot in Calcutta he was mobbed by Congress supporters; they danced around him as frenziedly as if the end of creation was nigh. There were eloquent speeches and encomia without end. The chorus was, 'Without heroes like you working for the country, the country has no hope.' Nabendu could hardly deny the truth of this, and so, all of a sudden, among all this hue and cry he found himself a national leader. When he entered the conference hall everyone rose to their feet and loudly shouted such queer foreign greetings as 'Hip hip hooray!' The Motherland blushed to the tips of her roots.

Her Majesty the Queen in due course had her birthday, but the prospect of a Rai Bahadurship for Nabendu had retreated and vanished like a mirage in the desert.

That evening Labanya Lekha invited Nabendu to her room, with great ceremony offered him a set of new clothes and with her own hands decorated his forehead with a blood-red *tilak* mark. After that, each sister-in-law hung around his neck a flower-garland of her own making. His wife Aruna Lekha, decked in a red sari and jewels, sat in her own room smiling shyly, looking radiant behind her veil of ornaments. Her sisters, pressing a particularly thick garland into her hands – which were hot with anxiety and chilly with embarrassment – tried to drag her to Nabendu, but she was unyielding; and so Nabendu's neck had to wait for its most important garland until the secret solitariness of night-time. The sisters-in-law told Nabendu, 'Today we've made you a real Raja. No one but you could have received such honour from all India.'

Whether or not this genuinely consoled Nabendu may be known only in his heart or perhaps by God. We must remain extremely doubtful on the point. Rather we believe firmly that Nabendu will be a Rai Bahadur before he dies, and that the occasion of his passing will be suitably marked by obituaries in the *Englishman* and the *Pioneer*. For now though, let us give 'three cheers' for Father Babu Purnendu Shekhar. Hip hip hooray! Hip hip hooray! Hip hip hooray!

# The Lost Jewels

My boat lay moored at the steps of a dilapidated ghat. The sun had just gone down.

On the roof of the boat the boatmen were engaged in their evening prayers. Their silent figures, kneeling and bowing, outlined against the dying glow of the western sky, seemed like a fleeting image. The unruffled surface of the river reflected every colour and every intensity in the spectrum of light, from palest gold to darkest steel-blue.

A decrepit old mansion with broken windows and tumble-down verandas looked down as I sat on the darkening stone steps of the ghat, which were cracking between the roots of a nearby banyan tree, and listened to the hum of the crickets. I was alone and felt a little forlorn. My eyes had become slightly moist with tears, when all of a sudden I was thoroughly startled by a voice asking, 'Sir, where are you coming from?'

I saw a man of half-starved appearance, obviously down on his luck. His face had that deprived look common among my countrymen when they take up service away from home. Above his dhoti he wore a greasy-looking coat of coarse Assamese silk. It seemed as if he was on his way back from a day's work, ready for his evening meal at home, and had decided to stop at the riverbank for a breath of air.

The stranger settled down beside me on the steps. I replied, 'I've come from Ranchi.'

'What do you do?'

'I am a merchant.'

'What kind?'

'I deal in myrobalan, silk cocoons and timber.'

'What name?'

I hesitated, then gave a name. But it was not my own.

Still the man's curiosity was not satisfied. He asked again, 'But why come to this place?'

'I said, 'For a change of air.'

This astonished him. 'Sir, I have been taking the air here for almost six years now, along with fifteen grains of quinine daily, and I am yet to see any good result.'

'Still, you must admit that after Ranchi this place is quite a change.'

'Indeed it is, that it most certainly is,' he said. 'Where will you put up here?'

Pointing to the ruined building above the ghat I said, 'There.'

I think the man suspected I was in search of buried treasure in the deserted mansion. But he kept his suspicions to himself and instead launched into a lengthy and loquacious tale of events which had taken place in the accursed building some fifteen years before.

I learnt that the man was the schoolmaster of the place. As he talked, I noticed an unnatural brightness in his large eyes which stared from their sockets in his wasted face beneath his enormous bald pate. He made me think of the Ancient Mariner of the English poet Coleridge.

The boatmen finished their prayers and began to concentrate on the cooking. The last gleams of light faded from the sky and the desolate mansion at the top of the ghat stood dark and motionless like a ghost of its earlier self.

The schoolmaster started to tell his story.

'About ten years prior to my arrival here, Phani Bhushan Shaha occupied this house. He had inherited the entire property and businesses of his uncle Durga Mohan Shaha, who was without a son.

'But, unlike Durga Mohan, Phani Bhushan was a man of the modern age. He had been educated. He spoke excellent English.

He even entered the business offices of English sahibs without removing his shoes. And he grew a beard in the modern manner. Thus there could be no hope of his advancing his career in the world of the sahibs. For anyone could see that Phani Bhushan was what is known as a New Bengali.

'And he had another handicap, this one domestic. His wife was a beauty. So, what with a college education and a beautiful wife, our old traditions stood little chance. In fact, if he was taken ill, Phani Bhushan used to call not for the village doctor but for the assistant surgeon, a sahib. The food, clothes and ornaments in his house all followed the same line of thinking.

'Sir, you are undoubtedly married, so I need hardly tell you that the average wife likes sour mangoes, hot chillies and a strict husband. The husband who is unfortunate enough to be deprived of his wife's love, will not necessarily be an ugly or poor man, but he will certainly be too considerate.

'You may ask why this should be. Well, the subject is one to which I have given much thought. When a person's propensity for something cannot be exercised, the person is not content. To sharpen its horns, the deer looks for the bole of a hardwood tree; the soft stem of a plantain gives it no satisfaction. Ever since the two sexes came into existence, women have been sharpening their skills of man-taming in every possible way. Thus the husband who tames himself of his own free will, leaves the wife unemployed: all those weapons she has inherited from generations of grandmothers – those centuries-old sobs, tantrums and snaring glances, as ancient as the gods – are rendered entirely futile.

'Therefore, in cases where the wife needs to express her love by enchanting her husband but the husband is too gentle to give her the opportunity, there is trouble in store for both of them, particularly from the wife.

'You see, under the spell of modern civilization men have forsaken their natural-born God-given barbarity, and the conjugal ties have become loosened. The luckless Phani Bhushan had emerged from the machine of modern civilization an absolutely faultless man – with the result that he was successful neither in business nor in his domestic life.

'Mani Malika, his wife, received caresses without her having to make any effort, Dacca muslin saris without having to shed any tears, and bangles without being able to pride herself on an emotional victory. Hence her woman's nature, and with it her capacity for love, atrophied. She only received, and never gave; while her innocent and foolish husband imagined that by giving, he would receive. His approach was a thoroughly misguided one.

'The upshot was, that Phani Bhushan came to be regarded by his wife as a mere machine for producing saris and bangles; a machine so well made that its wheels never needed a drop of oil.

'Phani Bhushan's birthplace was at Phulbere, the house here was his office. For reasons of business he spent most of his time here. His mother was no longer alive at the Phulbere house, though he had plenty of aunts and other relatives there. But Phani Bhushan had not married a pretty wife for their benefit, so he took Mani Malika away from them and kept her here in this house, alone. There is a key difference between a wife and other possessions, however: by keeping her away from everyone, all to oneself, one may lose her completely.

'Mani Malika did not talk much, nor did she have much to do with her neighbours, nor was it her custom to feed Brahmins in obedience to some vow, or give alms to local Vaishnava nuns. In her hands nothing was ever wasted, everything was most carefully saved, with the sole exception of the affection of her husband. And the really remarkable thing was that there was not the slightest hint of waste in her amazing beauty. People used to say that at the age of twenty-four Mani Malika looked as tender as she had at fourteen. Perhaps it is those with icy hearts, into which the pangs of love cannot penetrate, who stay freshest longest;

they are misers, who freeze their emotional as well as their physical assets.

'Like a creeper suffocating a plant, the Almighty had prevented Mani Malika from flowering, deprived her of offspring. In other words, God had kept from her a gift which she would have come to know as more valuable than the jewels in her iron safe; a gift which like the mild sunshine of an early spring morning would have thawed her heart and released its affection into the world like a fountain.

'But as far as her household duties were concerned, Mani Malika was a hard worker. She never kept more servants than was absolutely necessary, for she could not bear to pay anyone to do work she could do herself. With no worries about anyone and none of the distractions of love, she simply worked and saved, without anger or anguish; and with her constant good health, mental tranquillity and growing wealth, she appeared to reign over the house very firmly.

'For the majority of husbands this arrangement is enough – I should really say more than enough. It is akin to having lumbago – or rather, to not having lumbago; for as long as you have no pain in your waist, you do not think about your waist any more than you think about your arms and legs. So, in marital matters, there is no lumbago until a wife chooses to urge her love upon her husband at every moment of the day and night. Excessive devotion may be something glorious for a wife, we are told, but it is uncomfortable for a husband – at least that is my decided opinion.

'Surely, sir, it is not up to a man to put his wife's love in a jeweller's balance day in and day out. She should do her work, I should do mine – that is the long and short of it. Exactly how much has been left unsaid, the precise degree of feeling left unspoken and the precise position of every atom in a relationship, the Almighty did not give men the power to detect, because there was no need. It is only women who weigh up the tiniest discrepancies in a man's affections. They analyse mere words and extract the real meaning from them with sure and refined skill. For it is a man's love that gives a woman her strength, her capital in the business of life. If she can feel the way the wind is blowing and pick her moment to launch her boat, she will sail successfully. That is why God has installed love's compass in the hearts of women and not in those of men.

'Nowadays, though, men have acquired what God did not choose to give them. Poets are overriding the gods and putting this precious instrument, this compass, promiscuously into the hands of men. The Almighty is not to be blamed for creating men and women separate, but the fact is that civilization is obliterating the distinction: now women are becoming manly and men are becoming effeminate, and the home is perforce bidding farewell to peace and stability. Now, before they marry, both bride and bridegroom feel thoroughly disconcerted by the thought that they may be wedding their own sex.

'But sir, I think you are wearying of my discussion! You see, I am forced by circumstances to live alone, banished from the company of my wife, and here many profound social issues come to my mind which I cannot discuss with my pupils. As we continue talking, I shall present my ideas for your consideration.

'At any rate, although Mani Malika's cooking did not lack salt and her *pan* did not lack lime, her husband's heart was troubled by some vague anxiety. The wife had no particular fault, yet the husband was not happy. And so he went on pouring diamond and pearl jewellery into the cavity of her heart, thereby filling her iron safe but leaving her heart as empty as ever. Old Durga Mohan Shaha had known nothing of love's finer delights, had never yearned for them or given generously to his wife, yet he had received ample return from her. To be a success in business, one must not be a modern type of man, and to succeed as a husband one must be manly – of this you should have no doubt.'

As the schoolmaster said these words, there was a raucous howl from some jackals in a nearby thicket. The torrent of his talk stopped for a moment. It was as if some frivolous yokels had been listening all along to the schoolmaster's musings on conjugal morality and the over-civilized meekness of Phani Bhushan, and had suddenly burst into laughter. When the outburst had died down, the silence over both land and water lay deeper still: in the darkness the schoolmaster's eyes seemed to glow even brighter as he resumed telling his story.

'All of a sudden, Phani Bhushan struck danger in his tangled and extensive business affairs. What exactly had transpired, a layman such as I can neither grasp nor explain. But its effect was that without any warning Phani Bhushan found it difficult to obtain credit. He knew that if he could but raise a lakh and a half of rupees and flash them in front of the market, the danger would pass and his business would sail on smoothly.

'But the money was hard to come by. Were he to try to borrow it where he was well known, he feared that he would cause his business further harm; and so his thoughts turned to getting loans in unfamiliar places. But he knew that strangers would require security.

'Now of course jewellery is the best security because it avoids complex documents having to be signed, and makes the process of taking a loan quick and simple. So Phani Bhushan went at once to his wife. However, whereas most husbands can face their wives easily enough, Phani Bhushan could not. Unluckily for him, his love for her was of the variety celebrated by poets; it felt bound to tread circumspectly and could not speak plainly; like the attraction of the sun and the earth, it was strong yet kept its distance.

'But even heroes of romances sometimes get themselves into corners which compel them to mention to their beloveds such things as bills of exchange and promissory notes. Nevertheless, the tune sounds wrong, the tongue fumbles, and a note of unease disrupts what was formerly calm and orderly. The unfortunate

Phani Bhushan was quite incapable of saying bluntly to his wife, "Dear, I'm in need of money, bring out your jewels."

'He did ask her for them, but only with extreme delicacy. When Mani Malika responded by hardening her face and saying nothing, he felt the blow cruelly; but he did not hurt her back. For there was not a trace of masculine barbarity in him. Where he should have snatched by force, instead he suppressed his urge. Where love is the sole arbiter, one must not give way to force, even in times of disaster − that was what he believed. Had someone tackled him on the subject, most likely Phani Bhushan would have come out with some argument such as the following: "Just because the market won't give me credit for unfair reasons does not give me the right to rob it: if my wife will not trust me with her jewels of her own free will, I cannot grab them. Whether it be a business matter or an affair of the heart, force belongs only to the battlefield." But sir, was it to debate such fine-spun ideals that God endowed men with so much courage and strength? Have they the leisure to indulge the subtle nuances of such tender emotions, and does it befit them to do so?

'Whatever may be the case, Phani Bhushan, priding himself on being unable to touch his wife's jewels, left for Calcutta, in order to find other means of raising money.

'Now although, as a rule, a wife knows her husband better than a husband knows his wife, certain husbands have natures so refined they are not entirely perceptible even under a wife's microscope. Our Phani Bhushan was one such husband. Extremely modern men like him lie beyond the range of old-fashioned wifely wisdom. They belong to a new race of men, as mysterious as women. Ordinary men divide into three rough categories − barbarians, fools and blunt fellows − but these modern men fit none of the categories.

'And so Mani Malika felt a need for an adviser. Madhu Shudan was some kind of relative of hers, an assistant steward on Phani Bhushan's estate. His position had more to do with family ties than with hard work, which was not in his character: and he managed to save both his salary and even a little more.

'Mani Malika explained everything and finished up with, "Now what do you advise?"

'Madhu Shudan shook his head wisely; he did not like the look of things at all. Such wise characters never do. He said, "Babu will never be able to raise the money, in the end he will take your jewellery."

'Mani Malika, on the basis of her experience of men, thought this not only probable but very likely. Her anxiety became intense. She had no children, and though she had a husband, she did not feel his presence in her heart. And so the idea that her precious wealth, which she had been tending all these years almost like a growing child, which sparkled softly upon her breast, around her throat and on her hair – the very thought that all this might be flung into the bottomless pit of commerce in an instant, made her blood run cold. She cried out, "What is to be done?"

'"You must take the jewels to your father's house," the sage Madhu Shudan suggested. A plan had formed in his mind, in which a portion of the jewels, perhaps even the major portion, would fall to his lot. Mani Malika immediately consented.

'On a rainy night in late Asharh, the monsoon month, at this very ghat, a boat came to be moored. In the dense darkness before dawn, as frogs tirelessly croaked, shrouded from head to foot in a thick shawl, Mani Malika stepped aboard. The waiting Madhu Shudan rubbed his eyes and said, "Give me the jewel box." Mani replied, "Not now, later. Untie the boat."

'The boat became free and was pulled into the swift current.

'Mani Malika had spent the entire night draping her whole body, from top to toe, with jewels. If kept in the box, they might be snatched from her: that was her dread. But kept about her body she knew they could not be taken – without her first being murdered.

'Not having got near the box Madhu Shudan could not guess that beneath the thick shawl Mani Malika was guarding with her life that which meant more to her than life. For she may not have understood her husband Phani Bhushan, but Madhu Shudan she most definitely understood.

'He had sent a letter to the chief steward explaining that he was taking the mistress to her paternal home. The chief steward had been in Phani Bhushan's service since the days of his father and he was so indignant that he wrote a letter to his master. Though the quality of its grammar left something to be desired, it left the recipient in absolutely no doubt that to indulge a wife in this way did not befit a man.

'For his part, Phani Bhushan understood Mani Malika's motive only too well. And he felt terribly hurt: how could she still suspect him, despite his willingness to forgo her jewels and make desperate efforts to raise money by other means? He thought, even now she does not know me.

'Where he should have been enraged, he was only mortified. For is a man not God's rod of justice, on whom is bestowed the power to express divine wrath? – fie upon him if he fails to flash in anger at injustice done to anyone, including himself! In earlier times, the slightest provocation would make a man burst out in anger like a forest fire and a woman burst into tears like a monsoon rain cloud. But times seem to have changed.

'And so Phani Bhushan noted his wife's offence and yet told himself, "If that is your decision, so be it. I will carry on and do my duty." He should have been born five or six centuries from now, when psychic forces will prevail, but instead he had been deposited in the nineteenth century and married to a woman of atavistic mind. Phani Bhushan chose to write his wife not a single word on the subject of her departure, and resolved never to mention it to her. What a severe vow to take!

'About ten days later, after raising the necessary loan without too much trouble, Phani Bhushan reappeared at his house. By now, he imagined, Mani Malika would have dealt with her jewels and come home. Wondering if she would show any sign of repentance for her unnecessary and shameful act when she saw his success, he approached the door of the inner apartments.

'It was shut. He had the lock broken, entered the room and saw that it was empty. He opened the door of the iron safe and saw no trace of the jewels. His heart hammered. The world seemed without purpose, both love and money-making totally without meaning. For what is the point of our killing ourselves in trying to cage the world when the bird always escapes, never settles? Why do we persist in decorating each bar of the cage with rubies like heart's blood and pearls like teardrops? A lifetime's accumulation of possessions seemed suddenly pointless to Phani Bhushan, and he mentally gave the lot a tremendous kick.

'To begin with, his wife's absence did not trouble him much. He thought – when she's ready, she will return. But then his old steward came and said, "To do nothing is not right, you must seek news of the mistress." And so someone was despatched to the house of Mani Malika's people. Word came that neither Mani nor Madhu had been seen there.

'Then a search began in every direction. People made enquiries along both riverbanks. The police were given a description of Madhu, but they could find out nothing: neither which boat they had taken, nor who the boatman was, nor which route they had followed.

'One evening, with all hope now gone, Phani Bhushan entered his deserted bedroom. It was the time of Janmashtami, the festival of Lord Krishna's birth, and from the morning onwards rain had fallen incessantly. The festival was in full swing on some waste ground in the village; beneath a temporary thatched awning, everyone was absorbed in a theatre-cum-opera performance. The sound of singing was half-audible to Phani Bhushan through the drumming of the torrential downpour. He sat alone beside a window with a loose hinge – but his mind was not conscious of the moist breeze, the spray of the rain and the distant cries of the performers. Inside, on one wall of the room, hung garishly painted prints of the goddesses Lakshmi and Saraswati, while on a clothes rack a couple of towels and two saris, one striped and the other plain with a striped border, were laid out ready for use. In a corner of the room on a teapoy stood a brass tray with a few shrivelled betel leaves folded to make *pan* by Mani Malika's own hand. Inside a glass-fronted almirah her china dolls from child-hood days, her scent bottles and decanters of coloured glass, a pack of luxury cards, some large polished cowrie shells and even some empty soap boxes lay neatly arranged; and there, in the wall, in its appointed niche, stood her small kerosene lamp with its fancy round globe which she used to light every evening – its wick now dry and languishing. That insignificant lamp had been a silent witness of Mani Malika's last hours in this bedroom, thought Phani Bhushan. When someone goes away, abandoning everything, how her loving mark remains on her lifeless pos-sessions! Come Mani, come and light your flame once again, fill your room with light, stand before your mirror and put on one of those saris lying there so carefully folded by you – all your things are here, awaiting you. No one will demand anything from you, only come and infuse life into these scattered and orphaned objects with your undying youth and unfaded beauty; their inarticulate cries have made your room a funereal place.

'Evening became night, the heavy rain stopped, and there was a break in the singing at the all-night performance. Phani Bhushan sat on, quite still. The darkness beyond the window became so all enveloping and closely woven that he felt as if he were standing before the towering portals of Death itself – as if he had only to cry out and a vision of all the things that seemed lost for ever would be disclosed to him. On Death's jet-black expanse, that unyielding touchstone, did he see a very faint streak of gold?

'With this thought there came a sort of rapping sound, mixed with the jingle of jewellery. The sound seemed to advance up the steps of the ghat from the river. Water and darkness were as one. Phani Bhushan's skin tingled with excitement, and his eyes probed each square of darkness so eagerly they ached – but not a thing was visible. The more desperately he stared the denser seemed the darkness, and the more insubstantial the outside world. It was if nature, seeing a stranger attempting to peer into the abode of death at dead of night, had swiftly pulled a curtain over the entrance.

'The sound reached the top of the ghat. It began to advance towards the house. When it reached the door, it paused. The main door had been locked by the doorkeeper when he went off to see the opera. From outside it there now came a clatter of knocks and jingles as of ornaments frantically striking wood. Phani Bhushan could not restrain himself. Hastening through the lightless rooms and feeling his way down the darkened staircase, he arrived at the main door. It had been padlocked from the outside. He seized the handles with both hands and gave the door a violent shake: so great was the racket that it woke him. He realized he had sleep-walked. His whole body was drenched in sweat, his hands and feet were cold as ice and his heart was trembling like a lamp on the point of snuffing out. Now he knew that there was no sound outside, except the falling of rain, which had started again, mingled with the melodies of the village performers; he could hear children singing the last act before the dawn.

'But although it was all a dream, Phani Bhushan felt that he had come extremely close to something that vitally concerned him, the realization of his impossible yearning, of which he had been cheated, he felt, by the merest of obstacles. The pattering of the rain seemed to speak to him like some detached and far-off strain of raga Bhairavi: "Your awakening is but a dream, this world is but illusion."

The following day, the festival continued and the doorkeeper again took the night off. Phani Bhushan gave instructions that the door be left unlocked all night. The doorkeeper protested, "Sir, at festival time there are all sorts of people from all over the place about – it isn't safe to leave the door open." Phani Bhushan would have none of it. So the doorkeeper said, "I shall stay and keep watch all night." Phani Bhushan replied, "There's no need, go and listen to the show." This puzzled the doorkeeper, but he did as he was told.

'That evening, after extinguishing the lamp, Phani Bhushan took his place beside the bedroom window. The clouds covering the sky were swollen with rain and the outside world lay motionless as if profoundly expectant. Even the unceasing croak of the frogs and the songs and cries of the village performers could not disturb such stillness, but rather served to deepen it by their weird incongruity.

'It became late, the frogs and crickets and boys of the opera party finally fell quiet, and an even deeper darkness settled over everything. The hour was clearly nigh.

'As on the previous night, from the direction of the ghat the rapping and jingling sound was heard. But tonight Phani Bhushan did not look towards it. He had a fear that his very eagerness and anxiety would render his desires and actions fruitless, would somehow bewilder his powers of sight and hearing. With a supreme effort he controlled his restlessness and sat stock still, like a statue.

'The sound, resonant, ascended gradually from the ghat and entered the house through the open door. Then it could be heard winding its way up the spiral staircase. Phani Bhushan could barely keep his vow; his heart was palpitating like a small boat in a typhoon, his breathing was becoming laboured. When the sound reached the head of the stairs, it moved slowly along the veranda, and stopped outside with a jangling clank. It now lay just beyond the bedroom threshold.

'Phani Bhushan could stay seated no longer. Driven by

overmastering passion, he shot up like a lightning flash and yelled, "Mani!" The shriek awoke him and he heard the window panes rattle with its force. From outside once more he heard the croaking of frogs and the fatigued voices of boys singing in the village.

'Phani Bhushan struck his forehead in despair at his impatience.

'On the next morning, the festival broke up; and the market stalls and opera troupe moved on. Phani Bhushan gave orders that on the coming night no one but he would stay in the mansion. His servants concluded that their master intended to practise mystical Tantric rites. Throughout the day Phani Bhushan took no food.

'That evening, he assumed his usual seat in the totally deserted house. Tonight there were gaps in the clouds and through the clear rain-rinsed air, the stars shone with extraordinary brilliance. The moon was yet to rise. On the bursting river, now that the festival was finished, not a boat was to be seen; the villagers of the area were all plunged in sleep, after two days and nights of entertainment.

'Phani Bhushan, lying back in his chair and looking at the heavens, thought of the time when he was nineteen years old and studying in Calcutta: how at night he would lie out on the grass beside the tank in College Square with his head on his hands gazing at the eternal stars, and let his mind wander. He would see the glowing young face of the fourteen-year-old Mani in her lonely room at her in-laws' riverside house in the village, and feel a delicious sensation. In those days the flickering of the stars harmonized with the stirring of his young heart, as in the famous line from a Sanskrit drama about the "rhythmic movement of raga Bashanta", the raga of Spring! While today these same stars seemed to have inscribed in fiery letters across the sky another famous line, but from an ancient philosophical treatise: "How strange is this world!"

'As he gazed upwards, the stars seemed to fade away. A

darkness fell from the sky and rose from the earth like two black lashes closing over a weary eye. Phani Bhushan's mind was at peace. He felt an inward assurance that tonight he would attain his cherished goal; and that Death would finally vouchsafe its mystery to its devotee.

'As before, the sound made its way from the river up the steps of the ghat. Phani Bhushan, eyes now closed, sat in deep meditation. The sound entered the empty hallway, wound its way up the deserted staircase, passed along the veranda of the inner apartments, and paused at the bedroom door for a long time.

'Phani Bhushan's heart was racing and his whole body trembling, but this time he did not open his eyes. The sound crossed the threshold and entered the shadowy room. At each object in it – the clothes rack with its folded saris, the wall niche with its kerosene lamp, the teapoy with its tray of desiccated betel, the almirah with its various knick-knacks – the sound paused and hovered, until, at last, it came close to Phani Bhushan himself.

'Then he opened his eyes and saw in the faint light of the now-risen moon, standing in front of his chair, a skeleton. From top to bottom its bones glistened with gold and diamond ornaments: there were rings on its eight bony fingers and jewelled wheels on the backs of its bony hands, bangles on its bony wrists and bracelets on its bony arms, necklaces around its throat and a tiara on its skull. The ornaments hung loosely, but each was firmly attached. Most dreadful of all was the face: from its sockets two living eyes shone out, moist, with long thick lashes and black pupils and a fixed, unblinking stare. Eighteen years ago, Phani Bhushan had first seen those eyes in a brightly lit wedding hall to the accompaniment of raga Shahana, and they had been gorgeous and rapt. Seeing them now, at dead of night in the depths of the monsoon, lit by a dying moon, he felt his blood freeze. He made a desperate effort to close his eyes, but he could not; they remained wide open, as steady as the eyes of a corpse.

'Then the skeleton turned its gaze directly upon Phani

Bhushan's stupefied face and, noiselessly lifting its right hand, beckoned to him with its fingers. Four diamond rings flashed in the moonlight.

'Phani Bhushan stood up as if spellbound. The skeleton began to move towards the door, its joints and jewels uttering their harsh sound. Phani Bhushan followed like a marionette. They crossed the veranda, and in pitch darkness they wound their way down the spiral stairs, clanking and jingling at every step. Passing through the lower veranda, they entered the empty unlit hall and at last they reached the pebbled garden path outside the main door. Here, as they moved, the stones crunched beneath the bony feet; the moonlight struggled fitfully to reach the shadowy path through the overhanging thickets; and swarms of fireflies whirled in the humid scent of the monsoon night. Together they arrived at the top of the ghat.

'Here, at these very steps up which the sound had come, the jewelled skeleton commenced to descend – step by rattling step, its spine stiffly erect, its limbs rigidly inflexible. On the surface of the river's powerful current, a streak of moonlight could just be discerned.

'Phani Bhushan, obediently following, reached the water and dipped his foot. The instant he made contact, his drowsiness vanished. His guide too disappeared, and there remained only the silent trees brooding on the far bank of the river and the thin moon looking down in calm astonishment. A shudder convulsed Phani Bhushan's body and he fell headlong into the current. Though he knew how to swim, his limbs were not under his control: for a mere instant he stepped across the borderland from the world of dream into the world of wakefulness – and then he was plunged into abysmal sleep.'

★

Having finished his account, the schoolmaster at last fell silent. I was abruptly aware that the whole world had fallen still and silent too. For a long time I sat without saying a word, and in the darkness the schoolmaster was unable to see the expression on my face.

Then he said, 'You don't believe the story.'

I asked him, 'Do you believe it?'

He said, 'No, and I have several reasons for not believing. In the first place, Dame Nature does not write stories, her hands are already full with—'

'And secondly,' I interrupted, 'my name is Phani Bhushan Shaha.'

The schoolmaster was not in the least embarrassed: 'I guessed as much. And your wife's real name – what was it?'

I told him, 'Nritya Kali.'†

---

† 'Dancing Kali', an incarnation of goddess Kali who frequents the burning ghats and dances on the ashes of the dead. By mistake she dances on her sleeping husband, Lord Shiva. Nritya Kali is a highly improbable name for a Bengali woman of a respectable family.

# Purification

Many of the sins recorded in bold letters by old Chitragupta, who keeps the register at heaven's gate, are committed without the sinners themselves being aware of having sinned. But there are other sins which only we ourselves know about. The one I am about to describe is of this latter variety. By confessing it in advance, before I have to explain myself to Chitragupta, I hope to lessen my offence.

It took place yesterday, a Saturday afternoon. There was a Jain festival going on in our neighbourhood, and I was out for a drive with my wife Kalika. We had an invitation to tea from our friend, Nayan Mohan.

Kalika's name means literally 'a bud', and was chosen by my father-in-law; I am not responsible. It does not describe my wife's personality, which is actually a bold bloom, as one might say. So vigorously did she picket the selling of British cloth in Burrabazar not long ago, that her devotees decided to rename her Dhruba Brata, 'she of unwavering vows'. My own name is Garindra, which means 'lord of the mountains'. Not that my wife's followers take much notice of it; they know me simply as Her husband. I do have a small amount of significance, though, which I inherited by good fortune from my wealthy ancestors; and this the followers deign to notice when donation time comes round.

Marital harmony is best when a husband and a wife differ in character, as parched earth differs from a shower of rain. I am by nature easygoing, inclined to take life as it comes. My wife, by contrast, is very determined, and likes to get a grip on life. The very dissimilarity between us helps to preserve the peace of our household.

But there is one area of disagreement that continues to cause friction. In the opinion of Kalika, I am unpatriotic. Her belief in this opinion is so unshakeable that however many proofs of my patriotism I may give, she refuses to acknowledge it, because it does not wear the particular badges vetted by her party.

From childhood I have been a book lover; I buy books the moment they are published. And even my enemies would admit that I also read them. As for my friends, they know how endlessly I debate them; in fact my passion for discussion has driven all my friends away, bar one, Bon Bihari, who makes my Sundays lively. His name means 'forest roaming', but I have renamed him Kon Bihari – 'room roaming'. Some nights we are still talking on my roof terrace at two in the morning.

But the truth is, the present is not an auspicious time for book addicts. On the one hand there are the police, who regard the mere existence of a copy of the *Bhagavad Gita* in one's house as proof of sedition. On the other there are the patriots, to whom the cut pages of any foreign-published book signify treason in its owner. They regard me as a complete turncoat – no better than a black-jacketed, white-faced Little Englander. These days, even Goddess Saraswati's love of learning cannot protect her from patriotic suspicion of her white complexion. People are seriously suggesting that the divine water in her lake – which contains white lotus blossoms floating in it – far from soothing the Motherland's burning brow, is aggravating her condition.

Despite the good example set by my better half, as well as her ceaseless nagging, I have not taken to wearing home-spun khaddar. It is not that I have anything against khaddar, quality-wise or otherwise, or that I am fastidious about what I wear. Rather the reverse, in fact: I may be guilty of many other lapses from true patriotic deportment, but a refined sense of dress is not one of them. My clothes are as a rule shabby and baggy, my general appearance somewhat dishevelled. In the days before Kalika's modern transformation, I used to wear broad-toed shoes made by Chinese cobblers, which I would forget to have regularly polished; and I preferred loose *panjabis* to proper shirts, not minding in the least if they lacked a button or two. Indeed at one point these habits threatened to destroy our marriage.

Kalika used to tell me, 'Look, I feel ashamed to be seen with you in public.'

I replied, 'There's no need to be seen following me faithfully. Leave me behind when you go out.'

Though times have changed, my luck is unchanged. Kalika still says she is ashamed to go out with me. I did not wear the required uniform then, and I am not willing to wear her present allies' uniform today. Thus I am impartial in the shame I cause. And the fault lies in my whole personality. Whatever is the latest faction, I feel embarrassed to wear its sectarian colours; I cannot help the feeling. Whereas Kalika is incapable of accepting any dissenting opinion as final. Like a mountain stream constantly but vainly grinding away at a big rock, she cannot stop herself from confronting an opposing point of view; any contact with a position contrary to her own position seems to provoke an irresistible itch to respond.

Yesterday, while we were getting ready to go out to tea, Kalika launched an all-out assault on my non-khaddar outfit in a tone that was anything but sweet. My inveterate pride in logic would not permit me to listen submissively – an innate tendency in humans that leads only to futile debate. I hit back quite as hard as her with a caustic comment: 'Women like to pull a black-bordered sari around them, veil their god-given power of sight, and hitch themselves to convention. They feel safer when they obey than when they think. In every important matter, if they can avoid having to think and choose for themselves and instead confine themselves to the zenana of conformity, they are content. In our custom-riddled country the wearing of khaddar has become like the red *tilak* mark we daub on our foreheads and the garland we drape round our necks – a badge of virtue of the kind women seem to love.'

Kalika was almost fanatical in her fury. Her voice was so loud and agitated that the maidservant next door must have thought the mistress was berating the master about the inadequacy of some gold ornament he had given her. 'The sanctity of khaddar', said she, 'is such that when everyone will take to wearing it, and treat it as they now treat a bath in the holy Ganges, the country will be liberated. When reason joins force with habit, custom is formed. Thought, when it is sufficiently concentrated, is purifying. Man, with his eyes focused, achieves, but with his eyes wide-open, vacillates.'

Clearly these were epigrams from the lips of Professor Nayan Mohan, with their quotation marks worn away. Kalika had managed to make them her own quite easily.

'The silent man makes no enemies' – whoever coined that phrase was certainly not married. When I failed to reply, Kalika became incoherent with rage. 'Your mouth rejects caste distinctions,' she shouted, 'but the rest of you does nothing practical to remedy them. While we, by wearing the uniform of khaddar, have erased all distinctions, stripped them away to reveal the common core.'

I was about to say, 'My mouth does indeed reject caste distinctions, it has done so ever since it first relished chicken curry prepared by a Muslim cook. So my conversion was not verbal, like some people's, but oral – and it was most definitely an inner conversion. You see, to dress up old differences in new clothes is quite superficial; it may conceal the differences, but it cannot remove them.' But, having articulated this argument to myself, I lacked the courage to say it aloud. I am basically a timid fellow, who prefers to keep quiet. For I know from past experience that the arguments we have at home between ourselves Kalika carries like dirty washing to her friends, where they are ruthlessly beaten and mangled. From her visits to Professor Nayan Mohan, Kalika brings back counter-arguments which she hurls at me and follows with a burning, speechless look that says, 'Answer that, if you can.'

I was not at all keen to go to Nayan Mohan for tea that day. I knew what was in store for me in all probability, if not with absolute certainty: a nit-picking argument about the comparative roles in Hindu culture of tradition and originality, the irrational and the rational, and the reasons why our country is superior to all other countries – during which hot air would mingle with the steam rising from the teacups to create a thoroughly oppressive atmosphere. And what was more, some new books had just reached me from the bookseller and were lying beside my pillow waiting expectantly with their gold-blocked covers and uncut pages. I had taken a mere peep inside their still-veiled brown-paper packets; now, as we were about to depart, I felt an intense urge to pay court to them all. But I had no choice: if I did not go, I knew, from certain words, spoken and unspoken, that such a typhoon would blow that my health would be put seriously at risk.

Our motor car had travelled only a short way from the house, to the place just beyond the standpipe with the pantile huts (in one of which a pot-bellied, up-country confectioner always sits cross-legged, frying various unwholesome-looking savouries) – when we ran into a real hullaballoo. I could make out that some people from the neighbouring Marwari community were on their way to their temple in a procession, carrying expensive offerings, and that the procession had come to a halt. There were shouts and the sound of a thrashing. I supposed that some pickpocket was being beaten.

When, after repeated hooting of the car horn, we reached the centre of the hubbub we saw our old municipal sweeper being harshly attacked. Apparently, not long before, he had taken his bath in the standpipe, put on a clean wrap, and set off along the road with a bucket of clean water in his right hand and his broom under his arm. Dressed in a check-patterned vest, with his wet hair carefully combed and his fine-looking eight-or-nine-year-old grandson holding his left hand, he was looking handsome, a real picture. Then, by accident, he had brushed against someone or something in the crowd – hence this merciless thrashing. Now his grandson was weeping and imploring everyone, 'Don't hit him!' The old man, with folded hands, was crying out, 'I didn't see, I didn't think, please forgive me.' And the more he did so, the more the local devotees of non-violence hit him. The old man's frightened eyes were streaming with tears, and his beard was streaked with blood.

It was a quite intolerable sight. To argue with the mob was beneath me. I resolved that I must pick up the man in my car and demonstrate that I could not support piety of this kind.

Kalika noticed my agitation and immediately grasped what was in my mind. She gripped my arm and said urgently, 'What are you thinking of! He's a sweeper.'

I said, 'What if he is a sweeper, why should he be treated so unjustly?'

Kalika said, 'It's his fault. Why did he have to walk in the middle of the road like that? Would it have hurt his dignity to stay at the edge?'

'I don't know about all that, but I know I'm going to take him in my car.'

'In that case I'm getting out. I will not travel in the same car as a sweeper. A potter or weaver, perhaps, but not a sweeper!'

'Can't you see,' I argued, 'that he's just had a bath. He's wearing clean clothes. He's much cleaner than most of that lot.'

'Maybe, but he is a sweeper.'

Kalika commanded the driver, 'Ganga Din, get going!'

*

I was defeated. I am a coward. Over tea, Nayan Mohan advanced some profound sociological arguments against my position, involving the inevitable, indeed natural, inequality imposed upon men by their profession and which is inherent in the scheme of things. But I ignored him, and uttered not one word.

# The Parrot's Training

Once upon a time there was a bird. It was ignorant. It sang all right, but it never recited scriptures. It hopped, it flew, but it lacked manners.

Said the Raja to himself, 'Ignorance is costly in the long run. For fools consume as much food as their betters, and yet give nothing in return.'

*

He called his nephews into his presence and told them that the bird must have a sound schooling.

The pundits were summoned, and after deep deliberation went to the root of the matter. They decided that the ignorance of birds was due to their unsuitable habit of living in nests. Therefore, according to the pundits, the first thing necessary for the education of this bird was a proper cage.

The pundits had their rewards and went home happy.

*

A golden cage was built with gorgeous decorations. Crowds came to see it from all parts of the world. 'Culture, captured and caged!' exclaimed some, in a rapture of ecstasy, and burst into tears. Others remarked, 'Even if culture be missed, the cage will remain, to the end, a substantial fact. How fortunate is this bird!'

The goldsmith filled his bag with money and lost no time in sailing homewards.

Then a pundit sat down to educate the bird. With due deliberation he took a pinch of snuff, as he said, 'Textbooks can never be too many for our purpose!'

The nephews brought together an enormous crowd of scribes. They copied from books, and copied from copies, till manuscripts were piled to an unreachable height. Men murmured in amazement, 'Oh, the tower of learning, egregiously high! The end of it lost in the clouds!'

The scribes, with light hearts, hurried home, their pockets heavily laden.

The nephews were furiously busy keeping the cage in proper trim. As their constant scrubbing and polishing went on, the people said with satisfaction, 'This is real progress!'

Men were employed in large numbers, and supervisors were still more numerous. These, with all their cousins of differing degrees of distance, built a palace for themselves and lived there happily ever after.

*

But whatever may be its other deficiencies, the world is never short of fault-finders. They went about saying that every creature remotely connected with the cage was flourishing beyond words, except one – the bird.

When this remark reached the Raja's ears, he summoned his nephews and enquired, 'My dear nephews, what is this that we hear?'

The nephews said in answer, 'Sire, let the testimony of the goldsmiths and the pundits, the scribes and the supervisors, be taken, if the truth is to be known. Food is scarce with the fault-finders, and that is why their tongues have gained in sharpness.'

The explanation was so luminously satisfactory that the Raja decorated each one of his nephews with his own rare jewels.

*

At length the Raja, being desirous of seeing with his own eyes how his Education Department was busying itself with the bird, made his appearance at the Great Hall of Learning.

From the gate arose the sound of conch-shells and gongs, horns, bugles and trumpets, cymbals, drums and kettle-drums, tomtoms, tambourines, flutes, fifes, barrel-organs and bagpipes. The pundits began chanting mantras at the tops of their voices, while the goldsmiths, scribes, supervisors, and all their numberless cousins of differing degrees of distance, loudly raised a round of cheers.

The nephews smiled and said, 'Sire, what do you think of it all?'

The Raja said, 'Tremendous, terrific!'

'Sire, education that is based on a sound principle is also most enriching.'

Mightily pleased, the Raja was about to remount his elephant, when a fault-finder, from behind some bush, cried out, 'Maharaja, have you seen the bird?'

'Indeed, I have not!' exclaimed the Raja. 'I completely forgot about the bird.'

Turning back, he questioned the pundits about the method they followed in instructing the bird. It was demonstrated. The Raja was immensely impressed. The method was so stupendous that the bird looked absurdly unimportant in comparison. The Raja was satisfied that there was no flaw in the arrangements. As for any complaint from the bird itself, that was certainly not to be expected. For its throat was so choked with the leaves of books that it could neither whistle nor whisper. The entire learning process sent a thrill through anyone who saw it.

★

This time, while remounting his elephant, the Raja ordered the state ear-puller to give both ears of the fault-finder a thoroughly good pull.

Thus the bird tottered on, duly and appropriately, to the very verge of inanity. In fact, its progress was deemed extremely satisfactory. Notwithstanding, nature occasionally triumphed over nurture, and when the dawn light peeped into the bird's cage it sometimes fluttered its wings in a reprehensible manner. And, though this is hard to believe, occasionally it pecked pitifully at its bars with its feeble beak.

'What impertinence!' growled the head guard.

The blacksmith, with his forge and hammer, took his place in the Raja's Department of Education. Oh, how his blows resounded! Soon an iron chain was completed, and the bird's wings were clipped.

The Raja's brothers-in-law looked grim, and shook their heads, saying, 'These birds not only lack good sense, but also gratitude!'

With textbook in one hand and baton in the other, the pundits gave the poor bird what may fittingly be called lessons.

The head guard was honoured with a title for his vigilance, and the blacksmith for his skill in forging chains.

*

The bird died.

No one had the least notion exactly when this had occurred. The fault-finder was the first person to spread the rumour.

The Raja called his nephews and asked them, 'My dear nephews, what is this that we hear?'

The nephews said, 'Sire, the education of the bird is complete.'

'Does it hop?' the Raja enquired.

'Never!' said the nephews.

'Does it fly?'

'No.'

'Bring me the bird,' said the Raja.

The bird was brought, escorted by the head guard, sepoys on foot and sowars on horseback. The Raja poked the bird's body with his finger. Its inner stuffing of book leaves rustled.

Outside the window, a spring breeze murmured among newly budded *ashoka* leaves, and made the April morning wistful.

# NOVEL

Unlike the short story in Bengali, the novel was not the invention of Tagore; he was preceded by Bankim Chandra Chatterji, whose novels are still widely read in Bengal. But Tagore remains the only novelist in Bengali to have been read widely by non-Indians. Though he wrote thirteen novels, his reputation beyond India rests chiefly on just one, *The Home and the World*, published in Bengali in 1915–16 as a magazine serial, translated in 1919 into English and subsequently twenty other European languages, and powerfully filmed by Satyajit Ray in 1984. The original English translation is still in print.

When it first appeared, the novel was immediately admired by William Rothenstein, also by W. B. Yeats and Lady Gregory, and in Germany became one of Tagore's best-known books. 'You simply *must* read [it] – the finest novel I've read for a long time,' a friend told Albert Einstein. Hermann Hesse, reviewing it, referred to its 'purity and grandeur'. Bertolt Brecht noted in his diary: 'A wonderful book, strong and gentle.' But the Marxist critic Georg Lukács attacked Tagore for putting himself 'at the intellectual service of the British police' in his 'libellous pamphlet', 'a petit-bourgeois yarn of the shoddiest kind' containing 'a contemptible caricature of Gandhi'.

Lukács was ludicrously off-beam, since the book is set long before Gandhi's appearance on the Indian scene and was written two or three years before he became an Indian leader – but the vehemence of his criticism shows how this novel had an impact unusual among Tagore's fictional works. Bengalis, too, criticized Tagore severely for his unflattering portrayal of a Bengali revolutionary leader, Sandip, at the time of the 1905 Swadeshi

Movement, who manipulates Hindu symbols, deliberately stirs up anti-Muslim feeling and seduces the wife, Bimala, of his college friend, Nikhil. She, a traditional wife in purdah at the beginning of the novel, is so roused by Sandip's oratory that she emerges from purdah, supports the Cause emotionally and financially despite her husband's scepticism, and is eventually betrayed by Sandip and left totally humiliated.

The novel is about a triangle — and it is constructed in the form of three recurring, interwoven 'diaries', which describe the drama from the point of view of Bimala, Sandip and Nikhil — but what makes it unique is that Nikhil encourages Bimala's relationship with Sandip. For Nikhil, an idealistic zamindar, is really Rabindranath himself; from Nikhil's mouth come all those ideas of individual freedom and female emancipation that so appealed to the real Tagore. (Some of Nikhil's statements are actually the same, word for word, as statements by Tagore in essays on the revolutionary movement.) In the words of a *New York Times* writer, reviewing Ray's film in 1985,

> Such movements [as Communism, Islamic fundamentalism, or indeed the Swadeshi Movement] despise the Enlightenment ideal, still prized in the West, which takes the individual as the measure of things and resists abstractions that claim to go beyond the dimensions of man, the justification of cruelties to individuals for the sake of a faith or an ideology, the justification of pain in the present for the sake of a Utopian future or a paradisical hereafter. That central battle of our era may be glimpsed in *The Home and the World*.

There is this in the novel, and there is more. Into it Tagore packed all his tangled emotions about the Swadeshi Movement transmuted by his extraordinary western reception in 1912–13. The 'home' and the 'world' referred to his own mind divided against itself, to himself versus his school, to Shantiniketan versus Calcutta, to Bengal versus India, to India versus Britain, to the

East versus the West: the novel contains elements of all these clashes.

In selecting three extracts, one per protagonist, we have concentrated on the psychology of the triangle, rather than the plot. We have also looked for beauty of language. Though the translation (by Tagore's nephew Surendranath, revised by Rabindranath) is somewhat stilted and archaic as a whole, individual passages are fine pieces of literature. Nikhil's words, especially, express with real beauty what are some of Tagore's most profound thoughts and feelings.

# from *The Home and the World*

..................................................................................................................

## Bimala's Story

My husband was very eager take me out of purdah.

One day I said to him: 'What do I want with the outside world?'

'The outside world may want you,' he replied.

'If the outside world has got on so long without me, it may go on for some time longer. It need not pine to death for want of me.'

'Let it perish, for all I care! That is not troubling me. I am thinking about myself.'

'Oh, indeed. Tell me, what about yourself?'

My husband was silent, with a smile.

I knew his way, and protested at once: 'No, no, you are not going to run away from me like that! I want to have this out with you.'

'Can one ever finish a subject with words?'

'Do stop speaking in riddles. Tell me . . .'

'What I want is, that I should have you, and you should have me, more fully in the outside world. That is where we are still in debt to each other.'

'Is anything wanting, then, in the love we have here at home?'

'Here you are wrapped up in me. You know neither what you have, nor what you want.'

'I cannot bear to hear you talk like this.'

'I would have you come into the heart of the outer world and meet reality. Merely going on with your household duties, living all your life in the world of household conventions and the drudgery of household tasks – you were not made for that! If we meet, and recognize each other, in the real world, then only will our love be true.'

'If there be any drawback here to our full recognition of each other, then I have nothing to say. But as for myself, I feel no want.'

'Well, even if the drawback is only on my side, why shouldn't you help to remove it?'

Such discussions repeatedly occurred. One day he said: 'The greedy man who is fond of his fish stew has no compunction in cutting up the fish according to his need. But the man who loves the fish wants to enjoy it in the water: and if that is impossible he waits on the bank; and even if he comes back home without a sight of it he has the consolation of knowing that the fish is all right. Perfect gain is the best of all; but if that is impossible, then the next best gain is perfect losing.'

I never liked the way my husband had of talking on this subject, but that is not the reason why I refused to leave the zenana. His grandmother was still alive. My husband had filled more than a hundred and twenty per cent of the house with the twentieth century, against her taste; but she had borne it uncomplaining. She would have borne it, likewise, if the daughter-in-law of the Raja's house had left its seclusion. She was even prepared for this happening. But I did not consider it important enough to give her the pain of it. I have read in books that we are called 'caged birds'. I cannot speak for others, but I had so much in this cage of mine that there was not room for it in the universe – at least that is what I then felt.

The grandmother, in her old age, was very fond of me. At the bottom of her fondness was the thought that, with the conspiracy of favourable stars which attended me, I had been able to attract my husband's love. Were not men naturally inclined to plunge downwards? None of the others, for all their beauty, had been able to prevent their husbands going headlong into the burning depths which consumed and destroyed them. She believed that I had been the means of extinguishing this fire, so deadly to the men of the family. So she kept me in the shelter of her bosom, and trembled if I was in the least bit unwell.

His grandmother did not like the dresses and ornaments my husband brought from European shops to deck me with. But she reflected: 'Men will have some absurd hobby or other, which is sure to be expensive. It is no use trying to check their extravagance; one is glad enough if they stop short of ruin. If my Nikhil had not been busy dressing up his wife there is no knowing whom else he might have spent his money on!' So whenever any new dress of mine arrived she used to send for my husband and make merry over it.

Thus it came about that it was her taste which changed. The influence of the modern age fell so strongly upon her that her evenings refused to pass if I did not tell her stories out of English books.

After his grandmother's death, my husband wanted me to go and live with him in Calcutta. But I could not bring myself to do that. Was not this our House, which she had kept under her sheltering care through all her trials and troubles? Would not a curse come upon me if I deserted it and went off to town? This was the thought that kept me back, as her empty seat reproachfully looked up at me. That noble lady had come into this house at the age of eight, and had died in her seventy-ninth year. She had not spent a happy life. Fate had hurled shaft after shaft at her breast, only to draw out more and more the imperishable spirit within. This great house was hallowed with her tears. What should I do in the dust of Calcutta, away from it?

My husband's idea was that this would be a good opportunity for leaving to my sister-in-law the consolation of ruling over the household, giving our life, at the same time, more room to branch out in Calcutta. That is just where my difficulty came in.

She had worried my life out, she ill brooked my husband's happiness, and for this she was to be rewarded! And what of the day when we should have to come back here? Should I then get back my seat at the head?

'What do you want with that seat?' my husband would say. 'Are there not more precious things in life?'

Men never understand these things. They have their nests in the outside world; they little know the whole of what the household stands for. In these matters they ought to follow womanly guidance. Such were my thoughts at that time.

I felt the real point was, that one ought to stand up for one's rights. To go away, and leave everything in the hands of the enemy, would be nothing short of owning defeat.

But why did not my husband compel me to go with him to Calcutta? I know the reason. He did not use his power, just because he had it. . . .

★

This was the time when Sandip Babu with his followers came to our neighbourhood to preach Swadeshi.

There is to be a big meeting in our temple pavilion. We women are sitting there, on one side, behind a screen. Triumphant shouts of 'Bande Mataram'† come nearer: and to them I am thrilling through and through. Suddenly a stream of bare-footed youths in turbans, clad in ascetic ochre, rushes into the quadrangle, like a silt-reddened freshet into a dry river-bed at the first burst of the rains. The whole place is filled with an immense crowd, through which Sandip Babu is borne, seated in a big chair hoisted on the shoulders of ten or twelve of the youths.

'Bande Mataram! Bande Mataram! Bande Mataram!' It seems as though the skies will be rent and scattered into a thousand fragments.

† 'Hail to the Motherland', the rallying cry of the Swadeshi Movement.

I had seen Sandip Babu's photograph before. There was something in his features which I did not quite like. Not that he was bad-looking – far from it: he had a splendidly handsome face. Yet, I know not why, it seemed to me, in spite of all its brilliance, that too much of base alloy had gone into its making. The light in his eyes somehow did not shine true. That was why I did not like it when my husband unquestioningly gave in to all his demands. I could bear the waste of money; but it vexed me to think that he was imposing on my husband, taking advantage of friendship. His bearing was not that of an ascetic, nor even of a person of moderate means, but foppish all over. Love of comfort seemed to me . . . any number of such reflections come back to me today, but let them be.

When, however, Sandip Babu began to speak that afternoon, and the hearts of the crowd swayed and surged to his words, as though they would break all bounds, I saw him wonderfully transformed. Especially when his features were suddenly lit up by a shaft of light from the slowly setting sun, as it sank below the roof line of the pavilion, he seemed to me to be marked out by the gods as their messenger to mortal men and women.

From beginning to end of his speech, each one of his utterances was a stormy outburst. There was no limit to the confidence of his assurance. I do not know how it happened, but I found I had impatiently pushed away the screen from before me and had fixed my gaze upon him. Yet there was none in that crowd who paid any heed to my doings. Only once, I noticed, his eyes, like stars in fateful Orion, flashed full on my face.

I was utterly unconscious of myself. I was no longer the lady of the Raja's house, but the sole representative of Bengal's womanhood. And he was the champion of Bengal. As the sky had shed its light over him, so he must receive the consecration of a woman's benediction. . . .

★

It seemed clear to me that, since he had caught sight of me, the fire in his words had flamed up more fiercely. Indra's steed refused to be reigned in, and there came the roar of thunder and the flash of lightning. I said within myself that his language had caught fire from my eyes; for we women are not only the deities of the household fire, but the flame of the soul itself.

I returned home that evening radiant with a new pride and joy. The storm within me had shifted my whole being from one centre to another. Like the Greek maidens of old, I fain would cut off my long, resplendent tresses to make a bow-string for my hero. Had my outward ornaments been connected with my inner feelings, then my necklet, my armlets, my bracelets, would all have burst their bonds and flung themselves over that assembly like a shower of meteors. Only some personal sacrifice, I felt, could help me to bear the tumult of my exaltation.

When my husband came home later, I was trembling lest he should utter a sound out of tune with the triumphant paean which was still ringing in my ears, lest his fanaticism for truth should lead him to express disapproval of anything that had been said that afternoon. For then I should have openly defied and humiliated him. But he did not say a word, . . . which I did not like either.

He should have said: 'Sandip has brought me to my senses. I now realize how mistaken I have been all this time.'

I somehow felt that he was spitefully silent, that he obstinately refused to be enthusiastic. I asked how long Sandip Babu was going to be with us.

'He is off to Rangpur early tomorrow morning,' said my husband.

'Must it be tomorrow?'

'Yes, he is already engaged to speak there.'

I was silent for a while and then asked again: 'Could he not possibly stay a day longer?'

'That may hardly be possible, but why?'

'I want to invite him to dinner and attend on him myself.'

My husband was surprised. He had often entreated me to be present when he had particular friends to dinner, but I had never let myself be persuaded. He gazed at me curiously, in silence, with a look I did not quite understand.

I was suddenly overcome with a sense of shame. 'No, no,' I exclaimed, 'that would never do!'

'Why not!' said he. 'I will ask him myself, and if it is at all possible he will surely stay on for tomorrow.'

It turned out to be quite possible.

*

## Sandip's Story

Our work proceeds apace. But though we have shouted ourselves hoarse, proclaiming the Mussulmans to be our brethren, we have come to realise that we shall never be able to bring them wholly round to our side. So they must be suppressed altogether and made to understand that we are the masters. They are now showing their teeth, but one day they shall dance like tame bears to the tune we play.

'If the idea of a United India is a true one,' objects Nikhil, 'Mussulmans are a necessary part of it.'

'Quite so,' said I, 'but we must know their place and keep them there, otherwise they will constantly be giving trouble.'

'So you want to make trouble to prevent trouble?'

'What, then, is your plan?'

'There is only one well-known way of avoiding quarrels,' said Nikhil meaningly.

I know that, like tales written by good people, Nikhil's discourse always ends in a moral. The strange part of it is that with all his familiarity with moral precepts, he still believes in them! He is an incorrigible schoolboy. His only merit is his sincerity. The mischief with people like him is that they will not admit the finality even of death, but keep their eyes always fixed on a hereafter.

I have long been nursing a plan which, if only I could carry it out, would set fire to the whole country. True patriotism will never be roused in our countrymen unless they can visualize the motherland. We must make a goddess of her. My colleagues saw the point at once. 'Let us devise an appropriate image!' they exclaimed. 'It will not do if you devise it,' I admonished them. 'We must get one of the current images accepted as representing the country – the worship of the people must flow towards it along the deep-cut grooves of custom.'

But Nikhil needs must argue even about this. 'We must not seek the help of illusions,' he said to me some time ago, 'for what we believe to be the true cause.'

'Illusions are necessary for lesser minds,' I said, 'and to this class the greater portion of the world belongs. That is why divinities are set up in every country to keep up the illusions of the people, for men are only too well aware of their weakness.'

'No,' he replied. 'God is necessary to clear away our illusions. The divinities which keep them alive are false gods.'

'What of that? If need be, even false gods must be invoked, rather than let the work suffer. Unfortunately for us, our illusions are alive enough, but we do not know how to make them serve our purpose. Look at the Brahmins. In spite of our treating them as demigods, and untiringly taking the dust of their feet, they are a force going to waste.'

I went on: 'There will always be a class of people, given to grovelling, who can never be made to do anything unless they are bespattered with the dust of somebody's feet, be it on their heads or on their backs! What a pity if after keeping Brahmins saved up in our armoury for all these ages – keen and serviceable – they cannot be utilized to urge on this rabble in the time of our need.'

NOVEL – 343

But it is impossible to drive all this into Nikhil's head. He has such a prejudice in favour of truth – as though there exists such an objective reality! How often have I tried to explain to him that where untruth truly exists, there it is indeed the truth. This was understood in our country in the old days, and so they had the courage to declare that for those of little understanding untruth is the truth. For them, who can truly believe their country to be a goddess, her image will do duty for the truth. With our nature and our traditions we are unable to realize our country as she is, but we can easily bring ourselves to believe in her image. Those who want to do real work must not ignore this fact.

Nikhil only got excited. 'Because you have lost the power of walking in the path of truth's attainment,' he cried, 'you keep waiting for some miraculous boon to drop from the skies! That is why, when your service to the country has fallen centuries into arrears, all you can think of is to make of it an image and stretch out your hands in expectation of gratuitous favours.'

'We want to perform the impossible,' I said. 'So our country needs must be made into a god.'

'You mean you have no heart for possible tasks,' replied Nikhil. 'Whatever is already there is to be left undisturbed; yet there must be a supernatural result.'

'Look here, Nikhil,' I said at length, thoroughly exasperated. 'The things you have been saying are good enough as moral lessons. These ideas have served their purpose, as milk for babes, at one stage of man's evolution, but will no longer do, now that man has cut his teeth.

'Do we not see before our very eyes how things, of which we never even dreamt of sowing the seed, are sprouting up on every side? By what power? That of the deity in our country who is becoming manifest. It is for the genius of the age to give that deity its image. Genius does not argue, it creates. I only give form to what the country imagines.

'I will spread it abroad that the goddess has vouchsafed me a dream. I will tell the Brahmins that they have been appointed her priests, and that their downfall has been due to their dereliction of duty in not seeing to the proper performance of her worship. Do you say I shall be uttering lies? No, say I, it is the truth – nay more, the truth which the country has so long been waiting to learn from my lips. If only I could get the opportunity to deliver my message, you would see the stupendous result.'

'What I am afraid of,' said Nikhil, 'is that my lifetime is limited and the result you speak of is not the final result. It will have after-effects which may not be immediately apparent.'

'I only seek the result,' said I, 'which belongs to today.'

'The result I seek,' answered Nikhil, 'belongs to all time.'

Nikhil may have had his share of Bengal's greatest gift – imagination, but he had allowed it to be overshadowed and nearly killed by an exotic conscientiousness. Just look at the worship of Durga which Bengal has carried to such heights. That is one of her greatest achievements. I can swear that Durga is a political goddess and was conceived as the image of the *shakti* of patriotism in the days when Bengal was praying to be delivered from Mussulman domination. What other province of India has succeeded in giving such wonderful visual expression to the ideal of its quest?

Nothing betrayed Nikhil's loss of the divine gift of imagination more conclusively than his reply to me. 'During the Mussulman domination,' he said, 'the Maratha and the Sikh asked for fruit from the arms which they themselves took up. The Bengali contented himself with placing weapons in the hands of the goddess and muttering incantations to her; and as his country did not really happen to be a goddess the only fruit he got was the lopped-off heads of the goats and buffaloes of the sacrifice. The day that we seek the good of the country along the path of righteousness, He who is greater than our country will grant us true fruition.'

The unfortunate part of it is that Nikhil's words sound so fine when put down on paper. My words, however, are not meant to be scribbled on paper, but to be scored into the heart of the country. The pundit records his 'Treatise on Agriculture' in printer's ink; but the cultivator at the point of his plough impresses his endeavour deep in the soil.

★

## Nikhil's Story

During the day I forget myself in my work. As the late autumn afternoon wears on, the colours of the sky become turbid, and so do the feelings of my mind. There are many in this world whose minds dwell in brick-built houses – they can afford to ignore the thing called the outside. But my mind lives under the trees in the open, directly receives upon itself the messages borne by the free winds, and responds from the bottom of its heart to all the musical cadences of light and darkness.

While the day is bright and the world in the pursuit of its numberless tasks crowds around, then it seems as if my life wants nothing else. But when the colours of the sky fade away and the blinds are drawn down over the windows of heaven, then my heart tells me that evening falls just for the purpose of shutting out the world, to mark the time when the darkness must be filled with the One. This is the end to which earth, sky and waters conspire, and I cannot harden myself against accepting its meaning. So when the gloaming deepens over the world, like the gaze of the dark eyes of the beloved, then my whole being tells me that work alone cannot be the truth of life, that work is not the be-all and the end-all of man, for man is not simply a serf – even though the serfdom be of the True and the Good.

Alas, Nikhil, have you for ever parted company with that self of yours who used to be set free under the starlight, to plunge into the infinite depths of the night's darkness after the day's work was done? How terribly alone is he, who misses companionship in the midst of the multitudinousness of life.

The other day, when the afternoon had reached the meeting-point of day and night, I had no work, nor the mind for work, nor was my master there to keep me company. With my empty, drifting heart longing to anchor on to something, I traced my steps towards the inner gardens. I was very fond of chrysanthemums and had rows of them, of all varieties, banked up in pots against one of the garden walls. When they were in flower, it looked like a wave of green breaking into iridescent foam. It was some time since I had been to this part of the grounds, and I was beguiled into a cheerful expectancy at the thought of meeting my chrysanthemums after our long separation.

As I went in, the full moon had just peeped over the wall, her slanting rays leaving its foot in deep shadow. It seemed as if she had come atiptoe from behind, and clasped the darkness over the eyes, smiling mischievously. When I came near the bank of chrysanthemums, I saw a figure stretched on the grass in front. My heart gave a sudden thud. The figure also sat up with a start at my footsteps.

What was to be done next? I was wondering whether it would do to beat a precipitate retreat. Bimala, also, was doubtless casting about for some way of escape. But it was as awkward to go as to stay! Before I could make up my mind, Bimala rose, pulled the end of her sari over her head, and walked off towards the inner apartments.

This brief pause had been enough to make real to me the cruel load of Bimala's misery. The plaint of my own life vanished from me in a moment; I called out: 'Bimala!'

She started and stayed her steps, but did not turn back. I went round and stood before her. Her face was in the shade, the moonlight fell on mine. Her eyes were downcast, her hands clenched.

'Bimala,' said I, 'why should I seek to keep you fast in this closed cage of mine? Do I not know that thus you cannot but pine and droop?'

She stood still, without raising her eyes or uttering a word.

'I know,' I continued, 'that if I insist on keeping you shackled my whole life will be reduced to nothing but an iron chain. What pleasure can that be to me?'

She was still silent.

'So,' I concluded, 'I tell you, truly, Bimala, you are free. Whatever I may or may not have been to you, I refuse to be your fetters.' With which I came away towards the outer apartments.

No, no, it was not a generous impulse, nor indifference, I had simply come to understand that never would I be free until I could set free. To try to keep Bimala as a garland round my neck, would have meant keeping a weight hanging over my heart. Have I not been praying with all my strength, that if happiness may not be mine, let it go; if grief needs must be my lot, let it come; but let me not be kept in bondage. To clutch hold of that which is untrue as though it were true, is only to throttle oneself. May I be saved from such self-destruction.

When I entered my room, I found my master waiting there. My agitated feelings were still heaving within me. 'Freedom, sir,' I began unceremoniously, without greeting or inquiry, 'freedom is the biggest thing for man. Nothing can be compared to it – nothing at all!'

Surprised at my outburst, my master looked up at me in silence.

'One can understand nothing from books,' I went on. 'We read in the scriptures that our desires are bonds, fettering us as well as others. But such words, by themselves, are so empty. It is only when we get to the point of letting the bird out of its cage that we can realize how free the bird has set us. Whatever we cage shackles us with desire whose bonds are stronger than those of iron chains. I tell you, sir, this is just what the world has failed to understand. They all seek to reform something outside themselves. But reform is wanted only in one's own desires, nowhere else, nowhere else!'

'We think,' he said, 'that we are our own masters when we get in our hands the object of our desire – but we are really our own masters only when we are able to cast out our desires from our minds.'

'When we put all this into words, sir,' I went on, 'it sounds like some bald-headed injunction, but when we realize even a little of it we find it to be *amrita* – which the gods have drunk and become immortal. We cannot see beauty till we let go our hold of it. It was Buddha who conquered the world, not Alexander – this is untrue when stated in dry prose – oh when shall we be able to sing it? When shall all these most intimate truths of the universe overflow the pages of printed books and leap out in a sacred stream like the Ganges from the Gangotri?'

# POEMS

Tagore once told Edward Thompson, his biographer:

> I have come to the conclusion that translating a poem is doing it
> wrong, especially when the original belongs to a language which
> is wholly alien to the medium of its translation. Have you a single
> honest translation in English from poems written in any other
> European language, which occupies a decent seat in your litera-
> ture? Is not Dante in English a dead star which has its heavy load
> of materials and no light? You know most of the great poets of
> Europe through the experience of a large number of your
> countrymen who have read them in the original - their evidence
> being supplemented by translations which cannot but be inade-
> quate. Can you ever imagine the best passages of Keats, Shelley
> or Wordsworth in Bengali - and would it not be a pure act of
> mercy to leave them out if you must translate their poems?

Tagore was right, but we still believe that one can read his
poetry for both pleasure and insight into the rest of life and work,
provided the reader does not expect from him in English what
he or she expects from the best poetry of, say, Keats or Yeats,
and provided that the translator (who must be a native speaker of
English) chooses the poems of which the imagery and psychology
are not too alien to the reader.

The translators of this small selection are either Tagore himself
or the editors, with the exception of one poem translated by the
well-known south Indian poet A. K. Ramanujan working with a
Bengali poet. We believe that collaboration is the best solution
to the translation of Tagore, until such time as an English poet
acquires sufficient fluency in literary Bengali and knowledge of
Bengali culture and history to be able to judge the value of a

Bengali word or phrase with genuine confidence. For as Rabindranath himself humbly admitted to Ezra Pound: 'I do not know the exact value of your English words. Some of them may have their souls worn out by constant use and some others may not have acquired their souls yet. So in my use of words there must be lack of proportion and appropriateness perhaps.' (p. 156)

When Tagore collaborated face to face with W. B. Yeats and with Thomas Sturge Moore in 1912–13, the results were promising: *Gitanjali*, *The Gardener* and *The Crescent Moon*, three collections containing some poems that are still worth reading. But when he worked on his own, the results were mainly mediocre, judged as English poetry: very few of his poetry translations after *The Crescent Moon* are better than trite, and many are embarrassingly clumsy, whimsical or saccharine.

Ten poems taken from these three English collections apart, our selection is from the final third of Tagore's life, post-Nobel prize. They range widely in subject-matter, mood and style.

Some were prompted by known events. 'To Shakespeare' was composed in 1915 at the request of the Shakespeare Tercentenary Committee in Britain; 'Shah Jahan', after a visit to the Taj Mahal in 1914. 'A Skeleton' was written in Argentina in 1924 after seeing the bleached bones of some bovine creature on the pampas; 'Injury', in response to the bombing of Finland by Russia in 1940. A near-death experience in 1937 prompted 'The Borderland', and painful illness in 1940–41 the last poems in the collections known as 'The Sick-bed' and 'Recovery'. 'Last Writings 13' was almost the final poem of Tagore, written just ten days before he died.

The longest poem, 'Flute Music' (1932), could be said to have been prompted by Tagore's entire life. It contains a world of Bengali feeling, a distillation of seven decades of experience in urban and rural Bengal. It calls to mind almost inescapably that grimy garret above a smoky, noisy Calcutta railway yard to which Apu, the dreamy, impecunious would-be writer, brings his blooming, bejewelled, veiled village bride in Satyajit Ray's emotionally wrenching *Apur Sansar* (*The World of Apu*, 1959). With this poem (and others), Tagore lit the path for Ray to follow.

All the poems are presented in their entirety, except 'Shah Jahan'. The opening stanza of this long poem is magnificent, as befits the Mughal emperor who built the Taj Mahal, but the rest of the poem, though it contains some fine lines, is overblown. Rather than diminishing the impact of the first stanza with what follows, we have therefore stopped on the poem's most celebrated image.

# FROM *Gitanjali*

## 30

I came out alone on my way to my tryst. But who is this that
    follows me in the silent dark?
I move aside to avoid his presence but I escape him not.
He makes the dust rise from the earth with his swagger; he adds
    his loud voice to every word that I utter.
He is my own little self, my lord, he knows no shame; but I am
    ashamed to come to thy door in his company.

## 35

Where the mind is without fear and the head is held high;
Where knowledge is free;
Where the world has not been broken up into fragments by
    narrow domestic walls;
Where words come out from the depth of truth;
Where tireless striving stretches its arms towards perfection;
Where the clear stream of reason has not lost its way into the
    dreary desert sand of dead habit;
Where the mind is led forward by thee into ever-widening
    thought and action—
Into that heaven of freedom, my Father, let my country awake.

Deliverance is not for me in renunciation. I feel the embrace of freedom in a thousand bonds of delight.

Thou ever pourest for me the fresh draught of thy wine of various colours and fragrance, filling this earthen vessel to the brim.

My world will light its hundred different lamps with thy flame and place them before the altar of thy temple.

No, I will never shut the doors of my senses. The delights of sight and hearing and touch will bear thy delight.

Yes, all my illusions will burn into illumination of joy, and all my desires ripen into fruits of love.

I boasted among men that I had known you. They see your pictures in all works of mine. They come and ask me, 'Who is he?' I know not how to answer them. I say, 'Indeed, I cannot tell.' They blame me and they go away in scorn. And you sit there smiling.

I put my tales of you in lasting songs. The secret gushes out from my heart. They come and ask me, 'Tell me all your meanings.' I know not how to answer them. I say, 'Ah, who knows what they mean!' They smile and go away in utter scorn. And you sit there smiling.

# FROM *The Gardener*

## 49

I hold her hands and press her to my breast.
I try to fill my arms with her loveliness, to plunder her sweet
    smile with kisses, to drink her dark glances with my eyes.
Ah, but where is it? Who can strain the blue from the sky?
I try to grasp the beauty; it eludes me, leaving only the body in
    my hands.
Baffled and weary I come back.
How can the body touch the flower which only the spirit may touch?

## 75

At midnight the would-be ascetic announced:
'This is the time to give up my home and seek for God. Ah,
    who has held me so long in delusion here?'
God whispered, 'I,' but the ears of the man were stopped.
With a baby asleep at her breast lay his wife, peacefully sleeping
    on one side of the bed.
The man said, 'Who are ye that have fooled me so long?'
The voice said again, 'They are God,' but he heard it not.
The baby cried out in its dream, nestling close to its mother.
God commanded, 'Stop, fool, leave not thy home,' but still he
    heard not.
God sighed and complained, 'Why does my servant wander to
    seek me, forsaking me?'

# FROM *The Crescent Moon*

## *The Astronomer*

I only said, 'When in the evening the round full moon gets
    entangled among the branches of that *kadam*-tree, couldn't
    somebody catch it?'
But *Dada* laughed at me and said, 'Baby, you are the silliest child
    I have ever known. The moon is ever so far from us, how
    could anybody catch it?'
I said, '*Dada*, how foolish you are! When mother looks out of
    her window and smiles down at us playing, would you call
    her far away?'
Still *Dada* said, 'You are a stupid child! But, baby, where could
    you find a net big enough to catch the moon?'
I said, 'Surely you could catch it with your hands.'
But *Dada* laughed and said, 'You are the silliest child I have
    known. If it came nearer, you would see how big the moon
    is.'
I said, '*Dada*, what nonsense they teach you at your school.
    When mother bends her face down to kiss us, does her face
    look very big?'
But still *Dada* says, 'You are a stupid child.'

## *The Champak Flower*

Supposing I became a *champak* flower, just for fun, and grew on
    a branch high up that tree, and shook in the wind with

laughter and danced upon the newly budded leaves, would
you know me, mother?

You would call, 'Baby, where are you?' and I should laugh to
myself and keep quite quiet.

I should slyly open my petals and watch you at your work.

When after your bath, with wet hair spread on your shoulders,
you walked through the shadow of the *champak* tree to the
little court where you say your prayers, you would notice the
scent of the flower, but not know that it came from me.

When after the midday meal you sat at the window reading the
*Ramayana*, and the tree's shadow fell over your hair and your
lap, I should fling my tiny shadow on to the page of your
book, just where you were reading.

But would you guess that it was the shadow of your little child?

When in the evening you went to the cowshed with the lighted
lamp in your hand, I should suddenly drop to the earth again
and be your own baby once more, and beg you to tell me a
story.

'Where have you been, you naughty child?'

'I won't tell you, mother.' That's what you and I would say then.


## Authorship

You say that father writes a lot of books, but what he writes I
don't understand.

He was reading to you all the evening, but could you really
make out what he meant?

What nice stories, mother, you can tell us! Why can't father
write like that, I wonder?

Did he never hear from his own mother stories of giants and
fairies and princesses?

Has he forgotten them all?

Often when he gets late for his bath you have to go and call him
   a hundred times.
You wait and keep his dishes warm for him, but he goes on
   writing and forgets.
Father always plays at making books.
If ever I go to play in father's room, you come and call me,
   'What a naughty child!'
If I make the slightest noise you say, 'Don't you see that father's
   at his work?'
What's the fun of always writing and writing?

When I take up father's pen or pencil and write upon his book
   just as he does – a, b, c, d, e, f, g, h, i – why do you get cross
   with me then, mother?
You never say a word when father writes.

When my father wastes such heaps of paper, mother, you don't
   seem to mind at all.
But if I take only one sheet to make a boat with, you say,
   'Child, how troublesome you are!'
What do you think of father's spoiling sheets and sheets of paper
   with black marks all over on both sides?


## My Song

This song of mine will wind its music around you, my child,
   like the fond arms of love.
This song of mine will touch your forehead like a kiss of
   blessing.
When you are alone it will sit by your side and whisper in your
   ear, when you are in a crowd it will fence you about with
   aloofness.

My song will be like a pair of wings to your dreams, it will
transport your heart to the verge of the unknown.
It will be like the faithful star overhead when dark night is over
your road.
My song will sit in the pupils of your eyes, and will carry your
sight into the heart of things.
And when my voice is silent in death, my song will speak in
your living heart.

# FROM 'Wild Geese'

## 7 – Shah Jahan†

This fact you knew, Emperor of Ind, Shah Jahan,
That Time's stream carries off life, youth, riches, renown.
   Only your heart's grief
Could be eternal, that was your majesty's true belief.
   Your royal might, adamantine,
Would fade into oblivion like the crimson of the setting sun;
   Simply one great sigh
Would stay, forever-impassioned, rending the sky –
   That was your prayer.
   Diamonds, pearls, rubies glisten
Like the trickery of a rainbow on the empty horizon,
   Soon to vanish like mist
     Shedding just
   One tear droplet
On the cheek of Time, shining and undefiled –
This Taj Mahal.

## 15 – My Songs

My songs they are like water weeds,
Born in one place, but from it freed.
They have no roots, only flowers and leaves,
Which dance like sunbeams on the waves.

† opening stanza only

Dwelling nowhere, hoarding nothing,
They are unforeseen guests, ever roving.
When the river swells in a monsoon torrent,
And bursts its banks with its current,
My water weeds,
Mad with need,
Follow the floods
Along strange roads
From land to land;
Float into a myriad hands.

## 39 – To Shakespeare

When you arose, world poet, from behind the unseen
England found you within her horizon
And embraced you; took you to be her own,
Hers alone; she kissed your shining brow,
Clasped you a while within her sylvan arms, dandled
You a while hidden in her mist-mantle
In flower-covered dewy-green meadows
Where faeries played. As yet the isle's groves
Were not awake to hymn the poet-sun's true reckoning.
Then, gradually, at eternity's silent beckoning
You left the horizon's lap and through centuries ascended
To that zenith for which you were intended,
Your radiant throne at the centre of heaven,
Illuminating all minds; Hear how, after an aeon
The palm-groves on the shores of the Indian Ocean
Rustle their fronds and murmur their paean.

# A Skeleton

A beast's bony frame lies bleaching on the grass
      by the meadow path –
the grass that once had given it strength and tender rest.
The dry white bones seem like the hard laughter of Time
      which cries to me:
'Thy end, proud man, is one with the end of the cattle
      that graze no more,
for when thy life's wine is spilt to its last drop
      the cup is flung away with a final unconcern.'

'Hollow is thy mockery, Death' said I in answer,
Mine is not merely the life that pays its bed and board
      at close of day
with its bankrupt bones and is made destitute.
Never can my life contain to the full all that I have thought
      and felt, gained and given, listened and uttered.
Often my mind has crossed time's border,
Is it to stop at last for ever at the boundary of
      crumbling bones?

Flesh and blood can never be the measure of the truth that is
      myself;
the days and moments cannot wear it with kicks at every step
      as they pass on;
the wayside bandit, dust, dares not rob it of all its possessions.
Know that I have drunk the honey of the formless
      from the lotus of endless forms;

in the bosom of sufferings I have found the secret path
      of delight;
I have heard in my being the voice of Eternal Silence;
have seen the tracks of light across the empty desert of the
      dark.
Death, I accept not from thee
      that I am a gigantic jest of God,
that I am the annihilation built with all the wealth
      of the infinite.

# Flute Music

Kinugoala Lane
    A two-storey house
    Ground-floor room, bars for windows
    Next to the road.
    On the rotting walls patches of peeling plaster,
    The stains of damp and salt.
    A picture label from a bale of cloth
    Stuck on the door shows
    Elephant-headed Ganesh, Bringer of Success.
Apart from me the room has another denizen,
    Living rent-free:
    A lizard.
    The difference between it and me is simple –
    It never lacks food.

I earn twenty-five rupees a month,
    As a junior clerk in a trading office,
    Eat at the Duttas' house,
    Tutor their boy in exchange.
Then it's off to Sealdah Station
    To spend the evening.
    Saves the expense of lighting.
Engines chuffing,
    Whistles screeching,
      Passengers rushing,
        Coolies yelling,
          It's half-past ten
    When I head for my lonely, silent, gloomy room.

My aunt's village on the Dhaleshwari River.
    Her brother-in-law's daughter
Was all set for marriage to my unfortunate self.
Surely the signs were auspicious, I have proof –
    For when the moment came, I ran away.
The girl was saved from me
    And I from her.
She never came to this room, but she's never away from my mind,
    Wearing a Dacca sari, vermilion in her parting.


Monsoon lours,
    Tram fares go up,
    Often my wages get cut.
In nooks and corners of the lane
There pile up and rot
    Mango skins and stones, jackfruit peelings,
    Fish-gills,
    Corpses of kittens,
    And who knows what other trash!
The state of my umbrella is like
    The state of my wage packet,
      Full of holes.


My office clothes resemble
    The thoughts of a Vaishnava guru,
    Oozing and lachrymose.
The dark presence of the rains
    Hangs in my moist room
    Like a trapped beast
      Stunned and still.
Day and night I feel that the world
    Is half-dead, and I am strapped to its back.


At a bend in the lane lives Kanta Babu,

Long hair nattily groomed,
   Wide-eyed
      Refined of manner.
He loves to play the cornet.
Frequently the notes come floating
   Through the lane's stinking air.
   Sometimes at dead of night
   Or in the half-light before dawn,
   Sometimes in the afternoons
   When light and shadow coruscate.

Suddenly one evening
He begins to play in Shindhu Baroa raga,
   And the whole sky rings
   With the yearning of the ages.
Then in a flash I grasp
   That the entire lane is a dreadful lie,
   Insufferable, like the ravings of a drunk.
Suddenly my mind sees
   That Akbar the emperor
   And Haripada the clerk
   Are not different.
   Torn umbrella and royal parasol fuse
   In the pathos of the fluting melody
   Pointing towards one heaven.

   The music is true, the key
To that endless twilit witching
   Where flows the River Dhaleshwari
   Its banks fringed with dark *tamal* trees,
   Where
   In a courtyard
   She is waiting,
   Wearing a Dacca sari, vermilion in her parting.

# FROM 'The Borderland'

*8*

One by one the lamps on the stage blow out,
The meeting place empties, and a dark stain
Blots out my dream-images like deep sleep,
Hushes my mind like a raised forefinger. The guise
In which I have all along projected myself,
Since the curtain first rose, seems suddenly
Futile. The various marks of my individuality,
Embellished in many colours for the multitude,
Are obliterated; and I look into my depths
And am astonished — as is the boundless sky
When at the close of day, at sunset's obsequies,
It gazes at earth's darkling landscapes and is awed
By the luminous self-projection of its stars.

# Injury

The late afternoon glow is fading towards dark.
   The drowsy wind is slack.
A cart full of paddy-straw for far-off Nadia market plods
   Across the desolate fields.
   Behind the sheaves,
   Following, tied-on, a calf.
In the low-caste quarter on a bank
   Beside the tank
   Pundit Banamali's eldest son
   Sits all day with a fishing line.
High above him wild geese honk
   Flying from the river's dried-up bank
   To the lake, the Black Beel,
   In search of snails.


The sugar-cane is cut; beside its stubble
   Two friends indolently amble
   inhaling the scent as they pass
   Of rain-washed forest and grass.
      They are on holiday –
Met each other by chance in some village by-way,
   One of them being newly wed;
Their delight in talking seems to have no end.
All around, the *bhati* flowers are in the bloom of youth;
   In the maze of forest paths
      Their soft fragrance has wings
         Scattering the ecstasy of late spring.

While nearby in a *jarul* tree
    A cuckoo hammers its note dementedly.
    A telegram comes:
'Finland pulverized by Soviet bombs.'

FROM 'The Sick-bed'

## 21

Awakening this morning
In my vase I saw a rose:
The question came to my mind –
Through the cycling of time over aeons
This power that made you a thing of beauty
Shunning all distortion into uncouth imperfection,
Is it blind, is it abstracted?
– Like an ascetic who renounces the world,
the beautiful and unbeautiful without distinction –
Is it just logical, just physical?
Does not consciousness play its part?
There are those who argue and maintain
That in the court of Creation
Form and formlessness have equal rank,
No guards restrain them.
I am a poet, I do not debate,
I look at the world in its wholeness –
At the millions of stars and planets in the sky
Revolving in grandeur and harmony
Never losing the beat of their music
Never slipping into derangement.
When I look at the sky I see spreading petalled layers,
A vast and resplendent rose.

# FROM 'Recovery'

### 7

Brutal night comes silently,
Breaks down the loosened bolts of my spent body,
Enters my insides,
Starts stealing images of life's dignity:
My heart succumbs to the assault of darkness.
The shame of defeat,
    the insult of this fatigue,
Grow intense.
          Suddenly on the horizon,
Dawn's banner laced with rays of gold;
From a distant centre of the sky a shout:
    'It's a lie, a lie!'
Against the tranquil light of morning
I can see myself as a conqueror of sorrows
Standing on top of my fortress, my ruin, my body.

### 16

Day after day I sit silently,
Wondering what of life's gift remains to me
After all my saving and waste.
I spent so much in haste,
Have I received my due, given what I owed,
Kept some provision for the final road?
Some came near me, others went to far places;

Which of my melodies bears their traces?
To some I was unwittingly blind;
Their departing steps sound vainly in my mind.
Perhaps these unknowns went away unheard
But pardoned me without a word.
If I have made mistakes, will some be sore,
Aggrieved, even when I am no more?
Many threads have snapped in my life's patchwork
But there is no more time to repair any break.
In the love that has sustained my life to its end,
If any disrespect of mine has made a wound,
May Death's touch heal its pain —
On this thought I dwell again and again.

# FROM 'Last Writings'

## 13

The sun of the first day
Put the question
To the new manifestation of life –
Who are you?
There was no answer.
Years passed by.
The last sun of the last day
Uttered the question on the shore of the western sea,
In the hush of evening –
Who are you!
No answer came.

# EPIGRAMS

Many non-Bengalis first encounter Tagore through some epigrammatic remark. (They include Paul McCartney, the former Beatle, one of whose songs was based on a line by Tagore.) Several of Tagore's collections of verse contain epigrams, but only one, *Lekhan* (1927), published in English as *Fireflies* (1928), consists entirely of epigrams. The selection that follows is mostly from that book, with four epigrams from other sources.

According to Tagore, the epigrams in *Lekhan* 'had their origin in China and Japan where the author was asked for his writings on fans or pieces of silk'.

'I have created this world,' proclaims Time.
'And we have created you,' the clocks chime.

★

In a crack in the garden wall a flower
Blooms, nameless, lowly and obscure.
'Shame on this weed!' the plants tell each other;
The sun rises and calls, 'Are you well, brother?'

★

A holy topknot stated, shaking its tip,
'Whenever arms and legs act, they make some slip.'
'o unerring hairs,' arms and legs wryly remark,
'Mistakes occur because some of us must work.'

★

In the drowsy dark caves of the mind
dreams build their nest
with bits of things
dropped from day's caravan.

★

While God waits for his temple
to be built of love
men bring stones.

★

The blue of the sky longs for the earth's green.
The wind between them sighs, 'Alas.'

*

God honours me when I work,
he loves me when I sing.

*

I leave no trace of wings in the air,
but I am glad I had my flight.

*

The worm thinks it strange and foolish
that man does not eat his books.

*

My offerings are not for the temple
at the end of the road,
but for the wayside shrines
that surprise me at every bend.

*

Faith is the bird that feels the light
and sings when the dawn is still dark.

*

When I am no longer on this earth, my tree,
Let the ever-renewed leaves of thy spring,
Murmur to the wayfarer:
'The poet did love while he lived.'

# SONGS

*Rabindrasangit*, Tagore Song, means more to Bengalis than any other part of Tagore's life and work – and yet it is the least accessible of his achievements to those who do not know Bengali. There are nearly two and a half thousand Tagore songs. Their greatness lies in their perfect fusion of words and melody. It inspired Satyajit Ray, a composer steeped in the classical music of the West and the East, to say simply: 'As a Bengali I know that as a composer of songs, Tagore has no equal, not even in the West – and I know Schubert and Hugo Wolf.'

Arthur Fox Strangways, author of *The Music of Hindostan* (1914) – still among the best books on Indian music – founder of *Music and Letters* and sometime music critic of the London *Observer*, had this to say of *Rabindrasangit*:

> To hear him [Rabindranath] sing them is to realize the music in a way that is seldom given to a foreigner to do. The notes of the song are no longer their mere selves, but the vehicle of a personality, and as such they go behind this or that system of music to that beauty of sound which all systems put out their hands to seize. These melodies are such as would have satisfied Plato. 'I do not know the modes,' said Socrates, 'but leave me one that will imitate the tones and accents of a brave man enduring danger or distress, fighting with constancy against fortune; and also one fitted for the work of peace, for prayer heard by the gods, and for the successful persuasion and exhortation of men.'

Obviously, such songs cannot be translated into English literature, but this small selection may suggest a little of what Fox

Strangways felt when he heard Tagore sing. The first song, 'The flower says', was composed for Tagore's dance drama *Chandalika* (The Untouchable Maid), a drama based on an old Buddhist legend; we include only its first section. The second song, 'Well-beloved of the whole world', is a patriotic song. Tagore's patriotic songs were perhaps his greatest contribution to the 1905 Swadeshi Movement; later he composed the song, 'Jana Gana Mana', that became India's national anthem. The third song, 'Those who struck Him once', with its clear Christian message, is a heartfelt response to the horror of the Second World War and was composed on Christmas Day, 1939. The final song, 'The ocean of peace', Tagore composed in early December 1939, intending to sing it himself after the death of the boy Amal at the conclusion of *The Post Office*. When Rabindranath fell ill, and the performance had to be cancelled, he expressed the wish that this song be sung after his own death.

The flower says
Blessed am I
Blessed am I
Upon this earth . . .

The flower says
I was born from the dust
Kindly kindly
Let me forget it
Let me forget it
Let me forget.

Of dust inside me there is none.
No dust at all inside me
The flower says.

Well-beloved of the whole world,
O land of my forefathers,
my motherland.
Bathed in the orient sun
there you stand
bright and chaste.
The blue waters of the ocean
wash your feet.
In the soft-blown breeze
gently flutters your green mantle.
Your snow-crested Himalayan brow
is kissed by the heavens.
The first day dawned
in your sky.
Out of the heart of your hermitage
arose the first holy chants.
In your forest retreat were written
the first epics of wisdom and faith.
Hail, mother of abiding mercy,
sustainer of millions at home and abroad.
The holy waters of your Ganga and Yamuna
flow with your mother's milk
of living kindness.

Those who struck Him once
                        in the name of their rulers,
are born again in this present age.
They gather in their prayer halls in a pious garb,
they call their soldiers – 'Kill, kill,' they shout;
in their roaring mingles the music of their hymns.
While the Son of Man in His agony prays, 'O God,
fling, fling far away this cup filled with the bitterest of poison.'

The ocean of peace lies ahead of me.
Sail the boat, O pilot
You are my constant companion now.
Take me in your lap.
Along our journey to the infinite
The pole star alone will shine.
Giver of Freedom
Set me free.
May your forgiveness and compassion
Be my eternal resources for the journey –
May the mortal ties fall away,
May the vast universe
Hold me in embrace,
And with an undaunted heart
May I come to know the Great Unknown.

# Glossary of Indian/Bengali Words

Asharh – Bengali month corresponding to mid-June to mid-July.

*Ayurveda* – ancient system of medicine recorded in the *Vedas*.

Babu/*babu* – e.g. Rabi Babu. Form of address to a man implying formal/respectful distance from person addressed; a rough equivalent of Mr. On its own *babu* means a man from the leisured class or with pretensions to it, depending on context.

*bene-bou* [doll] – commonest type of clay doll in Bengal.

Bhadra – Bengali month corresponding to mid-August to mid-September.

*Bhagavad Gita* – poem forming part of the epic *Mahabharata*.

*bhai* – brother, friend.

chadar – length of cloth wrapped around the body; when not in use, folded and placed over the shoulder.

*champak* – species of magnolia, well known in Bengali folk literature.

*chapkan* – long, loose robe for men, chiefly used as part of official dress.

*chhatu* – fine flour made of maize, barley, etc.

*choga* – long-sleeved garment, like a dressing-gown, originally from Afghanistan.

*dada* – elder brother (*bara dada*, eldest brother; *meja dada*, middle elder brother).

*dai* – curds.

Devi/*devi* – e.g. Maya Devi. Form of address to a woman, usually married, implying formal/respectful distance; a rough equivalent of Mrs. On its own *devi* means a goddess.

dharma – religion (*sanatan dharma*, loosely, the most ancient form of Hinduism).

*didi* – elder sister.

*dhrupad* – style of Indian classical song.

*gayatri* – verse of the *Rig Veda* regarded as its most holy passage; comparable to the Lord's Prayer in Christianity. It is addressed to the old solar god Savitri.

*Jatakas* – any of the various stories of the former lives of the Buddha found in Buddhist literature.

*jatra* – theatre performances that tour the rural areas of Bengal, traditionally based on the Indian epics and folk tales.

*jhampan* – litter used for carrying people in the hills.

*kathaka* – bard, reciter.

*kirtan* – devotional songs in honour of Lord Krishna.

*luchi* – thin circular kind of bread prepared from refined flour and water and fried in ghee so that it blows up like a balloon.

Magh – Bengali month corresponding to mid-January to mid-February.

*Mahabharata* – one of the two ancient epics of India.

*maya* – illusion, the material world, physical or phenomenal nature.

*munshi* – secretary.

*pan* – 'betel': mildly addictive preparation of areca-nut, catechu, lime paste and other condiments, wrapped in the leaf of a betel tree; chewed all over India, especially as a digestive after meals.

*panjabi* – loose shirt worn in the hotter regions of north India, possibly imported into Bengal from the Punjab.

*parul* – species of trumpet-flower, well known in Bengali folk literature.

*pranam* – form of greeting to a respected older person in which one 'takes the dust of the feet'.

*puja* – worship, alone or in a group.

*Ramayana* – one of the two ancient epics of India.

*shandesh* – Bengali sweets made of milk solids and sugar, often perfumed.

*shakti* – power, the female principle taking part in the work of creation.

shastras – sacred Hindu writings and laws.

Shraban – Bengali month corresponding to mid-July to mid-August.

*tanpura* – four-stringed instrument with sympathetic strings, used as a drone accompaniment for the sitar and other instruments.

*tappa* – variety of amorous song.

*tilak* – mark painted or impressed on the forehead, generally of sectarian significance.

*Upanishads* – ancient Indian sacred texts, philosophical in nature, predated by the *Vedas*.

*ustad* – maestro in Indian classical music.

Vaishnava – pertaining to the worship of Vishnu, generally through ecstatic songs and other practices. Older Bengali literature was deeply influenced by Vaishnavism, propagated by Chaitanya.

*Vedas* – earliest and most sacred Hindu texts.

*yaksha* – earth-spirit, a kind of gnome or fairy.

zamindar – landlord, originally created by distribution of land revenue rights by the Mughals; later given ownership of the land by the British under the terms of the 1793 Permanent Settlement.

# Notes and Sources

The sources of all pieces included in this book are given below in the order in which the pieces are printed. Where a piece is a translation, and the translation is our own, we give the standard Bengali source. Where an existing translation has been used (usually with our revisions), we give the English source and the name of the translator, followed by a / and then the standard Bengali source. The latter is mainly the *Rabindra Rachanabali* (collected works of Tagore), abbreviated here to *RR*, followed by the relevant volume and page number.

The first date given is the date of composition of a piece. If this is not known, then the date of first book publication is given. Dates in Bengali have been omitted, to avoid confusion.

The notes are not intended to be exhaustive, only to answer the occasional vital question that may arise in the mind of a reader unfamiliar with Tagore's life, Bengal or Bengali. For a fuller discussion of many of the pieces in this book, see the editors' biography, *Rabindranath Tagore: The Myriad-Minded Man* and their edition of Tagore's *Selected Letters*.

## INTRODUCTION

*page 1* – 'It was Buddha' See p. 349.

*page 1* – 'Akhmatova' Quoted in Anatoly Nayman, *Remembering Anna Akhmatova*, trans. Wendy Rosslyn (London, 1991), p. 153.

*page 2* – 'He stopped at the thresholds' Quoted on the jacket of D. G. Tendulkar, *Mahatma, 1–8* (Bombay, 1951–54).

*page 2* – 'painted pict' Pound to Dorothy Shakespear, 4 October 1912, in *Ezra Pound and Dorothy Shakespear*, Omar Pound and A. Walton Litz (eds) (London, 1985), p. 163.

*page 2* – 'Briefly, I find' 'Rabindranath Tagore', *Fortnightly Review*, March 1913, p. 575.

*pages 2–3* – 'Great Sentinel' *Collected Works of Mahatma Gandhi, 21*, p. 288 (*Young India*, 13 October 1921).

*page 3* – 'Nehru' 'Prison diary with letters', *Selected Works of Jawaharlal Nehru, 11* (first series), pp. 671–72.

*page 4* – 'Listener' 24 August 1939.

*page 5* – 'More than any other thinker' Introduction to *Nationalism*, 2nd edn (London, 1991), p. 14.

*page 5* – 'It would be folly' *Ibid.*, p. 8.

*page 6* – 'I merely started' Letter to Patrick Geddes, 9 May 1922, in Supriya Roy, 'The Poet's town planner: remembering Patrick Geddes', *Rabindra-Bhavana*, Summer 1990, p. 13.

*pages 6–7* – 'Kingdom of the Expert' Letter to Elmhirst, 3 September 1932, in 'Tagore-Elmhirst correspondence', *Purabi: A Miscellany in Memory of Rabindranath Tagore 1941–1991*, Krishna Dutta and Andrew Robinson (eds) (London, 1991), p. 109.

*page 7* – 'This world is a human world' See p. 230.

*page 7* – 'Prigogine' Ilya Prigogine and Isabelle Stengers, *Order out of Chaos* (London, 1984), p. 293.

*page 7* – 'Dwelling on Shakespeare' *Creative Unity* (London, 1922), p. 61.

*pages 7–8* – 'letter … to Indira' 20 August 1892, *Glimpses of Bengal*, trans. Krishna Dutta and Andrew Robinson (London, 1991), pp. 76–77.

*page 11* – 'I can speak in English' Michael Madhushudan Dutta, quoted in *Modern Review*, April 1909, p. 315.

*page 11* – 'If you happen to use the wrong knife' See p. 101.

*page 12* – 'he tells of how Chatterton … inspired him' *My Reminiscences*, 2nd edn (London, 1991), pp. 103–04.

*page 14* – 'Robert Clive' *Ibid.*, p. 93.

*page 14* – 'human nature' *Ibid.*, p. 120.

*page 14* – 'Nirad C. Chaudhuri' *Thy Hand, Great Anarch!* (London, 1987), p. 607.

*page 15* – 'Tagore … told his daughter' Letter to Mira Devi, *Sharadiya Desh*, 1990, p. 42.

*page 16* – 'I leave no trace' See p. 382.


## DRAMA

*page 21* – 'Anita Desai' Introduction to *The Post Office*, trans. Krishna Dutta and Andrew Robinson (New York, 1996), p. viii.

*page 21* – 'Mahatma Gandhi' Letter to S. K. Rudra, 16 January 1918, *Collected Works of Mahatma Gandhi*, 14, p. 153.

*page 21* – 'Yeats' Preface to *The Post Office*, trans. Devabrata Mukerjea (London, 1914), p. vi.

*page 21* – 'Fly! Fly' Quoted in Prashanta Kumar Paul, *Rabijibani, 6* (Calcutta, 1993), p. 235. Tagore's comment was noted by Kali Mohan Ghosh in his diary.

*page 22* – 'Amal represents' *Letters to a Friend* (London, 1928), p. 172.

*page 22* – 'Jiménez' Tagore, *Obra escojida*, trans. Zenobia Camprubi Jiménez (Madrid, 1963), p. 1287.

*page 22* – 'Korczak' Cited in Bruno Bettelheim, *Recollections and Reflections* (London, 1990), p. 206.

*pages 22–23* – 'Elmhirst' 'On death', booklet on Dorothy Elmhirst prepared for her memorial service, 1968 (also printed in *Visva-Bharati Quarterly*, *29*, No. 4, 1963–64, pp. 284–88). Tagore made the response to Duke Gallarati Scotti in Milan on 28 January 1925; it was noted down by Leonard Elmhirst.

### The Post Office (1911)

Publication: *The Post Office*, trans. Krishna Dutta and Andrew Robinson (New York, 1996)/*Dak Ghar*, RR, *11*, pp. 379–406.

## MEMOIRS

*page 53* – 'most valuable and rich' Yeats to Macmillan, in Simon Nowell-Smith, *Letters to Macmillan* (London, 1967), p. 291.

*page 54* – 'In other parts of the world' *My Reminiscences*, 2nd edn (London, 1991), p. 186.

### My Reminiscences (1911)

Publication: *My Reminiscences*, trans. Surendranath Tagore, revised by Krishna Dutta and Andrew Robinson (London, 1991), pp. 17–18, 21–31, 59–79/*Jiban Smriti*, RR, *17*, pp. 263–64, 267–76, 304–23.

*page 59* – 'Day and night' 'Purano Bat' (The Ancient Banyan), RR, *9*, p. 91.

*pages 59–60* – 'The tame bird' 'Dui Pakhi' (Two Birds), *Shonar Tari*, RR, *3*, pp. 43–44.

*page 68* – 'Saradwata or Sarngarava' Two novices in the hermitage of the sage Kanva, mentioned in the Sanskrit drama *Shakuntala* by Kalidasa.

*page 69* – '*Gita Govinda*' Poem written in Sanskrit by Jayadeva, a Bengali then resident at the court of the last Hindu king of Bengal, who lost his throne *c.* AD 1200 to Muslim conquerors. The *Gita Govinda* has been called the Indian Song of Songs; it sings of the love of Krishna and Radha.

*page 72* – 'Satya' Satya Prashad Ganguli, a nephew of Tagore, though two years older than his uncle.

## My Boyhood Days (1940)

Publication: *My Boyhood Days*, trans. Marjorie Sykes, slightly revised by the editors (Calcutta, 1943), pp. 59–63, 82–91/*Chhelebela*, *RR*, *26*, pp. 615–17, 627–31.

*page 84* – 'Jyoti *Dada*' Jyotirindranath Tagore, a diversely talented elder brother of Rabindranath, who strongly influenced him as a boy and young man.

*page 84* – 'my second brother' Satyendranath Tagore, the first Indian to enter the Indian Civil Service.

*page 87* – 'Shahibagh' This palace was built in 1622 by Prince Khurram, later the emperor Shah Jahan.

*page 87* – 'The Hungry Stones' Recent translations of this famous story may be found in Tagore, *Selected Short Stories*, trans. William Radice, rev. edn (London, 1994), pp. 233–43 and in *Civil Lines, 1*, trans. Amitav Ghosh (New Delhi, 1994), pp. 152–68.

## TRAVEL WRITINGS

*page 95* – 'like a homesickness' Tagore to William Rothenstein, 1 June 1918, in *Imperfect Encounter: Letters of William Rothenstein and Rabindranath Tagore 1911–1941*, Mary M. Lago (ed.) (Cambridge (Mass.), 1972), p. 247.

*page 95* – 'It is not for me to travel about' Tagore to C. F. Andrews, 18 October 1918 [MS original at Rabindra Bhavan, Shantiniketan].

*page 96* – 'for want of ... common courtesy' *My Reminiscences*, 2nd edn (London, 1991), p. 115.

## Letters from an Exile in Europe (1879)

Publication: *Yurop Prabashir Patra*, RR, *1*, pp. 578–79 (first letter), pp. 553–60 (second letter); this translation by the editors.

## On the Way to Japan (1916)

Publication: 'On the way to Japan', *Visva-Bharati Quarterly*, *4*, No. 2, August–October 1938, pp. 102–06, trans. Indira Devi Chaudhurani, revised by the editors/*Japan Jatri*, RR, *19*, pp. 306–10.

*page 105* – 'Buddhist temple of Rangoon' The Shwedagon Pagoda, focal point of Rangoon.

## Letters from Java (1927)

Publication: 'Letters from Java', *Visva-Bharati Quarterly*, *6*, No. 2, July 1928, pp. 174–78 and *6*, No. 4, January 1929, pp. 373–79, trans. revised by the editors/*Java Jatrir Patra*, RR, *19*, pp. 507–25.

*page 113* – 'Victoria Memorial' One of Calcutta's great buildings, started in 1906 and opened in 1921.

*page 116* – 'Suniti' Suniti Kumar Chatterji, well-known Bengali philologist.

## Letters from Russia (1930)

Publication: *Letters from Russia*, trans. Sasadhar Sinha, revised by the editors, (Calcutta, 1960), pp. 1–5, 213–16/*Russiar Chithi*, RR, *20*, pp. 276–77 (does not include Tagore's interview with *Izvestia*).

## Journey to Persia (1932)

Publication: 'Journey to Persia', *Visva-Bharati Quarterly*, *2*, No. 4,

February 1937, trans. Surendranath Tagore, revised by the editors, pp. 78–80/*Parashya Jatri*, *RR*, *22*, pp. 438–42.


## LETTERS

*page 134* – 'Nirad C. Chaudhuri' *Thy Hand, Great Anarch!* (London, 1987), p. 602.

### Letter to Mrinalini Tagore (29 August 1890)

Publication: *Chithipatra*, *1*, pp. 3–5; this translation by the editors.

*page 136* – 'Beli and Khoka' Tagore's daughter Bela (Madhurilata) and son Rathindranath, then aged four and nearly two, respectively.

### Letters to Indira Tagore

Publication: *Chhinnapatrabali* (Calcutta, 1960), pp. 23–26 (25 January 1890), pp. 32–33 (19? January 1891), pp. 51–53 (June 1891), pp. 68–69 (4 January 1892), pp. 89–90 (12 June 1892), pp. 224–26 (5 September 1894), pp. 346–47 (12 December 1895); these translations by the editors. Abridged versions appear in *Glimpses of Bengal*, trans. Krishna Dutta and Andrew Robinson (London, 1991).

*page 147* – 'Arab Bedouin' Famous line from 'Duranta Asha' (Wild Hopes), *Manashi*, *RR*, *2*, p. 197.

*page 150* – 'The Postmaster' For a recent translation of this story, see *Selected Short Stories*, trans. Krishna Dutta and Mary Lago (London, 1991), pp. 25–32. The story was poignantly filmed by Satyajit Ray.

### Letter to William Butler Yeats (2 September 1912)

Publication: *Letters to W. B. Yeats*, *2*, Richard J. Finneran, George Mills Harper, William H. Murphy (eds) (London, 1977), pp. 251–52.

### Letter to Bertrand Russell (13 October 1912)

Publication: *The Autobiography of Bertrand Russell, 1872–1914* (London, 1967), p. 221.

*page 155* – 'your article' 'The essence of religion', *Hibbert Journal*, October 1912, pp. 46–62.

*page 155* – 'verse in the *Upanishad*' *Taittiriya Upanishad*, 2:9.

### Letter to Ezra Pound (5 January 1913)

Publication: Noel Stock, *The Life of Ezra Pound* (London, 1970), p. 110.

### Letter to Ezra Pound (5 February 1913)

Publication: MS original in Pound Papers, Beinecke Rare Book and Manuscript Library, Yale University.

### Letters to William Rothenstein

Publication: *Imperfect Encounter: Letters of William Rothenstein and Rabindranath Tagore 1911–1941*, Mary M. Lago (ed.) (Cambridge (Mass.), 1972), p. 140 (18 November 1913), pp. 143–44 (10 and 16 December 1913).

### Letter to Harriet Monroe (31 December 1913)

Publication: MS original in Monroe Papers, Joseph Regenstein Library, University of Chicago.

### Letter to Thomas Sturge Moore (1 May 1914)

Publication: *A Tagore Reader*, Amiya Chakravarty (ed.) (New York, 1961), pp. 23–24.

*Letter to Lord Chelmsford* (31 May 1919)

Publication: *Modern Review*, July 1919, p. 105.

*Letter to Romain Rolland* (14 October 1919)

Publication: MS copy at Rabindra Bhavan, Shantiniketan.

*page 166* – 'Review of Asia and Europe' Rolland never started this review.

*Letter to Charles Freer Andrews* (5 March 1921)

Publication: MS original at Rabindra Bhavan, Shantiniketan. An edited version appeared in *Modern Review*, May 1921.

*page 172* – '*Bara Dada*' Dwijendranath Tagore.

*Letter to Edward John Thompson* (20 September 1921)

Publication: MS original in Thompson Papers, Bodleian Library, University of Oxford.

*page 174* – 'your book dealing with myself' *Rabindranath Tagore: His Life and Work* (Calcutta, 1921). In 1926, Thompson published a much fuller study of Tagore.

*page 175* – '*Gitali*' Songs published by Tagore in 1914.

*Letter to Prashanta Chandra Mahalanobis* (September? 1921)

Publication: *Desh*, 24 May 1975, pp. 253–54; this translation by the editors.

*page 176* – '*Kshanika*' Poems published by Tagore in 1900. They were experiments in literary form, lacking the metaphysical content of Tagore's earlier verse.

*page 177* – 'Michael . . . Nabin Sen . . . Bankim' Writers in Bengali of the second half of the nineteenth century, whose work was based chiefly on epic or historical themes, romantic in tone; none of them used colloquial Bengali speech, as Tagore did.

### Letter to Victoria Ocampo (13 January 1925)

Publication: Ketaki Kushari Dyson, *In Your Blossoming Flower-Garden: Rabindranath Tagore and Victoria Ocampo* (New Delhi, 1988), pp. 390–92.

*page 181* – 'easy chair' In order that a convalescent Tagore should travel comfortably back to India from Argentina, Ocampo insisted that he take with him on board ship one of her chairs to which he had taken a special liking.

### Letter to Leonard Knight Elmhirst (7 November 1926)

Publication: 'Tagore-Elmhirst correspondence', *Purabi: A Miscellany in Memory of Rabindranath Tagore 1941–1991*, Krishna Dutta and Andrew Robinson (eds) (London, 1991), p. 101.

### Letter to Mahatma Gandhi (11 May 1933)

Publication: 'Letters to Mahatma Gandhi', *Rabindra-Biksha*, December 1991, pp. 22–23.

### Letter to William Butler Yeats (16 July 1935)

Publication: MS original in the collection of Michael Yeats.

### Letter to Jawaharlal Nehru (9 October 1935)

Publication: MS copy at Rabindra Bhavan, Shantiniketan.

*page 188* – 'Mahatmaji' From 1936, Gandhi raised money for Tagore's university, thereby rescuing it from collapse.

*page 189* – 'Sapru' Jurist and statesman important in the progress of British India towards self-government.

*page 189* – 'Indira' Indira Nehru was only briefly a student in Shantiniketan; she had to leave because of her mother's illness.

## Letter to Jawaharlal Nehru (31 May 1936)

Publication: 'A bunch of letters', *Visva-Bharati Quarterly*, *29*, Nos 2 and 3, 1963–64, p. 101.

## Letter to Yone Noguchi (1 September 1938)

Publication: 'Poet to poet', *Visva-Bharati Quarterly*, *4*, No. 3, November 1938–January 1939, pp. 202–05.

*page 195* – 'Okakura' Okakura Kakuzo, Japanese pioneer in reviving the Japanese people's interest in their own artistic heritage.

*page 195* – 'Spectator' 1 July 1938.

## Letter to Foss Westcott (16 June 1941)

Publication: MS copy at Rabindra Bhavan, Shantiniketan.

*page 196* – 'my recent reply to Miss Rathbone' 4 June 1941, later published in *Calcutta Municipal Gazette* (Tagore Memorial Supplement), 13 September 1941, p. 107.

# ESSAYS, STATEMENTS AND CONVERSATIONS

*page 202* – 'divine chastisement' *Collected Works of Mahatma Gandhi*, *57*, p. 44.

*page 202* – 'I have the faith' *Ibid.*, p. 165.

## East and West (1922)

Publication: *Creative Unity* (London, 1922), pp. 93–112.

*page 210* – 'Grogan and Sharp' Ewart S. Grogan and Arthur H. Sharp,

*From the Cape to Cairo: The First Traverse of Africa from South to North*
(London, 1900); preface by Cecil Rhodes. Tagore's quotations are among
the milder statements by the authors on the 'nigger question' in Africa.

*page 212* – 'Kasmai devaya' *Rig Veda*, 10:121.

*page 212* – 'the western poet' Rudyard Kipling, of course.

*page 213* – 'Hearken to me' *Rig Veda*, 10:13. 'I have known, from
beyond darkness' *Svetasvatara Upanishad*, 3:8.

## Poet Yeats (1912)

Publication: 'Kabi Yeats', *RR*, *26*, pp. 521–28; this translation by the
editors.

*page 219* – '*Bangadarshan*' Magazine started by Bankim Chandra Chatterji, later revived by Tagore as editor. Many of Bankim's novels were
serialized in *Bangadarshan*.

## On His Drawings (1930)

Publication: 'Dr. Rabindranath Tagore on his drawings', *Indian Art and
Letters*, *4*, 1931, pp. 69–72.

## On Music (1930)

Publication: *RR*, *28*, pp. 955–60 (slightly revised by the editors).

## On the Nature of Reality (1930)

Publication: 'Einstein and Tagore plumb the truth', *New York Times
Magazine*, 10 August 1930.

## The Bihar Earthquake (1934)

Publication: *Tagore and Gandhi Argue*, Jag Parvesh Chander (ed.)
(Lahore, 1945), pp. 169–70.

*The Problem of India* (1909)

Publication: *Modern Review*, August 1910, pp. 184–87.

*Ram Mohan Roy* (1933)

Publication: *Visva-Bharati News*, March 1933, p. 77. This piece was to mark the centenary of the death of Ram Mohan Roy.

*Hindu Scriptures* (1938)

Publication: Foreword to *Hindu Scriptures: Hymns from the Rigveda, Five Upanishads, The Bhagavadgita*, Nicol Macnicol (ed.) (London, 1938), pp. v–vii (slightly abridged by the editors).

*page 246* – 'Chandogya Upanishad' 1:4.

*A Poet's School* (1926)

Publication: *Visva-Bharati Quarterly, 4*, No. 3, October 1926, pp. 197–212.

*page 250* – 'Te sarvagam' *Mundaka Upanishad*, 3:2:5.

*page 258* – 'an English friend' Leonard K. Elmhirst, agricultural economist, who worked with Tagore from 1921 to 1924, and in 1925, with his wife Dorothy, founded the Dartington Trust.

SHORT STORIES

*page 265* – 'Anita Desai' Introduction to *Selected Short Stories*, trans. Krishna Dutta and Mary Lago (London, 1991), p. 16.

*page 265* – 'Satyajit Ray' Quoted in Andrew Robinson, *Satyajit Ray* (London, 1989), p. 47.

*page 266* – 'Khagam' Satyajit Ray, *Stories* (London, 1987), p. 3.

## The Conclusion (1893)

Publication: *Selected Short Stories*, trans. Krishna Dutta and Mary Lago (London, 1991), pp. 80–102/'Shamapti', *RR*, *18*, pp. 292–310.

*page 273* – 'Visvadip' 'The Light of the World'.

## The Raj Seal (1898)

Publication: *Noon in Calcutta: Short Stories from Bengal*, Krishna Dutta and Andrew Robinson (eds) (London, 1992), pp. 1–12, trans. by the editors/'Rajtika', *RR*, *21*, pp. 237–49.

*page 288* – 'Rai Bahadurship' Rai Bahadur was a minor title given from the middle of the nineteenth century to Hindu civil officers, such as deputy magistrates, for distinguished government service: it was a rough equivalent of OBE, Order of the British Empire.

## The Lost Jewels (1898)

Publication: 'Manihara', *RR*, *21*, pp. 249–65; this translation by the editors.

*page 316* – 'line from a Sanskrit drama' *Gita Govinda*.

*page 316* – 'ancient philosophical treatise' The philosopher is Shankaracharya.

## Purification (1928)

Publication: 'Shangskar', *RR*, *24*, pp. 215–19; this translation by the editors. The final paragraph incorporates an addition made by Tagore in his own translation of the story ('The Patriot', *Modern Review*, July 1928, pp. 1–3).

## The Parrot's Training (1918)

Publication: *The Parrot's Training*, trans. by the author, slightly revised by the editors (Calcutta, 1918)/*RR*, *26*, pp. 132–35.

# NOVEL

*page 333* – 'You simply *must* read it' Hedwig Born (wife of Max Born) to Einstein, 8 September 1920, in *The Born-Einstein Letters*, trans. Irene Born (London, 1971), p. 34.

*page 333* – 'Hermann Hesse' November 1920, in Martin Kämpchen, *Rabindranath Tagore and Germany: A Documentation* (Calcutta, 1991), p. 41.

*page 333* – 'Bertolt Brecht' 26 September 1920, *Diaries 1920–1922*, Herta Ramthun (ed.), trans. John Willett (London, 1979), p. 55.

*page 333* – 'Georg Lukács' *Reviews and Articles*, trans. Peter Palmer (London, 1983), pp. 8–11.

*page 334* – '*New York Times*' Walter Goodman, 7 July 1985, quoted in Andrew Robinson, *Satyajit Ray* (London, 1989), pp. 268–69.

### *The Home and the World* (1915–16)

Publication: *The Home and the World*, trans. Surendranath Tagore, revised by the author (London, 1919) pp. 11–17, 23–27, 182–88, 204–09/*Ghare Baire*, RR, 8, pp. 149–53, 157–60, 254–57, 266–68.

# POEMS

*page 353* – 'I have come to the conclusion' Letter, 16 April 1922 [MS original in Thompson Papers, Bodleian Library, Oxford].

*page 354* – 'Shah Jahan' A full translation of this poem appears in *Selected Poems*, trans. William Radice, rev. edn (London, 1994), pp. 78–81.

### *Gitanjali* (1912)

Publication: verse 30, *Gitanjali* (London, 1913), pp. 23–24 / *Gitanjali,*

RR, *11*, p. 79 (first published in 1910); verse 35, *Gitanjali*, pp. 27–28/ *Naivedya*, RR, *8*, pp. 56–57 (first published in 1901); verse 73, *Gitanjali*, p. 68/*Naivedya*, RR, *8*, p. 30 (first published in 1901); verse 102, *Gitanjali*, p. 93/*Utsharga*, RR, *10*, pp. 14–15 (first published in 1914).

### The Gardener (1913)

Publication: verse 49, *The Gardener* (London, 1913) p. 86/*Manashi*, RR, *2*, pp. 164–65 (poem written in 1887); verse 75, *The Gardener*, pp. 130–31/*Chaitali*, RR, *5*, p. 11 (poem written in 1896).

### The Crescent Moon (1913)

Publication: 'The Astronomer', *The Crescent Moon* (London, 1913), pp. 25–26/*Shishu*, RR, *9*, pp. 49–50 (poem written in 1903); 'The Champak Flower', *The Crescent Moon*, pp. 29–30/*Shishu*, RR, *9*, pp. 54–55 (poem written in 1903); 'Authorship', *The Crescent Moon*, pp. 58–59/*Shishu*, RR, *9*, pp. 35–36 (poem written in 1903); 'My Song', *The Crescent Moon*, p. 78/*Kari o Komal*, RR, *2*, pp. 62–63 (poem written in 1886).

*page 360* – 'Ramayana' The Bengali original has '*Mahabharata*' in place of '*Ramayana*'.

### Wild Geese (1916)

Publication: 'Shah Jahan', in Krishna Dutta and Andrew Robinson, *Rabindranath Tagore* (London, 1995), p. 192, trans. by the authors/ *Balaka*, RR, *12*, p. 14 (poem written in 1914); verse 15, *Balaka*, RR, *12*, pp. 34–35 (poem written in 1915) – this translation by the editors; 'To Shakespeare', in Krishna Dutta and Andrew Robinson, *Rabindranath Tagore* (London, 1995), p. 191, trans. by the authors/*Balaka*, RR, *12*, p. 65 (poem written in 1915).

### A Skeleton (1924)

Publication: 'The Skeleton', *Visva-Bharati Quarterly*, *3*, No. 1,

April 1925, pp. 36–37, trans. by the author/*Purabi*, RR, *14*, pp. 130–31.

## Flute Music (1932)

Publication: 'Flute Music', in Krishna Dutta and Andrew Robinson, *Rabindranath Tagore* (London, 1995), pp. 336–38, trans. by the authors/ *Punashcha*, RR, *16*, pp. 84–87.

## The Borderland (1937)

Publication: verse 8, *Prantik*, RR, *22*, pp. 11–12; this translation by the editors.

## Injury (1940)

Publication: 'Injury', in Krishna Dutta and Andrew Robinson, *Rabindranath Tagore* (London, 1995), p. 348, trans. by the authors/*Shehnai*, RR, *24*, pp. 132–33.

## The Sick-bed (1940)

Publication: in Krishna Dutta and Andrew Robinson, *Rabindranath Tagore* (London, 1995), p. 361, trans. by the authors/verse 21, *Rogashajyay*, RR, *25*, pp. 23–24.

## Recovery (1941)

Publication: verse 7, 'Eight poems and songs of Rabindranath Tagore', *Visva-Bharati Quarterly*, *1*, No. 1, 1985, p. 6, trans. A. K. Ramanujan and Naresh Guha, with one word changed by the editors/*Arogya*, RR, *25*, pp. 47–48; verse 16, *Arogya*, RR, *25*, pp. 55–56 – this translation by the editors.

## Last Writings (1941)

Publication: in Krishna Dutta and Andrew Robinson, *Rabindranath*

Tagore (London, 1995), p. 367, trans. by the authors/verse 13, *Shesh Lekha, RR, 26,* pp. 49–50.

## EPIGRAMS

*page 379* – 'Paul McCartney' His song 'Pipes of Peace' is based on Tagore's line: 'In love all of life's contradictions dissolve and disappear.'

*page 379* – 'According to Tagore' Introduction to *Lekhan,* written at Balatonfüred, Hungary, 7 November 1926.

Publication: the first three epigrams were published in 1899 in *Kanika, RR, 6,* pp. 25, 19, 21, trans. by the editors; the rest, except for the last one, were published in *Lekhan, RR, 14,* pp. 160, 162, 163, 165, 166, 171, 168, 172, trans. by the author; the last epigram was written in English and inscribed on a tablet beside Lake Balaton next to a tree planted by Tagore at Balatonfüred, Hungary, on 8 November 1926.

## SONGS

*page 385* – 'Satyajit Ray' Quoted in Andrew Robinson, *Satyajit Ray* (London, 1989), p. 47.

*page 385* – 'Fox Strangways' *The Music of Hindostan* (Oxford, 1914), p. 92.

Publication: 'The flower says', in 'Moods', *Visva-Bharati Quarterly, 40,* No. 4, February–April 1975, pp. 314–15, trans. John Boulton/*Gitabitan, 3* (Calcutta, 1966), p. 716 (composed for the dance drama *Chandalika* in 1933). 'Well-beloved of the whole world', in 'A sheaf of songs', *Cultural Forum,* November 1961, pp. 72–73, trans. Kshitis Roy/ *Gitabitan, 1* (Calcutta, 1967), p. 257 (composed in 1896/97). 'Those who struck Him once', *Poems* (Calcutta, 1942), p. 186, trans. by the author/*Gitabitan*, *3*, pp. 864–65 (composed on Christmas Day, 1939). 'The ocean of peace', in Krishna Dutta and Andrew Robinson, *Rabindranath Tagore* (London, 1995), pp. 369–70, trans. by the authors/ *Gitabitan*, *3*, p. 864 (composed in 1939).

# Books for Further Reading

A brief selection, all in English.

## BOOKS BY RABINDRANATH TAGORE

*Creative Unity* (London, 1922) (essays)

*Glimpses of Bengal*, trans. Krishna Dutta and Andrew Robinson, 2nd edn (London, 1991) (letters)

*The Home and the World*, trans. Surendranath Tagore, 2nd edn (London, 1985) (novel)

*I Won't Let You Go: Selected Poems*, trans. Ketaki Kushari Dyson (Newcastle upon Tyne, 1991)

*My Boyhood Days*, trans. Marjorie Sykes (Calcutta, 1943)

*My Reminiscences*, 2nd edn (London, 1991)

*Nationalism*, 2nd edn (London, 1991)

*The Post Office*, trans. Krishna Dutta and Andrew Robinson (New York, 1996) (play)

*Sadhana: The Realisation of Life* (London, 1913) (essays)

*Selected Letters*, Krishna Dutta and Andrew Robinson (eds) (Cambridge, 1997)

*Selected Poems*, trans. William Radice, rev. edn (London, 1994)

*Selected Short Stories*, trans. Krishna Dutta and Mary Lago (London, 1991)

*Selected Short Stories*, trans. William Radice, rev. edn (London, 1994)

*A Tagore Reader*, Amiya Chakravarty, (ed.) (New York, 1961)

*Towards Universal Man*, translated by various hands (Bombay, 1961) (essays)

# Books about Rabindranath Tagore

Dutta, Krishna and Andrew Robinson, *Rabindranath Tagore: The Myriad-Minded Man* (London, 1995)

Elmhirst, Leonard K., *Poet and Plowman* (Calcutta, 1975)

Hay, Stephen N., *Asian Ideas of East and West: Tagore and His Critics in Japan, China and India* (Cambridge (Mass.), 1970)

Kripalani, Krishna, *Rabindranath Tagore: A Biography*, 2nd edn (Calcutta, 1980)

Lago, Mary M., *Imperfect Encounter: Letters of William Rothenstein and Rabindranath Tagore 1911–1941* (Cambridge (Mass.), 1972)

Robinson, Andrew, *The Art of Rabindranath Tagore* (London, 1989) (reproduces paintings)

Tagore, Rathindranath, *On the Edges of Time*, 2nd edn (Calcutta, 1981)

Thompson, Edward J., *Rabindranath Tagore: Poet and Dramatist*, 2nd edn (New Delhi, 1991) (pbk reprint of 1948 edn)

Thompson, Edward P., *Alien Homage: Edward Thompson and Rabindranath Tagore* (New Delhi, 1993)

Tinker, Hugh, *The Ordeal of Love: C. F. Andrews and India* (New Delhi, 1979)

# Related Books about Bengal

Bose, Buddhadeva, *An Acre of Green Grass* (Calcutta, 1948) (review of Bengali literature)

Chaudhuri, Nirad C., *The Autobiography of an Unknown Indian* (London, 1951)

—— *Thy Hand, Great Anarch!: India 1921–52* (London, 1987)

Chaudhuri, Sukanta (ed.), *Calcutta: The Living City* (Volume 1, The Past; Volume 2, The Present and Future) (Calcutta, 1990)

Dutta, Krishna and Andrew Robinson, (eds), *Noon in Calcutta: Short Stories from Bengal* (London, 1992)

Ghosh, J. C., *Bengali Literature* (London, 1976) (reprint of 1948 edn)

Moorhouse, Geoffrey, *Calcutta: The City Revealed,* 2nd edn (London, 1983)

Ray, Satyajit, *Our Films Their Films* (New Delhi, 1976)

Robinson, Andrew, *Satyajit Ray: The Inner Eye* (London, 1989)

Sen, K. M., *Hinduism* (London, 1961)

Tagore, Debendranath, *The Autobiography of Maharshi Devendranath Tagore,* trans. Satyendranath Tagore and Indira Devi (London, 1914)

## HINDU SCRIPTURES AND SANSKRIT LITERATURE IN TRANSLATION

Basham, A. L., *The Wonder That Was India,* 3rd edn (London, 1967)

*The Bhagavad Gita,* trans. Juan Mascaró (London, 1962)

Brough, John, trans., *Poems from the Sanskrit* (London, 1968)

Coulson, Michael, trans., *Three Sanskrit Plays* (London, 1981)

Goodall, Dominic (ed.), *Hindu Scriptures* (based on an anthology by R. C. Zaehner) (London, 1996)

Kalidasa, *The Loom of Time: A Selection of His Plays and Poems,* trans. Chandra Rajan (New Delhi, 1989)

Narayan, R. K., *The Ramayana* (London, 1972)

—— *The Mahabharata* (London, 1978)

O'Flaherty, Wendy Doniger, *Hindu Myths* (London, 1975)

*The Rig Veda,* trans. Wendy Doniger O'Flaherty (London, 1981)

*The Upanishads,* trans. Juan Mascaró (London, 1965)